Grunwick

The Workers' Story

Jack Dromey & Graham Taylor

SECOND EDITION

Forewords by Tim Roache and Jack Dromey
Introduction by Graham Taylor

Lawrence & Wishart
London 2016

Lawrence and Wishart Limited
Central Books Building
Freshwater Road
Chadwell Heath
RM8 1RX

This edition © Lawrence & Wishart 2015
Edited by John Callow
Published in association with the GMB

Photographs: Andrew Wiard
Typesetting: e-type
Cover design: Andrew Corbett

ISBN 9781910448946

British Library Cataloguing in Publication Data.
A catalogue record for this book is available from the British Library.

Contents

EDITORIAL NOTE

A week is a long time in politics, and forty years is – in many respects – a different age. *Grunwick: The Workers' Story* was written at the cusp of societal, linguistic and cultural change, when considerations of race and gender were forcing their way onto the stage, as never before, and academics, as well as trade union activists and journalists, were compelled to fashion a new vocabulary that encompassed, and explained, new social movements, the dynamics of ethnic minority groups and the unique set of problems they faced, within a specifically British context.

As a consequence, some of the terms used in the first edition of the book appear dated, or clunky, when compared with the sophistication, and standardisation, of the language surrounding these themes and issues, that is employed today. While direct quotations from the participants in the Grunwick dispute have not been altered, some of the terms used in the narrative account of the strike have been updated in order to ensure that the text feels as fresh and approachable as when it was written. To give an example: 'racialism' – the standard term employed by British progressives in the late 1960s and 1970s – has been replaced by the more familiar, and now generally accepted, 'racism'. This term had its roots among academics and campaigners in North America in the same decades, but it did not cross the Atlantic and become part of general parlance in Britain, until the early 1980s.

John Callow

'We are the Lions, Mr. Manager!'

Tim Roache

When asked why his union had supported the strike at Grunwick, Len Gristey – the APEX area organiser – didn't hesitate for a moment. 'We could not walk away', he told reporters.

It was a simple statement made, in July 1977, against the backdrop of a year-long dispute that had captured the news headlines and polarised society, perhaps as never before, around the rights of new immigrants to Britain to dignity at work, to decent pay and to union representation.

Night-after-night, through the summer, the public had watched dramatic television footage of clashes on the picket lines, between snatch squads and regimented police lines, on the one side, and wave after wave of trade union members, pickets and protestors, on the other. Yet the strike had already been kept alive through a harsh winter. Each morning, another story had begun again, as the strikers, a group of predominantly Asian women, colourful saris often hidden beneath heavy woollen coats, would take up their posts on the picket lines, unbowed and unbroken in the face of intimidation, the threat of arrest and the sting of the cold.

Theirs was another kind of heroism, less obvious but, in its way, far more significant and remarkable. For they were challenging every assumption that had been made about them – in terms of their gender, ethnicity and supposed deference towards those in authority over them. In so doing, they not only changed the trade union movement but the whole of British society.

This is what Len Gristey had sensed and tried to communicate, as the press closed in and tried to bait him about the nature of a dispute that was beginning to look, after all, as though it might be lost. His words contained the essence of all that is best in the Labour and Trade Union Movement. For, what we do is not about cynical calculation, it is not about profit and loss, or momentary advantage. It is about decency. A decency that sees the value in every human being, regardless of their background or the colour of their skin. It is a sense of decency that unites in common cause and fights for universal values. It is the thing that brings us together, in the trade unions, and keeps us going through the hard times.

That is why, as General Secretary of the GMB (the union that APEX became part of), I am immensely proud of the story of the Grunwick workers. It is not some dry history, but a rallying cry, an inspiration and a point of departure. It makes us think – about ourselves and about the type of society in which we would wish to live – and, against the background of Brexit, new controversies about immigration and the resurgence of racism, in some respects it is more vital than ever.

This book is the primary source for the dispute and the surest guide to learning about what actually took place. This is history lived in the moment – raw and vital – told by the very people who made it. You'll find within it the stories: of Jayaben Desai, the pioneering organiser of Asian women in the workplace; of the nineteen-year-old student, Devshi Bhudia, whose refusal to be bullied triggered the strike; and of the thoughtful Mahmood Ahmad, who served as Secretary to the Strike Committee throughout the dispute. These were people who knew little of trade unionism before the Grunwick Strike but who quickly grew within it, as courageous and resourceful individuals who became adept at public speaking, the preparation and production of posters and leaflets, and the organisation of petitions, marches and countless meetings.

They had been employed by Grunwick in the belief that they would be easy to handle, to browbeat and to exploit. Yet, nothing could have been further from the truth, as they found their own distinctive voice in the course of the struggle to secure their rights. Even during the hardest of times, Jayaben Desai had the uncanny ability to evoke a mood or sum up a situation with a perfectly weighted turn of phrase. In this way, she had the measure of the most brutish and charmless of her managers, when she told him that: 'What you are running here is not a factory, it is a zoo. But in a zoo there are many types of animals. Some are monkeys who dance on your fingertips, others are lions who can bite your head off. We are the lions, Mr. Manager!'

Ranged against these 'lions' of the trade union movement was, however, a new type of employer, ruthless and implacable in defence of his 'right' to make the maximum amount of profit, regardless of the human cost, and behind him a new, highly ideological breed of hard right-wing politician, fanatically devoted to neoliberalism and the destruction of the hard-won freedoms of working people. Forty years on, we can see clearly how their demands for the restriction of picketing, an attack on the unions' political funds and finances and the ending of collective bargaining, served to shape the policies not only of the Thatcher years but also those of successive Conservative and coalition governments.

Today, the unions remain one of the major pillars of civil society. We haven't always got everything right, as this book shows, but we have consistently been on the side of the angels when it really counted – on issues such as economic and social equality, support for the NHS, the provision of a safety net of welfare that stretched from the cradle to the grave and opposition to racism and discrimination wherever, and whenever, they raised their ugly heads.

These are all good reasons for us to take heart and to celebrate our achievements. And there are few prouder, or more important, for today's GMB than the example of the activists who forged our modern union at the gates of Grunwick. This is their story, but it is also part of a larger, ongoing narrative that unites each and every one of us, as soon as we stop to think and choose to stand together against injustice and racism. As such, it speaks for us all and for the better, and fairer, days that lie ahead.

Tim Roache,
General Secretary GMB
20 August 2016

Grunwick: The Workers' Story

FOREWORD

Jack Dromey

The summer of 1976 was one of the hottest on record. In the sweltering conditions of the Grunwick film-processing plants in Chapter Road and Cobbold Road in Willesden, the predominantly newly arrived Gujarati workers from East Africa sweated under the yoke of company boss George Ward. Most of them had been expelled from East Africa where they were the mercantile, administrative and business class. They seethed with anger and humiliation. They were reluctant refugees from Uganda, Tanzania and Kenya, now treated with contempt.

'My Asians', as George Ward called them, received poverty pay for long hours. Forced to work compulsory overtime, humiliated women employees had to put their hand up to go to the toilet. Crude systems were put in place by a bullying manager, Malcolm Alden, to identify the slowest workers who would then be instantly dismissed. But those managers who would not have disgraced a nineteenth century mill owner reckoned without Jayaben Desai.

Four feet ten inches tall, she led the first walk-out on 23 August 1976. Born in Gujarat, she married a tyre-factory manager, Suryakant in Tanzania. A proud Hindu woman in her traditional sari, she had been schooled in the Indian independence movement and was inspired by Gandhi, as she came in turn to inspire millions. The fear of the sack was, she told Alden in defence of her fellow workers, 'like a sore on their necks'. 'What you are running here is not a factory', she said to a man eighteen inches taller, 'it is a zoo. But in a zoo there are many types of animals. Some are monkeys who dance on your fingertips. Others are lions who can bite your head off. We are those lions, Mr Manager!'

Thus began a strike that would make history, a walk-out by initially fewer than 100 workers. As they went out of the gate, she told the predominantly Gujarati women strikers 'this man [Alden] would not speak to white workers like he speaks to us'. Such, sadly, was the cold welcome to Brent and Britain of successive groups of immigrants who came to our shores. First, the Irish, then those from the West Indies and then the Asians who made up the population of Brent that was, by the 1970s, the most diverse in Britain. All had suffered prejudice. I remember my own father, an Irish road-digger from Cork, telling me what it was like to arrive in Kilburn and Cricklewood in the 1930s looking for lodgings, only to see those infamous signs in lodging house windows 'no dogs, no Irish'. Soon, as the Jamaicans arrived, it was to be 'no dogs, no blacks'.

The strikers' cause looked hopeless. But that reckoned without three things. Firstly, there was Brent, the most cosmopolitan borough in Britain, which had a strong Trades Council with deep roots in the local factories. Tom Durkin, an Irish carpenter, was its Chair, and I was proud to serve as its Secretary. And, very unusually for the time, the Trades Council had strong bonds with Brent's immigrant communities. The first Community Relations Council in Britain was born in Brent, the Willesden Friendship League, with fortnightly meetings of up to 200. Nelson Mandela addressed the then Willesden Trades Council before he returned to South Africa to serve twenty-seven long years in prison.

Secondly, there was the union, APEX, now part of the GMB. None of those who came out on strike were in a Union, but, again very unusually for the time, APEX took them in. APEX was not known for its militancy, but it backed the Grunwick strikers, giving them a home. Without this, the stand they took might have been over in days.

Thirdly, of course, there was Jayaben Desai and the Grunwick strikers. Those brave women and the men who stood with them, Vipin, Mahmood and Kamlesh, to name but a few. 'Mr Jack', Jayaben would often tell me, 'my English not good'. Yet she talked the language of Gandhi, with the burning sense of injustice of La Passionara, the great Republican leader in the war against fascism in Spain. Indeed, at times, she was almost Shakespearean. She had a way with words that captured the very essence of the human spirit.

But still, the odds were against them. What followed was truly remarkable, all the more so because of the sorry history of the ten years previous to the outbreak of the strike. Unions had not always been on the side of black and Asian workers. On the contrary. In 1968, Dockers and meat porters marched in support of Enoch Powell, following his infamous racist 'Rivers of Blood' speech. Workforces sometimes polarised along racial lines, and white Executives let down black or Asian workers in infamous disputes like those at Mansfield Hosiery Mills and Imperial Typewriters. Yet, defying all the odds, Grunwick was to see the biggest mobilisation in labour movement history around a local dispute of predominantly newly arrived Gujarati workers.

The strike was nearly won, when the then Union of Post Office Workers blacked the mail to Grunwick, bringing their mail-order film-processing business to a halt. The blacking was lifted when legal action was taken by the shadowy National Association for Freedom (NAFF), closely associated with the new Leader of the Conservative Party, Margaret Thatcher, and the emerging Tory ideological right. The strikers were in despair, but they were lifted to carry on the struggle by a magnificent speech to a packed Brent Trades and Labour Hall meeting by Jayaben. 'Who are we to give up? Never. We fight on', she said.

With APEX, the Strike Committee and the Trades Council then organised visits to well over 1000 workplaces in the months that followed, with Asian women in saris bringing home to the big battalions in the trade-union organised world of work, a dimension of exploitation that they never knew existed. Engineering and car plants, dockyards and steel mills, aircraft factories, the Grunwick strikers toured the length and breadth of the land. The strike for the basic human right to respect and union recognition became a cause célèbre in the trade union movement. It also transformed those stereotypes of the time that suggested that Asian workers were somehow 'passive and unorganisable' and forged a remarkable unity in a noble cause.

Then, what forced the dispute into the national headlines was what happened in the week of 13 June 1977. Local factories mobilised 100 workers a day as a show of support for the strikers. On the Monday, in what the police subsequently admitted was a 'disaster', eighty-four were arrested. Solidarity crystallised on the picket lines from all over Britain, with workers flocking to Chapter Road in ever greater numbers. By the Friday, 3000 joined the strikers. A mass movement was underway and that led to one of the most remarkable acts of solidarity in trade-union history.

At the local sorting office, the Cricklewood Post Office workers took unofficial action to black the mail to Grunwick for a second time, supported by their London District Council Officers, John Taylor and Derek Walsh, but defying the instructions of their Executive. All 100 were white, bar one West Indian. They were suspended and threatened with the sack. Yet for forty-four days they stood firm, led by Branch Chairman, Colin Maloney and Secretary, Archie Sinclair. Solidarity by white workers with Asian workers was, before then, without precedent.

Grunwick was now at the heart of a national and international mass movement from Belfast to Brussels. Rotterdam and French dock workers blacked all goods going to Grunwick. It was then, on 30 June, that the Labour Employment Secretary, Albert Booth announced a Court of Inquiry under Lord Justice Scarman. The Strike Committee warned of the dangers of losing momentum. Yes, we are confident that Scarman will recommend recognition and reinstatement of the strikers, we said. But we have to keep the pressure up, we argued. 'No employer has ever defied the recommendation of a Court of Enquiry', retorted Len Murray, TUC General Secretary. 'You don't know this employer and the emerging Tory right behind him', Jayaben and I warned. But the mass movement was nevertheless wound down, with the Cricklewood Post Office workers reluctantly ending their blacking of the mail after forty-four days.

Sure enough, George Ward then bluntly refused to accept the Scarman findings, which recommended recognition of APEX and the reinstatement of the strikers. The findings were morally but not legally binding. George Ward made his own infamous version of history, by becoming the first employer to reject the findings of a Court of Inquiry.

What followed were months of attempts to regain the initiative, but ultimately to no avail. The strikers fought on through a second bitter winter. But it became increasingly clear that the strike could not be won. It was on 14 July 1978, therefore, that the Strike Committee ended the strike. It was an emotional meeting but characterised by a strong view that no workers could ever have fought harder or longer. There was a sense of pride, yes; pride because theirs had been a noble cause and theirs was a sense of having made history.

Grunwick truly did make history. The strike saw the biggest mobilisation in labour movement history around a local dispute, with 20,000 descending on Chapter Road on 11 July 1977. Grunwick saw one of the most remarkable acts of solidarity in labour movement history with the brave stand taken by the Cricklewood post office workers. Grunwick put centre-stage the issue of the exploitation of immigrant workers, nailing the myth that Asian workers were passive and unorganisable. And Grunwick was a defining moment in the trade-union and political lives of tens of thousands, who came to the streets of Brent to back the Grunwick workers. Ultimately, we did not win, but you never lose a struggle like Grunwick. The legal right to union recognition was ultimately won under a Labour government, in a historic lasting legacy of the dispute.

Grunwick also saw, however, the emergence of the 'militant right'. The irony was that we were accused of being the militant left, when it was those emerging forces of the radical ideological right that were defying the one-nation Toryism, of Tory wets like their then Employment spokesman, Jim Prior. Prior wanted a negotiated solution and the acceptance of the Court of Inquiry. Grunwick was a harbinger of what was to come, the era of Mrs Thatcher, when trade unions came to be regarded as 'the enemy within'.

The history of Grunwick is remarkable, but Grunwick is not just history. Because, once again, the tensions of the 1970s are scarring our country. To their eternal shame, mainstream politicians put the politics of race and immigration centre-stage in the Referendum on the European Union. There is a growing xenophobia in a fearful and fractured country. Legitimate concerns are being exploited, concerns arising out of the exploitation of newly immigrated workers, and the undercutting of those who have been here for generations.

One of the few pillars left of social solidarity is the trade-union movement. Upon it falls a heavy duty to unite all workers around fair and equal treatment of all workers. That is why the determination of the GMB and its new general secretary, Tim Roache, to celebrate history and learn from it is so important. For they have captured what Jayaben said to me when we last met before she died. 'Mr Jack', she said, 'people will always want their freedom. As we have fought, others will fight. If we have inspired, I will die a happy woman.'

It was in that spirit that the words came back to me, when we scattered her ashes on the Thames, of the exchange between Lord Justice Scarman and that awful manager, Malcolm Alden, before the Court of Inquiry:

Malcom Alden: All of a sudden she [Jayaben Desai], kind of exploded and said 'I want my freedom. I am going. I have had enough'.

Lord Justice Scarman: Could you understand what she was shouting about?

Malcom Alden: 'I want my freedom' is the phrase that stands out in my mind.

Introduction

Graham Taylor

This book is being republished to celebrate the fortieth anniversary of the Grunwick strike, which began in August 1976. Anniversary events are being organised by a local group, Grunwick 40, and, while the strike itself was only a local event in the London borough of Brent, it unleashed passions that engulfed the whole country. Similarly, the anniversary is being celebrated by a trade union, the GMB (successor to the APEX union to which the Grunwick strikers belonged), with the celebrations including the reprint of this book. But the emotional appeal of this historic strike also stretched way beyond trade unions. The strike is still remembered after forty years, because it addresses deep questions. It is still posing questions to today's generation about the role in society of women, workers and immigrants. And the strike still carries, as it did from the start, a challenging message about the need for human dignity.

The first summer of the strike was the hottest August for twenty-nine years, and the beginnings of the strike were extremely haphazard, not to say chaotic. The strikers, as they said themselves, had no idea what they were doing. Nonetheless, even in those first few hesitant days, the strike was already accompanied by vivid scenes of passionate confrontation. For the next fifteen months, until the strike faltered, such images were to carry the name of Grunwick all around the world.

The debate about the strike was not always as broad as the issues it raised. The two questions usually asked in the 1980s were rather limited in scope: if the strike was a defeat, who was to blame? If it was a defeat, was it a total defeat or were there compensatory gains?

The first question can safely be left to the reader. The authors of this book were clear that 'it was the intervention of the right wing in the British labour movement' that was decisive. The Callaghan government felt that 'the electorate would be frightened off Labour if it had policies that were left-wing'. However, given the subsequent (some might say consequent) victory of Margaret Thatcher in the election of 1979, readers blessed with the benefit of hindsight may take the view that it was the intervention of the NAFF, backed by Thatcher, which was decisive.

With regard to the second question, the reader needs more help, since the effects of the strike naturally post-date the end of the book. Was defeat total? Or were there solid gains to justify the struggle? The indomitable leader of the strike, Jayaben Desai, had a clear-cut answer. She refused to concede that it was a defeat at all. From her ethical standpoint, what mattered most was whether George Ward, the proprietor of Grunwick, had secured a moral victory. She was sure he had not. History would one day vindicate her against Ward and his powerful backers. Jayaben said: 'I am proud of what I did. They wanted to break us down, but we did not break.' Union recognition and reinstatement were desirable ends for her but what mattered was that she had restored her own self-respect, and the self-respect of others.

Not everyone has Jayaben's faith in historical justice. Most people need the evidence of more immediate benefits. Paradoxically, the group that visibly seemed to benefit most from the strike were those who continued to work in the factory. For the NAFF and Thatcher, the struggle was ideological and they felt no expense should be spared to win. Thus, the company gave pay rises in November 1976 and April 1977, so as to retain the strikebreaking workforce, and rules about compulsory overtime were explained more clearly to staff in order to reduce clashes between managers and workers, which might otherwise have led to fresh walk-outs.

Some may well argue that looking for compensatory gains is whistling in the dark. It is generally accepted that the defeat at Grunwick was a major step forward for the right wing of the Conservative Party, that it contributed substantially to Thatcher's victory in the 1979 election, and that it was the 'dress-rehearsal' for her ruthless demolition of the trade-union movement in the 1980s.

In fact, however, there were gains from the strike that do stand up to scrutiny. On the trade-union level, Grunwick was the first strike where ethnic minority strikers received proper backing from trade-union officials. Further, the strike proved that white trade unionists were prepared to support black and Asian strikers. There had been a dispute in 1972 involving East African Asians at Mansfield Hosiery Mills in Loughborough. The workers had found themselves opposed by the white employer and yet not assisted by the white union officials. At Imperial Typewriters in 1974, an Asian workforce (mostly women) had also faced racism from both managers and white trade unionists. But, on Grunwick, the unions had an exemplary record.

This reversal in the trade-union position on racism contributed to a social revolution in Britain. The Grunwick picket lines and demonstrations lasted for months, and animated conversation in highly charged circumstances broke down barriers between men and women, black and white, straight and gay, young and old. The feeling of togetherness, transcending all social divisions, often translated into personal feelings of liberation and self-confidence. Even years afterwards, Grunwick strikers reported positive feelings about their participation. They cherished the feelings of human warmth and solidarity that had emanated from total strangers on the picket lines and in relation to the strike, and recollected fondly the friendships they had forged, as it were, on the barricades. Their new self-confidence often had concrete outcomes. One Grunwick striker described how, when made redundant from her next job without adequate notice, she sought advice from the Citizens Advice Bureau, took on her employer for unfair dismissal, and won the case.

Jayaben Desai herself was already active before the strike, in the Indian community in Wembley where she lived, but after 1978, she further developed a women's group for the Brent Indian Association, continued her teaching of Gujarati, taught dressmaking (she was a trained tailor) and participated in the Gujarati Literary Academy. After she learnt to drive, at the age of sixty, she once again caused controversy. She encouraged other Indian women to drive, thus provoking angry clashes with fathers and husbands.

Other women strikers, in the wake of the strike, also took up social work. Jayaben said she noticed an improvement in race relations – Indian women were now looked on with more respect by white society. On the other hand, according to a leading member of the Wembley Gujarati community, Vipool Kalyani, the position of women inside the community has improved only a little since 1978. Although Jayaben has been praised in many films and books, and been honoured by the trade-union movement (including a gold medal in 2007 from the GMB union), some Gujarati men still refuse to honour her because they disapprove of forceful, independent women. She remains to this day a prophet not fully honoured in her own community.

After the thirtieth anniversary celebration of the strike, held at Brent's Tricycle Theatre in September 2006, renewed debate about the strike began to open up. By that time the strike had become part of history and was ready for retrospective analysis, chiefly from feminist- and class-based perspectives.

Before that, some interesting documents appeared from the Special Branch files, published in response to a Freedom of Information request. The files helped the reputation of the strikers, by vindicating them from the accusations of violence with which they had been besmeared by the right-wing press. The police were clear that the violence came from interlopers (political extremists) and not the 'genuine pickets' (with official armbands). Of course, the strikers would have added that some of the worst violence came from the police themselves, as was well-attested.

In 2008, a brilliant new film was produced by Chris Thomas, *The Great Grunwick Strike 1976-78: A History*. It ends at a GMB conference addressed by Gordon Brown. The film took the line that the strike was betrayed by trade-union and Labour leaders but it also adopted a new approach, by going back to the words of the original strikers by interviewing them again after thirty years. Thomas had already made two films about Grunwick, *Standing Up* (1977) and *Look Back at Grunwick* (1978), but this film was superior in terms of its analysis and human interest.

It was from 2009 onwards, that an academic reassessment of the strike began to appear. Linda McDowell, Ruth Pearson and Sundari Anitha (who wrote the entry for Jayaben Desai in the *Oxford Dictionary of National Biography*) had been researching other strikes involving Asian women. These included the Burnsall strike in Birmingham (1992), the Hillingdon Hospital cleaners strike (1995), the Lufthansa Skychef strike (1998) and finally the Gate Gourmet strike (2005), which involved women workers producing airline meals for British Airways at Heathrow Airport. To illustrate the trend of their research, they mounted an exhibition, *Striking Women*, at the Women's Library in London. Jayaben Desai attended. They followed up with a series of articles in 2010-14 on the relationship between class, gender, ethnicity and trade unions. A book on these strikes by

Ruth Pearson and Sundari Anitha is due to be published in 2017 by Lawrence and Wishart.

Their articles argued that, though Grunwick was celebrated as a turning point in trade-union history, little had been written about the original perspectives of the women workers involved. Their feeling was that, while the strike became a struggle for union representation once the strikers had contacted APEX, it was important to remember that in the eyes of those workers it was above all a struggle for dignity and fair treatment in the workplace. Although the trade union movement initially backed the strikers 100 per cent, it ultimately withdrew its support, which the women regarded as a betrayal. In their article in 2012, they also noted that in writings about these disputes 'ethnicity always seems to outweigh class and gender' but usually workers suffered injustice on all three counts.

The trend in much of the research on strikes since 2007 (another example is the recent article by George Stevenson on the Trico strike in *Labour History Review*), is towards a return to the words and experiences of the strikers themselves. This can only be healthy. The trade-union movement naturally pushed its concerns for better pay and conditions, and naturally wanted to recruit from the unorganised ethnic minorities but the result was that class and gender were often given less prominence than pay demands and race. In fact, all four were important and the academic research has usefully corrected a longstanding imbalance.

Jayaben Desai united in one person these very issues of gender, race and class, and she did not ignore pay either. Indeed, she went further and called for freedom from all oppression ('I want my freedom'). She walked out in 1976 for self-respect, pride and dignity. She did not wish to be humiliated by anyone with power over her, whether as an Indian, a woman or a worker. She seems to have been born a fighter against injustice. In 2011 at a meeting in Willesden Library a very old man recounted what he said was his clearest memory of Jayaben as a child. When she was only six or seven, he said, the boys were taught how to ride and repair a bicycle but the girls were not. Jayaben demanded to know why this was and, when given a dismissive reason, refused to accept it. Everyone was astounded. In the book she reacts in a similarly spontaneous fashion to perceived racial discrimination ('this man wouldn't speak to white workers like he speaks to us') and as a socialist in reaction to class privilege ('It is their money against our pride'). Over all this, however, there stands an overarching ethical framework: 'The strike is not about the money. This is what Ward will never understand. The strike is for our human dignity – and we cannot live without it.'

I was inspired to write this book by Jayaben Desai, and I sent off a proposal to Lawrence & Wishart in July 1977. I wanted her never to be forgotten. Jack was brought in as co-author for his invaluable trade-union expertise and for his outstanding role in the strike. All through the winter of 1976-77, I had stood on the picket line in Chapter Road with Jayaben, and had been writing down, for publication in articles, the torrent of colourful words and phrases that she effortlessly produced. I remember interviewing her on the picket-line in November 1976, when she made one of her most famous statement: 'What you are running here is not a factory but a zoo'. It seemed as if everything she said was a memorable quotation.

Jayaben died on 23 December, 2010. I wrote in my obituary: 'Jayaben was unbowed by defeat. She had fought to the end, unlike some, and could hold her head up high … She was part of a movement for human rights which stretched from Rosa Parks to Nelson Mandela, and that movement was victorious' (*Morning Star* 8-9 January 2011). She subscribed to the beautiful Hindu idea that rivers unite the human race by all flowing into the common ocean. Some of her ashes were therefore scattered in Kailas, in Tibet, in China, near the sources for four rivers, including the Indus and the Ganges. The Kailas Mountain is said, after all, to be the abode of Lord Shiva, the destroyer of all ignorance and illusion. Other ashes were scattered in the pilgrimage centre of Allahabad in India, a confluence of three rivers. Finally, some ashes were scattered just east of Cherry Garden Pier in Rotherhithe on the Thames, just in front of the place where the only statue in London stands to a woman trade unionist, Ada Salter, another heroine of the GMB.

What was left behind in the ruins of the Grunwick strike was inspiration, and this inspiration came largely from one woman, Jayaben Desai. Though a Shivaite, she was also a universalist. When in old age she and her husband travelled across Asia, from Moscow to Mongolia and China, she took care always to light a candle in every church, temple or mosque they came across. But the greatest candle she lit was in the streets of Willesden, outside the Grunwick factory. It was the candle of human dignity. The other candles have long since flickered and failed, but the light of the Grunwick candle will shine brightly into the future, inspiring indomitable resistance in new generations of exploited workers, women and ethnic minorities.

1978 Foreword

This is the only book on the Grunwick strike approved by the Strike Committee. In a letter to the publishers, the Committee wrote:

> This book is the inside story of the strike and we recommend our supporters to read it. It faithfully reflects our experience during an epic struggle that we so nearly won. This book is essential reading for all those who want to understand the lessons of the Grunwick strike, a strike that brought out the very best and the very worst in our trade-union and labour movement.

The book is written from the point of view of the trade-union movement. Both of the authors are trade unionists who participated actively and personally in solidarity action with the strikers. The book has been checked for its accuracy and interpretation by representatives of the Strike Committee and by other trade unionists who were closely involved. We would like to thank in particular Kamlesh Gandhi, Mahmood Ahmad and Jayaben Desai, the Chairman, Secretary and Treasurer respectively, and Bill Henwood and Vipin Magdani of the Strike Committee, as well as Tom Durkin and Ken Gill.

Despite our total commitment to the cause of the strikers, we believe this book accurately records all the important facts of the Grunwick strike and that history will bear out its interpretation. We have taken care to mention all the major arguments put by the company and, where we think that the union side erred or exaggerated its case, we have said so. The quotations from the Scarman Court of Inquiry are based on the transcript of an independent firm, W. A. Gurney and Sons of 39 Victoria Street, Westminster; quotations from the Scarman Report itself are from its official publication (HMSO, August 1977). Any incident described or any quotation made which is not given a reference is from the personal experience of one of the two authors. The quotations from newspapers during the mass picket (see Chapters 11-13) are taken from the issues of the following day.

Finally, we must thank our publishers for giving us the opportunity to give this account of Grunwick, and for their understanding over many months for two authors who had to try and coordinate their thoughts and views in the middle of the very conflict they were attempting to describe. Responsibility for the final version rests, of course, with none of the people we have thanked but only with ourselves.

June 1978

Chronology

1964-5	Grunwick Processing planned and launched.
1972	Grunwick moves to Willesden (Cobbold Road).
1973	The first dispute for union recognition at Grunwick after some members of the Transport & General Workers Union (TGWU) were made redundant.
1975	Grunwick leases premises at Chapter Road from Brent Council.

1976

20 August	The first walk-out.
23 August	The strike begins: the first picket of Grunwick since 1973.
24 August	Sixty strikers join the Association of Professional, Executive, Clerical and Computer Staffs (APEX). Management offers to take back strikers provided they drop the idea of a union: they refuse.
31 August	Advisory Conciliation and Arbitration Service (ACAS) offers mediation. The company refuses.
1 September	Grunwick receives official letter from APEX, seeking a meeting.
2 September	Grunwick sacks the 137 strikers.
14 September	Jayaben Desai taken to hospital after management car passes over her foot. Police refuse to act.
20 September	Police arrest picket for obstruction.
23 September	Woman hospitalised after being knocked down by management car.
5 October	Roy Grantham of APEX calls for court of inquiry.

15 October   Lobby of Parliament. APEX officially refers the dispute to ACAS upon the advice of the Secretary of State for Employment.

1 November   Union of Post-Office Workers (UPW) blacks Grunwick mail. Police arrest nine pickets.

4 November   Debate in Parliament on Grunwick. UPW forced to abandon blacking under threat of legal action and in return for a promise from Grunwick to cooperate with ACAS.

25 November Grunwick increases wages by 15 per cent.

12 December Len Murray supports strikers at Brent Trades Hall.

29 December ACAS despairs of winning Grunwick's cooperation for a ballot of the workforce.

1977

10 March   Final ACAS report finds in favour of the strikers and recommends recognition of APEX. But police arrest four more pickets and Grunwick says it will take ACAS to court and have the report declared invalid.

23 March   General Council of the TUC effectively turns down the first request by APEX for the blacking of essential services. An Industrial Tribunal rules it has 'no jurisdiction' to say whether the strikers were sacked fairly or unfairly.

1 April   Grunwick implements promised wage increase of 10 per cent.

27 April   Over 1400 march through Willesden in support of the strike.

3 May   Middlesex Crown Court finds arrested pickets innocent and censures the police. Police are ordered to pay costs.

19 May   Three government ministers join the picket line.

13-17 June   Mass picket called, for one week only.

13 June   Police arrest eighty-four pickets on the first day.

14 June   Bus used to drive 'loyal workers' through the picket

line; eleven more 'loyal workers' join the strikers in the first two days.

15 June   On the advice of the UPW's London District Council, the Cricklewood sorters launch the unofficial blacking of Grunwick mail.

21 June   Labour MP Audrey Wise arrested on the picket line.

23 June   Arthur Scargill (President of the Yorkshire Miners) arrested. PC Trevor Wilson hit by a bottle – a tragedy for the strikers, exploited to the full by the media.

30 June   Booth announces the Scarman Court of Inquiry.

10 July   'Operation Pony Express' by the National Association For Freedom (the NAFF).

11 July   Nearly 20,000 in demonstration against the company. Seven more 'loyal workers' join the strikers. At Chapter Road the company bus is prevented from entering for the whole morning.

12 July   High Court decision (Widgery) in favour of ACAS, against Grunwick.

29 July   Black Friday. Postal workers vote to end their blacking. Strikers vote to call off the 8 August mass picket. Appeal Court (Denning) overturns the High Court decision of 12 July: ACAS report now declared invalid.

25 August   Scarman Report published. Calls for union recognition and reinstatement while criticising the mass picket and the postal blacking. Welcomed as a victory by APEX.

31 August   Grunwick rejects the Scarman Report.

6 September   Unanimous agreement to step up the campaign against Grunwick after short debate at the TUC Congress.

29 September   Strike Committee calls for new mass picket on 17 October.

17 October   Mass picket 5000 strong.

7 November   Mass picket 8000 strong: 113 arrests; 243 pickets injured.

21 November   Hunger strike outside the TUC by Jayaben Desai, Vipin Magdani, Johnny Patel and Yasu Patel.

14 December   House of Lords confirms 29 July decision against
              ACAS. APEX responds by making a second reference
              to ACAS.

1978

14 May   National conference in Wembley called by the strikers.

15 May   Ward rejects the ACAS proposal for a ballot of the
              workforce to be conducted by Grunwick's own
              solicitors. He dismisses ACAS as the 'Association of
              Comrades for the Advancement of Socialism'.

14 July   Strike Committee announces end of strike.

1

Inside 'The Zoo'

From the very beginning, even before it entered the political arena, the Grunwick Strike was a trade-union phenomenon. Within eight days of the first walk-outs it won the official backing of a union that had no previous tradition of militancy. Less than a week from its recognition, it drew stormy applause from a TUC conference committed to moderating workers' pay demands. Although only a local dispute, the strike seized the headlines of press, radio and television in under three months and was international news within ten. Though the strike was earnestly debated in the highest courts of the country, though hundreds of pickets were arrested, though thousands of police were deployed in street battles, the strike was started, almost fortuitously, by six individuals who had never been trade-union members, had never been on strike and who barely knew what a union was.

It was consistently a record-breaking strike. It was the most militant in British history by a white-collar union. It attracted over 550 arrests, more than any dispute since the General Strike of 1926. Although not a national strike, it forced a panic-stricken government to set up a Court of Inquiry. It even made post-war history by bringing five hundred MPs to attend the House of Commons on a Friday afternoon.

Many commentators have attempted to explain what it was in the atmosphere of August 1976, or in the nature of the strike, that enabled this tiny dispute to attract worldwide interest and support. As we shall see, much of the answer lies in high politics but partly it lies in the history of Grunwick.

'Grunwick Processing Laboratories Ltd' was formed in March 1965 by three men, Anthony Grundy, George Ward and John Hickey, hence the name, 'Grunwick'. They started off at Loudoun Road Mews, St John's Wood, with Grundy attending to sales, Hickey to production and Ward supplying the money from capital accumulated after three years' work in Brazil.

At first Grunwick's operations were confined to 'processing' (that is, developing and printing) black-and-white films for photographers. Later, the company made 'mail order' the central part of its business, moved into the processing of colour films and won customers in the Netherlands, Belgium and West Germany as well as in Britain. Amateur photographers were encouraged by various marketing devices (such as free film offers) to post their films to the company which would process them in its 'laboratories' and then return them as soon as possible. The company was successful because of its rapid turnaround of film, its quality of work and its cheap rates.

As photographers turned to more expensive colour film, the company prospered and grew. By 1972 it was able to move to a site off Cobbold Road, Willesden, where its small fleet of blue vans and its colour film-processing departments are now based. In 1973, Grunwick merged with another small company, Cooper and Pearson, situated in Chapter Road, Willesden, a family business dating back to 1946. So rapid was the company's progress on the mail-order side of the business that, by 1974, it had to rent the thirteenth floor of Station House, Wembley, in order to house a large computer. To cope with the summer rush – one hot weekend could overwhelm them with work – it took to hiring students when business reached a peak.

The company's last expansion came in October 1975 when it leased premises from Brent Council on Chapter Road, next to the Cooper and Pearson building. It was this small complex of buildings that was to become familiar on television screens all over Europe as the scene of confrontation between pickets and police.

Chapter Road is normally a quiet road by London standards. Its main advantage was probably its proximity to the Cobbold Road processing plant, only half a mile away on the other side of Willesden High Road. The fact that the new premises were only a few paces from Dollis Hill tube station must have seemed an added attraction. The management was not to know that this convenience would make it an easy meeting place later for thousands of trade unionists from all over Britain.

The company lavished expense on its new project. It spent £70,000 modernising the Chapter Road premises before opening them for business in April 1976. The company was consolidated in Willesden by transferring the computer and the clerical staff from Station House, Wembley, to Chapter Road. The modernised premises – with a sign at the front still saying 'Cooper and Pearson' – housed the now greatly expanded Mail-Order Department. By August 1976, when the strike broke out, Grunwick employed about 480 people in all, with the majority of staff working at Cobbold Road but with Chapter Road not far behind. Of the 160-170 staff in Chapter Road about a hundred were concentrated in the Mail-Order Department. This department was the very heart of the business, where Grunwick secured its extraordinary returns upon capital invested, through the elimination of retailers by direct mailing to the customer. It was here that the strike which amazed the country first broke out.

The staff in 'mail order' in 1976 were nearly all immigrants, mostly East Africans of Indian origin whose native language was, in the majority of cases, Gujarati. Many were also women, some dressed in saris, some in European clothes. In August, there were additionally large numbers of students, also East Africans as a rule. Of the total weekly-paid workforce of 429 when the strike began about 140 were students, some of whom worked in the Mail-Order Department.

The trouble began not on Monday 23 August 1976, the official anniversary of the strike, but on the previous Friday afternoon. Devshi Bhudia was a young worker, aged nineteen, not a student, who had joined the staff of Grunwick in September 1975. At about 9.30 a.m., according to his own account, Bhudia, who was already discontented with pay and conditions, fell into an argument with the manager of the Mail-Order Department, Malcolm Alden. The manager wanted Bhudia to supervise the students in his work area, but Bhudia would agree only if he was given extra money. The manager was not pleased by his unexpected resistance but, on the other hand, Bhudia, as everyone agreed, was a good worker. Alden therefore ordered Bhudia to get on with it, but also promised a possible rise at a later date. There the matter rested.

Later that day, around lunchtime, Bhudia was suddenly presented with thirteen crates of new work, mail for despatch which had to be sorted and batched according to destination, for the computer. Alden asked how long a crate took and was told that it would take ten minutes for one person. He gave Bhudia and those working under him one hour to complete the thirteen crates. Alden had a reputation as a tough manager, as a sacking manager, and as a manager who did not take kindly to the sort of resistance Bhudia had put up in the morning. Bhudia feared he had deliberately been set a difficult target and at the end of the hour would be called to Alden's office and, like so many before him, be dismissed for 'unsatisfactory work', behind closed doors, with no means of appeal.

Bhudia was personally not too concerned about being sacked, but he and his friends had been bitter for some time about what they regarded as the 'bullying tactics' of the management. Bhudia had become so discontented that he had gone to the length of getting another job. It was that card up his sleeve which had given him the courage to stand up to Alden in the morning. But it was not enough just to leave. The students thought it was selfish just to walk out without making an effort to improve conditions for the rest of the workforce. In a discussion a week or two before, they had decided to protest if the opportunity presented itself. As one of Bhudia's friends, Chandrakant Patel, was later to tell the Court of Inquiry, the protest he now made was not just to relieve his own feelings, it was 'because I couldn't stand the grievances which people had in the firm'.

Malcolm Alden, the Mail-Order Department manager, was thirty-two and had just that month been appointed a director of the company, having joined Grunwick in 1970 as a data-processing manager. He projected an aggressive manner that played a significant role in the dispute. On the picket line in the winter months it was to be Alden, pale-faced and intense, who took the lead in baiting the pickets on duty. It was Alden who would hurl the pickets' placards into the gutter, yelling at the bespectacled Manji Varsani: 'Keep that off our property, four-eyes!' It was Alden who later drove the blacklegs' bus. His rigorous time-saving on behalf of others was less strictly applied to himself, for on most afternoons in the winter of 1976-7 he could be seen in the yard of Chapter Road glowering at the pickets who would nudge visitors and whisper: 'That's Alden. He does this all the time. He's the one who started the strike.'

Alden was very conscious that the Mail-Order Department was the most labour intensive at Grunwick. It was also the department which was vital to the quick turnaround of film that Grunwick's competitiveness required. His policy was, therefore, in his own words to the Court of Inquiry, to 'press' the workforce in that department. He devised a scheme of individual output records for each worker so that productivity could be raised by identifying the slower workers, and he backed up his pressure with dismissals or threats of dismissals, so that in 1976 the labour turnover in his department, at a time of high unemployment, was some hundred per cent turnover per year.

Lord Justice Scarman's Court of Inquiry later felt obliged to devote a separate paragraph of its report to the managerial style of Malcolm Alden. Scarman characterised it as follows: 'Mr Alden was doing his duty as he saw it: he was a tough manager determined to maintain a high level of productivity. He believed in discipline and believed that it was his discipline that mattered.'

One of the witnesses at the Court, Jayaben Desai, had put the matter more starkly: Alden 'wanted to put such an impression on the staff that everybody would be scared by him. That was his attitude from the first … Anybody, any time, we expected our sack.'

This fear of dismissal was one of the fundamental grievances at Grunwick. Devshi Bhudia has related how, not long after he started at the firm, a lad working near him had been fired and his girlfriend had walked out in a futile protest. According to the evidence of a supervisor, Rajeshwari Patel, sackings in the Mail-Order Department averaged about two per month in 1975-7. She guessed that problems with the compulsory overtime were the main reason but she was unsure because she was never told why the workers she supervised were dismissed. In the last six weeks before the strike, out of a total workforce of 102 in Mail-Order, nine were sacked and eighteen left. In annual terms, that is a labour turnover of 230 per cent. Psychologically, however, the effect on the workers was even more damaging than the figures indicate; as they were never told the reason for a sudden departure, they assumed that nearly all of those who left had in fact been sacked.

There was one grievance, however, which many workers rated as more deeply felt than either the job insecurity or the harsh discipline: the nature of the compulsory overtime. Of course, all the Grunwick workers had accepted compulsory overtime when they took their jobs. There was a question about it on the application form and a contract to sign later on. There is also no doubt that, on a basic starting pay of £28 for a forty hour week for process workers and £25 for thirty-five hours for clerical workers, all the employees needed overtime – at one and a quarter times the basic rate for the first six hours and time and a half thereafter – if they were to take home a reasonable wage. What new recruits did not reckon with, however, was the disruption of their private lives that could be caused by long hours imposed at short notice. As Indira Mistry, who worked sixty-five hours per week in the summer, told the Scarman Inquiry: when she took the job, she had certainly accepted 'compulsory overtime' but not overtime compulsory 'till ten o'clock at night'.

Malcolm Alden was usually uncompromising on overtime because he was determined to handle all the work that came into Mail-Order that day. Jayaben Desai explained Alden's attitude to compulsory overtime as follows: Mr Alden would say, 'Look, you have a contract and you have signed this contract and you have to do what we want. We do not want to listen to your problems.' Indira Mistry, for example, was refused permission to attend a relative's wedding on a Saturday. When the workers drew up a petition seeking permission to leave work in time for a Hindu festival at 8 p.m., Alden, they alleged at the Court of Inquiry later, just tore it up. Again, this grievance played its part in Bhudia's rebellion. It was compulsory overtime at short notice applied once too often that had caused him and his friends to hold their subversive discussion the week before.

Petitions and complaints were not easy, however, for discipline was strict. Wage rises, time off and remission from compulsory overtime were all quite possible but, as their introduction was at the discretion of management, they formed a huge incentive to conform to management's demands. Holidays in the summer months were also at management's discretion. Devshi Bhudia had received a week's holiday that summer, but he was acknowledged by management to be a good worker. Smoking was forbidden. At one stage, visits to the toilet were strictly rationed. According to Indira Mistry's evidence she once spent six minutes in the toilet and was told by a manager, Mr Luther: 'that's five minutes off your pay'. As for time off, she explained: 'We had to have a good reason to get off earlier – a very good reason. If your reason was going to the doctors or the dentists it is not a good reason for Mr Alden ... He used to say, if you were sick and wanted to go off earlier: "Why don't you be sick during Saturdays or Sundays instead of working hours?"' When she was sick and stayed away, Alden didn't believe her doctor's certificate. Instead he gave her the benefit of his own ascetic philosophy: 'If I had a throat infection I would come to work'.

The unease that spread among the Grunwick workers in August 1976 was intensified by one of the hottest summers in British history. The drought was so severe that the Government had to appoint a special minister to deal with it: Denis Howell, Minister for Sport, and President of a white-collar union called APEX. This appointment did

nothing, however, for the workers in Chapter Road, where the promised air-conditioning unit had still not been delivered by 20 August.
They laboured in the heat of the Mail-Order Department week after
week, nearly a hundred immigrants, working in rows at long tables,
in a room with no windows, constantly overlooked by a management
whose glass-fronted offices faced onto the workroom. The management
claimed proudly that their offices represented 'management-from-the-
front', a situation where managers were always visible and accessible
to the workforce. To the workers it looked as if the glass was there to
make their every move visible and accessible to the management. They
found this increasingly unbearable in the sticky heat, which was quite
unlike that of East Africa. The workers were 'boiling' inside Chapter
Road, Jayaben Desai told Scarman, and 'one girl, when she asked to
keep the door open of the office, Mr Alden he made her cry and said
"Who are you telling me my job? I know what to do".'

The heat, added to a draconian discipline that frowned upon
too much laughing or talking, gradually generated a claustrophobic
feeling. It was this ugly sense of being enclosed and hemmed in, of
being physically imprisoned, that was to make one placard in particular a special favourite in the first week of the strike; 'GRUNWICK
IS A ZOO' was all it said. It was a simple slogan which summed up a
deeply-felt reaction.

Devshi Bhudia, Chandrakant Patel, Bharat Patel and Suresh
Ruparelia knew nothing of trade unions. Another worker, Sunil Desai,
had mentioned the phrase to them but as Sunil had little understanding
himself of trade unions the subject had soon been dropped. The four
friends therefore decided that, as nothing could be done constitutionally, their protest would have to be of an irregular nature. In any case,
for the two who were students, there was little personal risk, as they
would be leaving in a couple of weeks to return to their studies. So the
four made a pact that Friday afternoon. They would work as slowly as
possible right under Alden's nose. The crux of the pact was that when
Alden sacked one of them, as they felt sure he was about to do anyway,
the other three would walk out in protest. It is a revealing comment on
Grunwick management that four youths could predict accurately that
they would react only in such an extreme fashion.

Alden watched their go-slow but, as he was talking to Kenneth
Pearson, another director, it was not until 3.30 that he called Bhudia
into his office. The thirteen crates had still not been sorted. There was

a row between Bhudia and Alden, and Bhudia was sacked. Bhudia came out, picked up his newspaper and walked out of the building. His three workmates then crossed over to Alden's office and told Alden they thought Bhudia's dismissal was unfair, and that they were therefore resigning in protest.

Outside the Chapter Road gate the four rebels stood around in a group talking angrily. It soon became apparent that, having made their high-minded protest, they were at a loss what to do next. All they had achieved by sacrificing their jobs and at least two weeks' pay was probably nothing more than a minor disruption of Alden's schedule, soon put right by a little extra overtime. After much discussion they still failed to come up with any really practical proposals, apart from letting down the tyres on Alden's Jaguar, a course of action they rejected.

The Grunwick Strike could easily have ended right there, with four frustrated young men arguing on the pavement of Chapter Road; if unexpected reinforcements had not come to their aid they would probably have drifted home. Indeed, even if an experienced trade unionist had chanced to walk by, the young men would not have been much encouraged. They could have been advised only that Grunwick was a most unlikely place for any strike at all. Anyone acquainted with industrial relations would have argued that smallish companies were harder to organise than big, that women were less experienced in trade unionism than men, while first generation immigrants were normally too grateful to have jobs, or too lacking in confidence, to hope to lead an effective struggle.

It was through inexperience, therefore, that the young men stayed at the gate. Instead of drifting away they stayed put. That was their contribution to history. They did not know that their desperate action would prepare the way for an all-out strike. They did not realise that Grunwick was a time bomb of grievances and they were the fuse.

2

On The Track

One of the features of the Grunwick Strike that undoubtedly fixed attention upon it, was the fact that the strike force was composed almost entirely of immigrant labourers. Of those immigrants, the vast majority were the so-called 'East African Asians' and, of those East Africans, about half had arrived in Britain from Uganda, the rest coming from Kenya and Tanzania. Their role in the Grunwick Strike was – at a time when the labour movement was combatting racism not only outside but also inside its own ranks – to explode the prevalent myth that first generation immigrants are incapable of struggling for workers' rights. Their involvement in the strike reassured those who feared that immigrants undermined the pay and conditions for which British trade unionists had struggled over 200 years.

The 'East African Asians' were by origin 'British' Indians, many of whom had been taken by the rulers of the British Empire to East Africa when India was still a colony. They differed considerably from other immigrants to Britain in a number of important respects. For one thing, they were better educated than earlier immigrants, who had mainly come to Britain from the West Indies, India and Pakistan to escape low living standards and high unemployment. For another, when the 'Asians' were forced to leave East Africa they arrived in Britain not in a period of an expanding economy and high employment, as did immigrants in the 1950s, but in a period of mass unemployment and ongoing and rising racism. Lastly, unlike most other Commonwealth immigrants, they migrated to Britain not voluntarily but under compulsion. They were therefore often not willing immigrants but reluctant refugees.

The 1890s was a worrying time for the Empire. In 'British' Sudan, north of East Africa, British troops were 'forced' to slaughter 40,000 rebels in one battle. To the south, the discovery of gold and diamonds had created an explosive situation in 'Rhodesia', where white aggressors claimed to have killed 10,000 black people in four days. Uganda's Lake 'Victoria', source of the Nile, was held to be strategically vital to this bloodbath. So it was that in the decade before 1903 a railway track was built, linking Lake Victoria to British warships on the coast. The railway was delayed at first because the native labour of Kenya was insufficiently skilled to build the track. The British authorities therefore imported labourers across the Indian Ocean from Gujarat in the north-west of India. The Gujaratis belonged to a civilization much older than Europe's. Not far to the north of Gujarat, at Harappa and Mohenjo-Daro in Pakistan, are the first cities known in history. The capital of Gujarat itself, Ahmadabad, now a huge textile centre three times the size of Manchester, was part of a culture dating back to a time when Britain was still an underdeveloped country of illiterate tribes. These were the 'East African Asians'.

Thousands of Gujaratis and other Indians had to be brought in to build the railway which would supposedly keep the Nile forever British. Although many of the original workers returned to India, thousands came in their wake to service the railway community. The military, perhaps like Grunwick management later, believed the Gujaratis would prove more docile and industrious than the local tribes. They certainly proved to be industrious. Once the railway was built, no doubt with compulsory overtime, the 'Asians' soon became the artisans, craftsmen and shopkeepers of East Africa, forming a middle class between the new white landowners and the unskilled black-Africans.

When Kenya, Uganda and Tanzania achieved independence in the early 1960s, the imported 'East African Asians' hoped to be assimilated in these new countries. It was not to be. The British authorities, following the divide-and-rule policy so successful in Ireland, Cyprus, Palestine, Malaya and India, had been careful to encourage animosity between the Africans and the Gujaratis. In time, Gujarati clannishness in a foreign land had come to be seen by the underprivileged black-Africans as an economic obstacle second only to that of the white colonists. When independence came, the 'Asians', fearing the worst, opted to retain their British passports.

The 'Asians'' fears were soon realised in all three countries, although it was Kenya, the most right-wing, which first forced them to leave in large numbers in the late 1960s. The climax was reached in January 1971 when tanks under the command of Idi Amin captured

Kampala, the capital of Uganda, and overthrew the government of Milton Obote. Uganda had been moving in a socialist direction and Obote, so as to be less dependent on Britain and the USA, had been drawing closer to the USSR. The British businessmen and military officers, whom Obote had unwisely allowed to remain in Uganda, therefore welcomed the black nationalism of Amin for, whatever it was, at least it was not socialism. In London, Edward Heath promptly showed the Conservative government's approval by making Britain the first country to recognise Amin's regime.

Within twelve months of his coup the huge and apparently jovial figure of Idi Amin had announced that Ugandan 'Asians' with British passports would be expelled from Uganda. Driving out 'Asians' was not an original idea. As early as 1968, Jomo Kenyatta of Kenya had panicked 'Asians' into fleeing by declaring they would never receive Kenyan citizenship and by placing restrictions on their trading activities. Amin's originality lay not in the idea but in the speed and ruthlessness of the mass expulsions between August and October 1972. Of the 40,000 'Asians' expelled that summer, just over 27,000 disembarked in Britain. Some went to India, though they were foreigners there. The rest joined thousands of Kenyan 'Asians' already settled in Britain as a result of pressure from Kenyatta. The Ugandan 'Asians' dispersed all over Britain, but the largest number settled in the outer London borough of Brent, in the areas of Wembley and Willesden, where they took unskilled and semi-skilled jobs with companies like Grunwick, ironically alongside the railway track of the Bakerloo line.

Could they not have stayed in Uganda and thus have avoided reliving the 1890s? The difficulty was that Amin was a particularly unpleasant imperial product whose notoriety dated back to the 1950s. Trained in Wiltshire, England, Amin had served with the British King's African Rifles during the 'Mau Mau' rising in Kenya. Unlike Julius Nyerere of Tanzania and Kenyatta of Kenya, Amin had stood not on the side of his own people but on the side of the imperial forces. Over 10,000 black-Africans were killed by the British 'security forces' with which Amin served, and over a thousand 'Mau Mau' were executed. In return the 'security forces' lost 600 uniformed men and 1700 civilians. When Idi Amin seized power in 1971 with Heath's blessing, the 'Asians' decided not to stay and argue.

They would certainly not have migrated to Britain – and to lower standards of living – had they been given security in Uganda. The borough of Brent was in industrial decline in 1971, while Uganda was economically prosperous. Unlike the Ugandan capital, Kampala, which had tripled its population since Uganda's independence in 1962, Brent had lost nearly 40,000 people in the same period. While Kampala was adding tree-lined avenues of white, modern buildings to its multicoloured array of mosques and church steeples, the grimy streets of Willesden were breaking out into a grey rash of derelict shops, disused factories and abandoned houses. Kampala lies only twenty-one miles north of Lake Victoria, not far from the source of the White Nile. The blue surface of the vast lake is encircled by lush vegetation of greens and yellows. The greyish-brown dilapidation of Willesden is another world.

Unlike some other immigrants, therefore, the East Africans were compelled to settle in Britain. Their resentment at the treatment they had received was heightened by the welcome awaiting them. Amin's actions, together with Heath's Immigration Act of 1971 and the speeches on race of Conservative MP Enoch Powell, had already triggered off a new wave of racism in Britain itself. The National Front, a neo-fascist party, looked as though it might become an electoral force. To their dismay the Ugandan 'Asians', who had been shuttled from country to country like so much excess baggage, now found themselves less than wanted in the very country that had guaranteed them protection in 1962. They had no reason to be grateful to Britain, whose rulers had used them as pawns for a hundred years. On the contrary, they were suspicious of what was in store for them next. Between Idi Amin and the National Front there is only the deep blue sea.

The PEP report of 1974 showed that of all the immigrant groups in Britain, the East African Asians had the highest qualifications and education but the lowest average earnings. They were mainly middle-class people forced to do unskilled or semi-skilled work. This may have played a large, though largely unstated, role in the origins of the Grunwick Strike. In the incidents recounted by some of the strikers there is a strong feeling of humiliation and a certain contempt for the managers, many of whom the strikers regarded as relatively unskilled at their jobs.

During the course of the dispute, these cultural forces occasionally surfaced. One day a white racist yelled abuse at a young woman on the picket line. His advice to her – to get back to her own country – was well-loaded with epithets she could not have discovered in the *Oxford*

English Dictionary. Would she tell him, perhaps, that for her there was no country to go back to? Before she could reply another woman, Jayaben Desai, had intervened. 'Do not argue with that man', she said proudly. 'He has no knowledge of history.'

3

The Strike Breaks Out

About two-and-half hours after the first walk-out, Jayaben Desai was packing up her work to go home. She was not aware of Bhudia's walkout but had been disturbed that afternoon when, in a separate incident, her son, Sunil Desai, had been harshly rebuked for talking too noisily. Although upset, she had put the incident to the back of her mind. She had lived through many worse injustices during her time at Grunwick.

Jayaben Desai is a slightly-built, middle-aged Indian woman, four feet ten inches high. She often dresses in a brightly-coloured sari and has warm, intelligent eyes separated by the traditional red spot worn by Hindu women who are not widows. Her English is good but she often talks so rapidly and with such feeling that she drives the English words out without waiting for syntax or grammar. Her powerful and attractive personality, her loving concern and her fierce pride later captured the imagination of the trade-union movement. The very idea of a shop steward in a sari was a novelty. Female, immigrant, of small stature, she came to typify the Grunwick Strike in the public mind. The sight of her diminutive figure, with a yellow cloak thrown over her shoulders, remonstrating with hundreds of blue-uniformed police officers who, in helmets, stood half as tall again, was enough to capture the front page of even the most hostile newspaper. Even at the Court of Inquiry she stole the show, defeating Grunwick's lawyer in two sharp skirmishes and earning the admiration of Lord Justice Scarman. She shattered forever in Britain the stereotype of the passive, obedient, Asian woman who is nothing more than a chattel to the male.

Like most of the strikers, Jayaben Desai is Gujarati by origin. Unlike the others she was actually born in Gujarat, then the province of Bombay. She married a Gujarati from Tanzania, Suryakant Desai, and lived in Tanzania for many years. Her husband was manager for a tyre company. When they arrived in Britain in 1969, they had to start all over again, he finding a job as an unskilled labourer for Desoutter Engineering in Wembley, she working on a sewing machine in a Harlesden workshop. With her husband improving his earnings, she was able to stay at home for a couple of years looking after her two children, but the need for extra money and the boredom of home eventually drove her to bag-filling at Grunwick, part-time in the evenings from 5 to 10 p.m. She found the job convenient in a period of worsening unemployment and, having worked part time for a couple of months, she signed up at Grunwick, Wembley as a full-time worker in the September of 1974.

Throughout the strike, after she had become nationally famous as the most militant representative of the women strikers, she always looked back on the assistant manager of the Mail-Order Department, Peter Diffy, as 'a nice person' and 'a fair man'. Diffy had joined Grunwick in 1971 from Kodak, and had read economics at London University. The labour turnover in his customer relations section was negligible compared to the Mail-Order Department as a whole.

Her relationship with Malcolm Alden was not so idyllic. When she signed her contract, she had wanted to read it first. Alden did not want valuable work time wasted. 'Sign it now and read it lunchtime', he said. Then there was the affair of the toilets. As she told the Court of Inquiry in her usual graphic fashion:

> One day I was going at nine o'clock because I have started eight o'clock on the job. I was passing from the gate and I saw Mr Alden entering in that office and I asked him 'Good morning, Mr Alden'. Instead of his reply he asked me: 'Where are you going?' I say I am going to ladies' and he said: 'Look, from now on, from this day, if you want to go in ladies' then you have to take permission from me, from Mr Diffy, or Mr Mike [Rickard] or Mr Dennis'!

It seemed to her that Alden lacked respect for the workers but she was not one to be easily rebuffed. On one occasion she asked Alden: 'Can't you say to me politely something?' He replied sharply: 'Don't tell me what to do'.

In her opinion Malcolm Alden's approach was to put maximum pressure on the workforce in terms of discipline. She told Lord Justice Scarman: 'First off, people were scared to go to him. That was his attitude. A person like me – I am never scared of anybody.'

Jayaben Desai was always vocal for her own rights and for those of others, even though there was no action she could take in a non-union company. Her forthright behaviour was noticed by the highest management but as she, like Bhudia, was a good worker, she was to some extent tolerated. In 1977, when George Ward, Grunwick's managing director, was speaking on Capital Radio, he portrayed her as 'a very difficult employee'. Her immediate manager, Peter Diffy was, in Ward's eyes, 'the kindliest manager we have'. Yet, as he explained: 'In the winter Mrs Desai would complain that it was too cold, so Mr Diffy would find her a heater. In the summer Mrs Desai would complain that it was too hot. Mr Diffy would find her a fan.' It was certainly true that Mrs Desai and Mr Diffy usually worked well together.

The whole of Jayaben Desai's history was remote from any tradition of passive obedience. At school she and her group of girl friends, in the midst of the movement for Indian independence, had been very self-reliant in their views. She remembers vaguely the imprisonment of Nehru and Gandhi by the British authorities. Gandhi was also a Gujarati and, after his assassination in 1948, she remembers hearing his lectures on philosophy broadcast over the Indian radio. Sometimes there is an echo of Gandhi in her thinking. 'Remember,' she once told a reporter, '... that all this industrialisation is still only materialistic. It brings happiness, yes, but it brings a misery too.'

Jayaben Desai was totally unprepared for what happened next on that Friday afternoon. It was not Alden and not Diffy, but a supervisor who started the final sequence of events. As she was tidying away, he confronted her with: 'Who told you to pack up?' The abrupt question revived all the indignation slumbering for two years. She always did her work and she did it well. Never before at Chapter Road had she been asked whether she had permission to leave. She believed that she had agreed to move from Wembley, near her home, to Chapter Road, only on condition that she was given no more compulsory overtime. Were the management now going back on their word?

Her reaction can easily be depicted merely as a complaint against compulsory overtime, but this would oversimplify the origins of the Grunwick Strike. Jayaben Desai had never objected to compulsory overtime in itself. What she objected to was the short notice and the atmosphere of fear in which the overtime was imposed. As she was to tell Lord Justice Scarman: the Grunwick workers endured long hours of standing for low rates of pay and all the while the constant fear of dismissal nagged away 'like a sore on their necks'.

Peter Diffy arrived on the heels of the supervisor at the most inopportune possible moment. He brought some cheques to be returned, another half an hour's work, so she could not in any case go home. This new work, she thought, would keep her past 7 p.m. At Chapter Road she had so far avoided working beyond that time. Why was she being treated like this all of a sudden? She raised her voice. All might still have been well had Malcolm Alden not decided at this juncture to exert his authority.

When Alden ordered the two of them, herself and Diffy, to accompany him into Diffy's office it suddenly occurred to her, with a shock, that perhaps she had also been marked down for the sack. She resolved that she would avoid at all costs that ultimate humiliation.

Even then, the situation could possibly have been resolved. A supervisor had spoken a little roughly. A manager had produced, at very short notice, what he deemed unfinished work. Neither of these factors, however, caused the final rupture. It was the fear of unjust dismissal preying upon the mind of Jayaben Desai and of all the mail-order workers that was decisive.

Jayaben Desai explained it to the Court of Inquiry:

Then I say, 'Look, Mr Alden, why you bring me in the office? I am here to explain something and I want to know what is going on. If you want to shout at me I am not prepared to listen to what you are talking about. If you are prepared to listen to me I am prepared to listen to you as well, but if you shout like that to me I am not talking to you.'

Alden then said: 'I warn you'. Jayaben Desai had heard management claim that workers dismissed were first given a warning. Alden's three words rang alarm bells in her head: 'Anybody, any time, we expect our sack'. But she was no lamb for the slaughter: 'I stopped him in the middle and said, "Look, I do not want to work with you. I do not want your warning ... Please give me my cards straight away."'

Although this pre-emptive resignation seemed to turn the tables on what she imagined, rightly or wrongly, to be Alden's intention to sack her, she still had a problem to solve. If she walked out now, she believed the management would give the impression that she had been sacked or forced to resign. This she would not tolerate either. She therefore pulled open Diffy's door and yelled in Gujarati to the workers outside that she was leaving voluntarily: 'My friends, listen to this. What is happening to me today will happen to you tomorrow. This man wouldn't speak to white workers like he speaks to us. He says he is giving me the sack but I am leaving myself. I do not want to be given his sack.'

Having begun, she thought she might as well make a good job of it before she left. She addressed all the workers within earshot, mainly in Gujarati: 'Listen, my friends ... You have to understand what is the treatment you are getting from these people. I am asking this in front of Mr Alden and I am asking him, why he is not employing any white girls in this department.' That was how she recalled it at the Scarman Inquiry. Nor was that the end of it, for she had yet to touch upon the industriousness of the Gujaratis and the nature of their exploitation:

> Look, we are hardworking people and we are working with loyalty and these people ... are taking advantage of us. We have small money and they are taking hard work from us – standing on our backs all the time and taking work by forcing us with a small amount of money. I am leaving myself and you have to understand that I am here to clear it that I am leaving myself. Do not understand he sacked me. That is why I am asking him in front of you: 'Please give me my cards'.

Alden and Diffy stood helplessly by as Jayaben Desai, soon joined by her son, Sunil, harangued their workforce. When she finally walked out, she left Malcolm Alden with this parting shot, reported later in the *Morning Star:* 'What you are running here is not a factory, it is a zoo. But in a zoo there are many types of animals. Some are monkeys who dance on your fingertips, others are lions who can bite your head off. We are those lions, Mr Manager.'

Outside the two Desais encountered the four pioneers of the Grunwick Strike still doggedly picketing the gate, as they had been since earlier that afternoon. Stacey, the Personnel Manager, was talking vaguely to the four about intercession with Alden, but the two new recruits to the walkout now transformed the situation. The six fired each other up, with anger and indignation. Jayaben Desai scathingly dismissed Stacey from her presence: 'You are not here to help these boys. You were sent here to calm them down. Where were you inside the factory when they had problems and grievances? It is only now you appear and tell us "I am the Personnel Manager" – now, when it is too late!'

The Desais raised the discussion above the level of Alden's car tyres. Jayaben had walked out intending to get another job as a sewing-machinist but she was now full of concern for the five boys and their revengeful tone. She searched her mind for a constructive channel of protest and the phrase 'trade union' came into her head. The boys made her think. Without them, she says, there probably would never have been a Grunwick Strike.

That night Jayaben Desai discussed trade unionism with her husband. He repeated the analysis of Grunwick that he and Sunil had discussed briefly before – that nearly all the endless frustrations which consumed so much energy at Grunwick were trivialities resolved every day in other companies by a competent trade union.

That weekend, on the initiative of Sunil Desai, the trade unionists in search of a trade union prepared a petition for a management that did not like petitions, and placards for a strike that did not yet exist. On the Monday morning, the Grunwick directors were disconcerted to find a number of pickets on the Chapter Road gate urging workers to show their support for trade unionism by signing a petition. Nearly every member of the Mail-Order Department signed.

It was high time to find out exactly what a trade union was. Sunil Desai therefore rode off on his bicycle to the Wembley Citizens' Advice Bureau for information on how to start a strike. This was not the sort of request the CAB handled every day but they tried to be helpful. They advised Sunil that the appropriate union was probably APEX, the Association for Professional, Executive, Clerical and Computer Staffs. They also supplied Sunil with the telephone number of the TUC and of the Secretary of the Brent Trades Council, Jack Dromey.

When Sunil phoned the TUC later that morning, an assistant confirmed that APEX was the appropriate union to approach. Sunil was anxious, however, to do more than contact APEX and the TUC. By organising the petition, he realised, he had alerted the management. He knew that organisation inside the factory was impossible because of the restrictions on talking. He therefore decided to call for a walk-out immediately, before those who had signed the petition could be identified and sacked. 'If we hadn't walked out on the

Monday afternoon', says Sunil, 'there would never have been a union at Grunwick'.

The management had been none too worried over the weekend. After the Desais had left, Malcolm Alden had called the remaining staff together and told them that, if others also harboured grievances, they had better leave there and then. No one had volunteered. He and Diffy were therefore flabbergasted when at 3 p.m. on the Monday afternoon over fifty workers suddenly walked out of Chapter Road and assembled at the gate. The petition for a trade union was to be backed up by a show of strength.

Even now the Grunwick Strike was still not really off the ground. It was still only a walk-out from Chapter Road. The management could hope to contain the explosion, some even talked of reinstating Jayaben Desai and Devshi Bhudia. After all, Cobbold Road, the heart of the company's production, was untouched. What the management failed to reckon with, however, was the liberating effect of the walk-out itself. As the strikers marched out into Chapter Road, they brought with them, into the open, all the longstanding grievances of the Grunwick workers. To the dismay of the directors, they massed in the middle of Chapter Road and then moved off towards Dudden Hill Lane. They were going to march on the Cobbold Road laboratories.

The Cobbold Road premises of Grunwick are at the end of a cul-de-sac behind the Rolls-Royce bodywork factory known as Mulliner Park Ward. It is the centre of Grunwick's colour-processing and is broken down into departments for preparation, splicing, processing itself, printing, negative-cutting, photo-cutting and despatch. It also has a transport department of about twenty drivers who collect and deliver film, from and to, chemists all over London. The company's blue vans visit the chemist shops twice or even three times a day.

The road leading to the company is not a public highway but an access road into the industrial estate. Approaching Grunwick, it is only about thirteen metres wide from factory wall to factory wall. As the strikers advanced, the besieged management decided to lock all the doors and forbid any conversation between strikers and the workers inside. The strikers, still Grunwick employees, had friends inside and expected to speak to them. Some working inside, tipped off by Sunil Desai at lunchtime about the march, were also waiting expectantly for contact to be made. What happened next is unclear. The strikers shouted, but the management turned on music inside so loudly that the workers could not hear. One striker is said to have attempted to crawl through a window, but was forcibly expelled. According to Devshi Bhudia, a woman called Nilam Patel was threatened with a broken bottle by one of the drivers guarding the entrance. One manager alleged that windows were broken as strikers stoned the premises. According to other witnesses, a manager slapped a woman's face and she smashed the windows, in retaliation, with an iron bar. The police arrived. Order was restored. The strikers retreated back to Chapter Road. Only seven or eight from Cobbold Road had joined their ranks but, as the next three days were to prove, they had well and truly planted the seeds of revolt.

Much later, Grunwick was to claim that the violent scenes at Cobbold Road ended all hope of compromise with the strikers. At the time, management took no such stand. When the evangelists returned to Chapter Road, Alden and others renewed their efforts to secure their return to work. Alden met Bhudia, Chandrakant Patel and the striking supervisor, Rajashweri Patel. According to her, Alden offered them reinstatement and they accepted – providing they could have a union. Alden's reply was that they could come back as individuals but not as a union. Already, even at this early stage, the demand for a union was the main stumbling block.

On Tuesday morning, the strikers leafleted both buildings. The leaflets called for a meeting of all Grunwick workers – the first mass meeting of the Grunwick Strike – that lunchtime in the car park of the White Hart public house. Jack Dromey and some local APEX members would be there to advise them.

The Cobbold Road management did not stand idle. They seem to have taken a tougher stand than Alden and Diffy. A petition for a union similar to the one that circulated at Chapter Road was seized by the Cobbold Road management. John Hickey, thirty-eight, was a founder-director of Grunwick and, with the managing director away in Ireland, was the senior director in charge. On Tuesday, he tried to stem the tide by declaring that a trade union would never be tolerated inside Grunwick, so any walk-out was futile. According to Delcie Claire, Hickey declared his animosity towards trade unions. He had started from scratch and had worked very hard to get where he was and he was not going to let a union come and dictate to him. According to Joyce Pitter and Kalaben Patel, Hickey added that he would close the company down rather than let a union inside.

John Hickey was not a management expert but a technical man. At the Court of Inquiry, under cross-examination, he was unable to define what 'collective bargaining' meant. He could not even tell the court whether Grunwick held membership of an employers' association. It emerged that he thought 'industrial relations' was something to do with the hiring of staff. Nor did he know, at the start of the strike, what the 'Advisory, Conciliation and Arbitration Service (ACAS)' was. In other words he was ignorant of basic industrial relations concepts, which most senior management and any active trade unionist would have regarded as lesson number one.

Before the Tuesday lunchtime, Chapman, the works manager, asked some of the Cobbold Road workers to report back to him on the White Hart meeting. According to Noorali Valliani, who worked in the printing department, Chapman asked him to persuade those who had walked out to relent. Noorali Valliani returned with bad news for Chapman and Hickey. The strikers were certainly ready to come back, but only with a trade union to negotiate their grievances. Hickey told Valliani he did not want a union in the firm.

By Tuesday evening, it was clear that no compromise was possible. The decision to join a union was formalised. Sunil Desai had arranged a meeting with an APEX official, Len Gristey. Through Jack Dromey and an APEX representative on the Trades Council, Eric Boon, they arranged for APEX application forms to be available at the Trades Hall. Over sixty strikers turned up at the Hall and they elected a delegation to meet Gristey. They were impressed. By the end of Tuesday the sixty had joined APEX.

Meanwhile, at the Cobbold Road plant, many workers could not understand why they should not have a trade union if they wanted one. After all, according to Kalaben Patel, they had similar problems with Chapman as the Chapter Road workers had with Alden. They also had a grievance about working in the darkroom, which was unpleasant over long periods, and earned them no extra pay. When word filtered through about the formation of a union on the Tuesday evening, the stage was set for a walk-out from Cobbold Road. At about eleven o'clock on the Wednesday morning the walk-out began. It was led by Noorali Valliani, a Pakistani technician who had been in a union at Rank, and Vipin Magdani who, although lacking any union experience, was able to win over many workers in his section because of his conscientiousness and hard work.

Just as in the case of Chapter Road, the management's reaction was to try to secure a return to work. Hickey and the Personnel Manager, Stacey, asked representatives of the strikers out for lunch in Kingsbury Park. Five workers went: Noorali Valliani, Vipin Magdani, Gasper Fernandes, Kantilal Patel and Paul Vig. They asked the five what concessions management might make, short of trade-union recognition, which might entice those on strike to return. The workers told them that the very least was the removal of Chapman and Alden from their positions. Hickey promised to phone the managing director, still in Ireland, and ask his opinion that night.

On Thursday, the Cobbold Road workers learnt that there was to be no compromise. Chapman and Alden were to stay. It had to be. If they had been able to sack the managers they would not have needed a trade union. More workers now joined the strike, so that by Friday afternoon, 137 workers were on strike out of a total workforce of 480 and a total weekly-paid workforce of 430 (176 male, 254 female).

In the propaganda war later, the management often pointed out that the strikers were not an overall majority, but this glosses over the fact that while many did not dare to go on strike, they were prepared either to join the union secretly, as some did, or at least let others join. On Jayaben Desai's petition, there were the names of people who supported a union but lacked the courage to come out on strike. In any case, the argument is specious: no union starts with a majority. And if there is no freedom to organise inside the workplace the minority can only win majority support with extreme difficulty. Moreover, APEX was not claiming to represent all grades. Its claim was for recognition for the weekly-paid staff. Drivers and warehousemen were certainly excluded, and possibly others; their place was in the Transport and General Workers Union (TGWU) not APEX. As for the similar 'numbers' argument that most of the original strikers were students, this is clearly disproved by figures used at the Court of Inquiry: about 140 staff were students out of 429 weekly-paid (about 33 per cent) while of the 137 on strike forty-six were students (also about 33 per cent). The students were no more and no less militant than the rest.

The Grunwick management and APEX were now on a collision course. On Friday 27 August, Len Gristey sent a letter to Hickey asking for talks. Monday being a Bank Holiday, it arrived on the

Tuesday 31 August. On that day, the Grunwick board met and on the Wednesday, the company took legal advice for the first time. It was publicly announced on the Wednesday by APEX that the strikers would receive strike pay, i.e. the strike was 'official'. On the very next day, 2 September, the company prepared dismissal notices, which were sent out by hand. The 137 workers who had walked out were all sacked and at the same time Hickey sent his reply to Gristey rejecting APEX'S claim for recognition.

Anyone studying the above timetable of events cannot possibly accept the company's subsequent claim that the sacking of the workers had nothing to do with the formation of a trade union. According to the management, the 137 (ninety-one permanent staff and forty-six temporaries) were sacked for breach of contract in walking out, irrespective of whether they were in a union or not. Yet neither in the Chapter Road nor the Cobbold Road walk-out was a single worker sacked. On the contrary, management pleaded with those who walked out to return. Only after they joined the union were they dismissed.

The company has also claimed that the 137 could never be reinstated because they participated in violence outside the Cobbold Road building. As most of the 137 were at that stage quietly working away *inside* the Cobbold Road building and were not even on strike, such statements are nonsensical. No individual was sacked for misconduct in Cobbold Road, nor did the company prosecute anyone for the violent behaviour they only later blamed on the workers. The Scarman Report summed it up neatly:

> Although there was some violence, it was short-lived – no more than an explosion of excitement following upon the Chapter Road walk-out. We do not believe it was, or ought to have been, a major factor in the determination of the company's attitude towards the strikers or of its actions in dealing with the union.

It was clear to the trade-union movement that the workers were sacked after Len Gristey's letter reached Grunwick. The movement therefore took up the cause of the strikers as a 'recognition issue'. No one asserts that the strike was started by trade unionists – far from it. But the demand for a trade union summed up all of the grievances they felt, and was the only demand whose satisfaction would remedy their plight. As Len Murray, General Secretary of the TUC was later to tell them: what trade unionism means is self-respect, 'the right to answer the gaffer back'. It was precisely that right, precisely that self-respect, which had been totally lacking at Grunwick.

4

'The Happy Family'

What is a strike? What causes a group of workers to abandon a safe routine and a regular wage, to risk their jobs in the midst of unemployment, to cast away all those economic and social ties that bind millions of others to their work every day? It cannot be for a few pennies or because of a row with the boss. For a strike may be the most courageous and independent action of a whole lifetime, an action that has to be justified day in and day out to sceptical relatives and, in the end, defended against the inevitable hostility of the privately-owned press.

The causes of the Grunwick Strike are not immediately obvious. Superficially, by 1976 the company seemed to have built up a prosperous and powerful position. By 1972, *Which?* was naming 'Bonuspool' (launched by Grunwick in 1968 as their first mail-order enterprise) as the best buy in the British photo-processing market. From a pre-tax profit of £13,500 in 1969, Grunwick had advanced to £126,719 in 1973-4 and to £210,687 in 1975-6. These profits were lucrative for the shareholders because the small size and the nature of the company meant that it paid very little in tax. The company's growth was remarkable: from about 100 employees in 1973, it mushroomed into a workforce exceeding 400, thus becoming a medium-sized firm in general terms and the largest film-processing company in Britain, apart from the multinationals. By June 1977, Grunwick, although strikebound, was described by *Which?* as the most efficient and the least expensive of all the film-processing companies.

George Ward, the Managing Director, was in a particularly happy position. With his relatives, he controlled 51 per cent of 'GP Combined', the holding company that embraces the operating names of Cooper & Pearson, Bonuspool Ltd, Trucolor Free Film Laboratories Ltd and Monkolor. In August 1976 there had been no major unrest in the company for over three years and increasing unemployment seemed to guarantee that no unrest was likely. The business was thriving. No wonder, as Ward told Capital Radio in 1977, he looked upon Grunwick at that time as one 'happy family'. Clearly, with soaring profits and a labour force of vulnerable immigrant workers unaware of trade unionism, it was a remarkable achievement by the Grunwick management to produce a strike at all.

The Conspiracy Theory

Ward himself had an explanation which he often repeated throughout the strike. He believed political troublemakers and agitators had conspired against him. Like all autocrats, Ward, unable to accept any criticism of his own regime, resorted to a theory of conspiracy. He told the *Kingsbury News* that the strike was instigated by the left-wing Brent Trades Council and in his book, *Fort Grunwick*, Ward blamed the strike on a local Communist, Tom Durkin, 'and his friends'. Such accusations come strangely from Ward as, in point of fact, the only political organisation directly involved in the strike was – as we shall see – imported by Ward himself that November.

The Court of Inquiry rightly paid no attention to Ward's 'theory'. For a start, the Brent Trades Council was not asked by Sunil Desai to intervene in the dispute until Tuesday 24 August, when the decisive steps had already been taken. Whatever Ward may think, the Citizens' Advice Bureau and the switchboard of the TUC are by no means tools of revolutionary communism. What is more, if Tom Durkin and Jack Dromey had been Sunil Desai's secret mentors, Ward can rest assured that the events of Monday 23 August, would have been better organised than they were.

As for the strikers themselves, they had little or no political affiliation. In East Africa, the British Empire had insulated them effectively from socialist ideas. The British imposed heavy censorship in Kenya and Uganda and no one was allowed to travel to Eastern Europe, the USSR or China. None of the Strike Committee belonged to a political party.

Low Pay?

Was the original cause of the strike low pay? This was a plausible explanation to make; over the years, the media, unwilling to accept that there is a fundamental defect in the social system, have accounted for strikes by projecting the stereotype of the 'greedy worker'. Although research has shown that since 1945 only a little over half of all strikes have been concerned with demands for higher pay, many newspapers continue to argue that it is greed for money which leads workers to abandon £60 per week jobs for £10 per week strike pay. As Frederick Engels pointed out a century ago, the reverse is often true: workers go on strike even in the knowledge that they have little or no chance to win, merely to assert their humanity against forces apparently beyond their control. The point when a worker succumbs to the desire for money is when he abandons his newfound freedom and agrees to return to work.

If the Grunwick Strike had hinged on the question of money, that would, of course, have been no surprise. Grunwick's expansion had not exactly benefited all the workforce equally. In the year ending 31 March 1976, Ward and his family received after-tax profits of nearly £70,000 on top of Ward's own pre-tax salary of £163 per week. This, it has to be remembered, is in addition to expenses, including company cars. A new employee at Grunwick, on the other hand, would in 1976 have started on a basic wage of £28 for a forty-hour week, and over eighty hours per week of hard work would be required in order to reach the national average wage at that time of £72. To reach Ward's salary it would have been necessary to work overtime, without eating or sleeping, for more than the 168 hours in a week.

In Greater London at the time of the strike, a full-time, female, manual worker averaged £44.20 for thirty-nine hours' work. A full-time, female, non-manual worker averaged £55. Yet at Grunwick in 1976, Indira Mistry, for thirty-five hours' basic, was earning £29 per week before tax. According to George Ward himself, in the *Willesden and Brent Chronicle* of November 1976, the average pay at Grunwick for both men and women was only £34 per week including overtime and before deducting income tax of around 30 per cent. With rent for the cheaper family flats in London then about £18–£20, this was clearly not an adequate wage. As Stephen Sedley, the Trades Council's lawyer told the Court of Inquiry in 1977: 'The short home truth is that neither this year nor last year could the average human being live on a take home pay packet produced by a gross wage of £35 a week'. Mahmood Ahmad, Secretary of the Strike Committee, remarked later that there never would have been a Grunwick Strike if the workers in 1976 had received the rates paid to blacklegs in 1977.

However, wages were not the main cause of the strike, although they were a very important underlying factor. For one thing, the women workers at Grunwick found £34, overtime or not, an essential addition to the family income at a time when the Government was enforcing lower living standards. It was tolerable, providing another person in the household was also working. Second, because they were not white (only one of the original strikers, a woman, was white), they also looked upon Grunwick as a haven from a growing rate of unemployment which, in Brent, or elsewhere, discriminated against black and Asian faces. Third, the work at Grunwick was, compared to the local engineering factories, neither so noisy nor so dirty. The students, who worked in large numbers at Grunwick during the peak period in the summer, also confirmed that Grunwick meant useful money for a short period, if racial prejudice precluded the possibilities of a better job. The wages were bad, but unemployment was worse.

Jayaben Desai certainly never conformed to the 'greedy worker' stereotype. One day, on the picket line, she watched Ward drive his car over a placard saying: 'End Slave Labour: £28 for a forty hour week'. She exclaimed angrily: 'But it is not just for the money – that is what Ward will never understand! It is for our human dignity!' Then she added by way of explanation: 'It is the Wards who love too much the money, not us. This strike – it is their money against our pride.'

Racism?

If the fundamental cause of the strike was not wages, was it racism or feminism? It is easy to fall into oversimplifications on such matters. Nonetheless, at the Court of Inquiry, Stuart Shields, the APEX lawyer, listing the causes of the Grunwick Strike, did start with 'the vulnerable labour force'. The whiteness of the all-male senior management in contrast to the black and Asian mostly-female picket line was undoubtedly one of the most prominent features of the strike.

Whether the individual managers were racist is hard to say. Pickets allege that Ward boasted: 'I can buy a Patel any time for £15'. On 8 May 1977, Ken Pearson was alleged to have told Vipin Magdani: 'I hate you Asians. I hate you. But I'm prepared to be nice to those inside to get my work done.' The management has denied these remarks. More evidence, however, appeared in the *Wembley Observer* of 15 March 1977, when a reporter was told by blacklegs, not strikers, that at Grunwick white workers got a better deal than black. One of the blacklegs, Hildegaard Watte, an immigrant from East Germany, said of the strikers in the same article: 'I couldn't give a damn for them. They walked out without any reason. They are all Indians. There is no white person amongst them.'

The strikers were convinced that at least some of the managers were racist. They even drew up placards for their marches through Willesden: 'I can buy a Patel for £15. NOT ANY MORE!' Another placard drew a parallel between Grunwick and the bloody protests in Soweto, South Africa, against apartheid: 'Grunwick–Soweto: ONE STRUGGLE!' In the autumn of 1976, representatives of the Grunwick Strike Committee marched in a large anti-racist demonstration in central London, organised by the TUC and the Labour Party.

Back in 1974 when Jayaben Desai first started work in Station House, Wembley, the majority of the workers were white women. She was not the only one who noticed the deterioration in the supervision, and in the real wages, as the proportion of immigrant employees increased. Some strikers allege that supervisors turned away white job applicants in 1975-6, but the company strenuously denies that it discriminated against white applicants in favour of more profitable black and Asian workers. According to the company, their workforce merely reflected the high proportion of immigrants in the local areas. George Ward told the Court of Inquiry that everyone in Grunwick had the opportunity to progress through the company 'regardless of race, colour or creed'.

The trade-union side maintained that the company took advantage of unemployed immigrants who were desperate for work. Stephen Sedley, lawyer for Brent Trades Council, pointed out the hollowness of the company's argument in relation to the population of Brent: no more than 20 per cent of Brent's population is black or Asian whereas the proportion in Grunwick's weekly paid workforce was over 90 per cent. There was no doubt in the minds of APEX that the company had achieved record profits in 1975-6 by means of exploiting immigrants. As Roy Grantham, General Secretary of APEX, told the TUC conference on 7 September 1976: 'Here is a clear case of a reactionary employer taking advantage of race and employing workers on disgraceful terms and conditions'.

George Ward?

One of the ambiguities facing the accusation of racism, is that George Ward is himself Anglo-Indian. Managing director of Grunwick and chief spokesman for the company, he was born in New Delhi in 1933, and first came to England in 1938 with his father who, according to the *Daily Telegraph,* was a 'very rich man'. Like many Anglo-Indians Ward had a Roman Catholic upbringing, attending a Jesuit school in Calcutta and then a school run by the Irish Christian Brothers in Darjeeling. In Willesden, he was nicknamed 'the Pope of Chapter Road'; Ward had first met Grundy and Hickey, his original partners, at a priory. He is still, like Roy Grantham, his trade-union enemy, a regular churchgoer.

The Wards did not stay long in the England of 1938, where war was imminent. They swiftly returned to India where, however, the war caught up with them when the Japanese invaded from the east. After the loss of the family investments, his father's death, and Indian independence, Ward returned to England in 1948. His family were understandably not to be reconciled to their depleted social status, and high hopes were placed in young George. In his book, *Fort Grunwick* (1977), Ward's ambition is a constant factor, with the phrase 'to get ahead' recurring again and again. The first stage of Ward's rise to the top was completed in 1959 when he qualified as a chartered accountant.

Ward, however, found working his way up in Britain a difficult task, partly due to racial discrimination. So from 1960-3 he worked in Brazil and there accumulated the nest egg which helped launch Grunwick Processing soon after. In his book he compares Brazil favourably over Britain because of Brazil's freedom for employers without restriction from trade unions. Roman Catholic, multi-racial, Portuguese-speaking – the language of many Catholics in India – Brazil contained some features similar to British India in the 1930s.

Ward's background is, however, unclear to those ignorant of the Anglo-Indian community. Anglo-Indians do not generally identify with India or with Indian culture, but with the English upper classes. Anglo-Indians are mostly Christian, not Hindu or Buddhist. English is their first language. They often regard themselves as white, not black. As Sheila Patterson describes them in *Immigrants in Industry* (1968): 'Very often Anglo-Indians do not like to admit that they are anything but English. When they come to the UK they regard it as returning home in the same way as an ordinary Englishman does … they do not usually regard themselves as immigrants'.

In manners, appearance and speech Ward is every inch an Englishman, and it is significant that he left India in 1948, in the very aftermath of Indian independence. This alone implies that Ward did not align himself with the progressive aspirations of Nehru and Gandhi but with the departing British Empire.

Ward has consistently identified himself with the class that imposed an empire on one quarter of humanity. For example, Ward once spoke of the strikers' 'Bombay violence' in Chapter Road, and in the *Observer* of 26 June 1977 described the march on Cobbold Road on the first day of the strike as behaviour in 'Bombay fashion'. The explanation of this phrase seems to be that under the British Raj, Bombay was the capital of Bombay Province, the province that included Gujarat, home of Mahatma Gandhi and the movement for Indian independence. Ward did not identify with that tradition: 'The Anglo-Indians', he says in *Fort Grunwick,* 'were the children of the Raj'.

Oppressed Women?

Apart from racial disadvantage, the Grunwick workers were also a 'vulnerable labour force' because of the preponderance of women. About 59 per cent of the weekly-paid staff were female and so were over 60 per cent of the strikers. The reason for the high number of women strikers was that the rigorous supervision affected women most of all. It often conflicted severely with their domestic ties – fetching their children from school, cooking meals for their husbands.

Most of the directors, in contrast, sent a company driver to fetch their children from school. Yet when women with sick children asked for time off, they were told: 'This is not a holiday camp'. Sometimes, the women had planned to collect children from nursery when extended overtime was suddenly imposed. If permission to go was refused, they had to work on, worrying about the fate of the infants once the nursery had closed. Or they argued with the manager and got the sack.

In his book, Ward unwittingly reveals the plight of the Grunwick women in his praise for a blackleg, Azadi Patel. He describes how she used to get up at six o'clock each morning 'to cook her husband's lunch' (perhaps because he had no canteen at work); then she used to take her son 'to the childminder' (presumably because there was no nursery); and then she used to join the blacklegs' bus.

On 26 February 1977, Jayaben Desai addressed a women's rally at the Alexandra Palace. She claimed: 'The women were treated particularly badly in the company. We had to put our hands up to go to the toilet. Pregnant women were not allowed to go to the antenatal clinic and women were refused time off to take their sick children to the doctor ... We were insulted if we did not work harder. All this and more was suffered in silence by the Asian women of Grunwick.'[1]

The women strikers at Grunwick compensated for their previous reticence once the strike had begun. Often at the strikers' meetings, the women voted more militantly than the men. In India, women take on a great deal of responsibility. It is the only country in the world where women die younger than men. Hinduism has female goddesses who are by no means passive. As Jayaben Desai told Nell Myers of the *Morning Star:* 'In India there have always been strong women, making decisions, participating in politics and business and so on. But our culture teaches us too that we follow our husbands and raise our children. And this can make us shy and afraid of trouble. It took time, at Grunwick, to get angry all together.'

In verbal skirmishes on the picket lines, the women, no longer fearing the sack, gave as good as they got. Sometimes the managers made remarks about their saris or about the sex lives of the younger women. One manager leered at Jayaben Desai: 'You can't win with that sari on. Why don't you change into a miniskirt?' 'I'll tell you something, manager,' she retorted, 'Mrs Gandhi wears a sari and she runs a country of 600 million people. You can't even run a little factory.'

The 'Conditions'

The main cause of the Grunwick Strike was, however, not directly to do with money, racism or the women's question. The main cause was the 'conditions of work', which meant the terms and conditions of employment, enforced, as they were, by strict management.

Of the conditions of employment, the most important was undoubtedly the compulsory overtime. Kamlesh Gandhi, chairman of the Strike Committee in 1977-8, when asked on television for the causes of the strike, put compulsory overtime as number one. Of course workers were paid the normal hourly rate times one-and-a-quarter and, as the management were fond of pointing out, in the winter they were sometimes able to go home half an hour or an hour early without losing money. It is also true that the workers needed the money – so low was the basic – and therefore complained sometimes if there was no overtime available. Nonetheless, the long extra hours, imposed as late as 5.30 or 6, disrupted private life out of all proportion to the pay. It was this that caused Laurie Pavitt, Labour MP for Brent South, to allege in Parliament that Grunwick was a 'sweat shop' lifted straight out of the Dickens era.

There was also discontent about the holiday entitlement, inferior to that of Grunwick's nearest competitor – Tudor Processing in Cricklewood – and which also had to cope with a seasonal rush. After 1974, when Grunwick switched over increasingly to immigrant labour, holiday entitlement was actually reduced. Many workers had only two weeks' holiday and holidays in the summer were entirely at management discretion. As Roy Grantham, a trade-union official since 1949, told the Court of Inquiry, 'I think this is to my knowledge the only case that I have ever known of a company actually going backwards in terms of company holidays'.

Of course the management side at the Court of Inquiry tried to rebut these charges. They produced Bipin Patel, a Kenyan Asian medical student, to testify that he had always been granted time off whenever he asked for it, and Azadi Patel, a Ugandan Asian, who claimed she had never been forced to do overtime against her will. However, the union side produced twice as many witnesses to the contrary.

Bad Management?

The conditions of employment were not decisive by themselves. What caused such indignation was their application by certain managers in a dictatorial fashion. There was 'bad management' at Grunwick but the 'bad management' varied from section to section. In the Mail-Order Department there was clearly an atmosphere of job insecurity bordering on hysteria. Devshi Bhudia and Jayaben Desai, both level-headed, both good workers, were nonetheless, at the critical moment, both 'expecting our sack'. Creating such an atmosphere in a company of low-paid workers is equivalent to filling a room with gas: a single spark may cause the explosion. Not only that but according to Alden at the Court of Inquiry the labour turnover of 100 per cent in his department – a major indication of management failure – was typical of the company as a whole. The atmosphere was further poisoned by the fact that workers' prospects, bonuses and rises were not based on any structure but were at the discretion of managers. Even directors of the company, such as Hickey and Alden, had obviously never opened a book on management in their lives.

The Court of Inquiry concentrated heavily on these classic symptoms of bad management, but was particularly disturbed by the lack of any mechanism for ventilating grievances, real or imaginary. There was a Works' Committee founded by Stacey, the Personnel Manager, but its reputation was minimal. In Mail-Order, Devshi Bhudia and his friends did not even know there was a Works' Committee. They should have elected a representative to it but, as Alden explained later, he could find no one who would stand as a candidate so he nobly assumed that office himself. In this way, it came about that Malcolm Alden, invigilating from his glass box, became the workers' official representative on the Works' Committee! No wonder the Grunwick workers were astounded in 1977 to read the firm's claim in the press, that it was championing 'individual freedom' in Britain against 'corporatism'.

Some narrow the charge of 'bad management' to one man: Malcolm Alden himself. Raschid Muhammed, the company's assistant accountant, expounds this view very strongly. According to him, there had been complaints made to Diffy about Alden's behaviour and he compared Alden unfavourably to his own boss, Mr Byrne, whom he described as a 'gentleman'. Muhammed pointed to the high labour turnover in Alden's department as proof. Raschid Muhammed even claimed to have warned Ward about Alden some time before the strike: 'With Alden's attitude,' he told Ward prophetically, 'you will have a big problem on your hands'.

Such an analysis, however, cannot explain how 137 workers went on strike, many of whom had never worked for Alden, nor how it was that they remained on strike for over eighteen months. Nor should it be forgotten that at Cobbold Road they demanded the removal of Chapman, the works' manager. The truth probably is that Alden and Chapman had the 'dirty jobs' of getting production out and for this task aggressive supervision was held to be necessary. As Malcolm Alden quite rightly told Scarman: 'the workers knew there was a terrific pressure of work and knew that I was the figurehead, as it were, causing these pressures'.

Some blame George Ward on the grounds that he was in ultimate charge and in 1976 let things slide. Ward had started a hobby for himself – racehorses. By the time of the strike he was said to have owned eleven horses, some worth as much as £40,000 each, and his horse trainers, on £60 per week, were paid double the basic pay of the Grunwick workers. Many strikers did not believe he was on holiday in Ireland at the time of the strike: they believed he was touring Ireland looking at horses. Jayaben Desai reckoned that Ward 'was more interested in his horses than his workers'. Ward virtually admitted his declining interest in Grunwick to Lord Justice Scarman: at the beginning of 1976, he said, he had decided to take a back seat in the running of the company and let the younger managers have a chance to develop.

Yet the theory that blames it all on Ward is even less convincing than the one which blames Alden. Of all the Grunwick management, Ward was indisputably the most capable. Moreover, most of the strikers' grievances date from before January 1976, when Ward's process of delegation began.

The blame for the harsh conditions at Grunwick is placed more generally than on the behaviour of two men. Grunwick inhabits a world of multinational monopolies such as General Motors and, in photofinishing, Kodak. In such an atmosphere, characterised by the Labour MP for Brent East, Reg Freeson, as 'giantism', small entrepreneurs are hard pressed and have to exploit their workers much more keenly than their giant rivals, who will otherwise eliminate them through economies of scale or sheer promotion. Given such assumptions, the Grunwick managers were behaving quite logically. To recruit over 200 immigrant women, drain every last ounce of work out of them, sack those who complain and send the rest home with barely enough money to pay the rent – that was a reality of the system. Alden and Chapman had to hammer the work through – from their point of view, there was no time for messing about with management theory or supervisory finesse. As another director, Fanning, put it so delicately to one of his drivers, in Slattery's evidence: if you don't like it you can 'fuck off out'.

Even as the strike proceeded, Brent Trades Council found it becoming clearer and clearer that Grunwick was not unique or even rare. There are 800,000 small and medium firms in the UK about the size of Grunwick, and they employ 3.2 million workers. Far from it being an isolated case of 'bad management' Brent was shown to be covered with Grunwicks – a veritable plague of Grunwicks was rampant throughout the borough. As the strike won more and more publicity, requests for information about trade unionism poured into Brent Trades Hall from all over Brent. In the evening, workers who had just finished work, nearly all black or Asian, nearly all working for smallish companies, would walk hesitantly into the Trades Hall. They arrived in the Hall anxious and fearful, whispering even inside the office, loath to divulge names, in fear of dismissal and unemployment. It was around the same time that Callaghan and President Carter were criticising the violations of human rights in the poorer countries of the world.

A Proud Workforce

Why had those workers not acted before? That brings us to one final ingredient in the Grunwick Strike not so far mentioned – the strikers themselves. It was not just the nature of the management but also the resistance and self-confidence of the strikers that produced a strike at Grunwick but not elsewhere in Brent. Ward had gained in the short term from the persecutions of Amin and Kenyatta, but in the long term he had imported industrial dynamite into his company. He forgot the golden motto of British India, divide to rule; he allowed Gujarati-speaking Indians numerically to dominate the weekly-paid work force, instead of keeping them to a third or a half, which would have kept the workers divided. The Gujaratis were intelligent, confident workers with a sense of community. The quality of this labour was a bargain in 1974 but a powder keg by 1976.

The Grunwick strikers acted against all expectations. Immigrants had been imported and employed by British companies since the 1950s, precisely because it was thought that they accepted low pay and bad conditions and would never go on strike. *But the Grunwick immigrants went on strike.* Women workers were expected to be so tame and obliging that Grunwick took on women at low pay even before they tried employing immigrants. *But the women at Grunwick proved to be at least as militant, if not more militant, than the men.* Finally, in 1975-6, the Government had persuaded the TUC to back a wage freeze, under the guise of the 'Social Contract' which reduced trade-union activity so much, that there were fewer strikes in 1976 than at any time for twenty-three years. The trade-union movement was in retreat. *The Grunwick strikers broke that spell.*

It was because of this quality of self-confidence amongst workers expected humbly to touch their forelocks, that the 11 million-strong trade-union movement rallied to their support. British employers had grown accustomed to making use of black people, exploiting women and taking the ignorant for a ride. This time they had picked the wrong bunch.

NOTES

1. Ward has stressed that asking permission to visit the toilet was imposed only when the firm was in Wembley. He claims it was to prevent workers 'making love' in the firm's time (*Fort Grunwick,* p. 25).

5

The Movement Mobilises

Few strikes for union recognition have attracted such wide and quick support as that at Grunwick. One reason was fortuitous: the Trades Union Congress of 1976 began on Monday 6 September, just two weeks after the strike began. Another was that the strikers' confidence in the justice of their cause was rapidly transmitted to the movement by their union, APEX, and the local Trades Council in Brent.

APEX is a union for 'white collar' workers, one of many that have expanded rapidly in the post-war boom in the organisation of such workers. Formerly the Clerical and Administrative Workers Union (CAWU), it moved 'upmarket' in 1972 to capture those in the professional and executive grades of industry who were beginning to feel vulnerable without the protection of union organisation. Its name changed to the Association of Professional, Executive, Clerical and Computer Staffs. By 1976, membership had increased by 20,000 to 142,000, of which half were women, considerably more than the average union female membership of one third. Despite its recent growth, APEX is an old association, founded in 1890.

Unlike many of the white-collar unions, APEX is well-known for its unashamed, right-wing political stance; Roy Grantham established its credentials before the Scarman Court of Inquiry when he said that his union had been one of the few to support entry into the Common Market and that APEX was a firm supporter of the Social Contract. It practices widespread proscription and insists that candidates for office declare their political affiliations. Not all its members have come out of the same mould. The old Bolshevik, Maxim Litvinov, had in exile been a member of CAWU's ancestor, the National Union of Clerks.

The response of APEX to the walkout at Grunwick was, however, exemplary. Within three days, it accepted into membership strikers who had never paid a penny to the union. In eight days, the strike was declared official and the union paid out the first strike pay of £8 per week on 17 September, backdated to 31 August. Soon after, the strike pay was increased to £12 per week and was supplemented by weekly payments from the local strike fund of between £2.50 and £6 according to the needs of individual strikers. The strikers were suitably impressed at the swift and generous actions of a union none of them had ever heard of a few weeks earlier. According to Vipin Magdani, they were amazed to receive strike pay. They had never heard of that either.

Roy Grantham, the General Secretary of APEX, is a shrewd man with a gift for explaining trade-union issues with extreme lucidity. A trade-union official with substantial experience, General Secretary for six years, an official since 1949, and a member of the TUC General Council from 1972 until 1975, Grantham took to the rostrum of the Trades Union Congress on 7 September and delivered a powerful speech on behalf of the strikers. While he estimated that the film-processing industry had enormous potential for recruitment, he showed in his speech his genuine contempt for an employer who had taken advantage of black workers. He overstated the numbers of those on strike, but the fault was not his. In the confusion and excitement of the first ten days of the strike, his officials on the ground had exaggerated the extent of the walkout. The response to Grantham's impassioned plea was instant. Tom Jackson, the General Secretary of the Union of Post Office Workers (UPW), promised his union's help.

By 14 September, Grantham recognised that he had a hard fight on his hands. He had sought the help of the Advisory, Conciliation and Arbitration Service within days of the walkout. ACAS was asked to bring the two parties together around the negotiating table. The company, as in 1973, the year of the first Grunwick strike for union recognition, refused to talk to anyone. Thus, on that day, Grantham wrote to Tom Jackson and asked for the official support of the UPW, whose members at Cricklewood had already refused to cross the picket lines. On 6 October, Grantham went further still. He wrote to Len Murray and asked for the support of the TUC. He knew that the solidarity required to affect a company like Grunwick must be of a very high level, and would require the active assistance of Congress House and the General Council. No union would have bettered the actions of APEX thus far.

Grantham saw the first priority as the reinstatement of his 137 sacked members. His argument was based upon custom. It was not without precedent in Britain for strike action to precede union membership, but it was unusual for workers on strike to be sacked and stay sacked. Most peace settlements where strikers had been sacked started with the reinstatement of those dismissed. Recognition and the tackling of the grievances of the strikers came second in the list of objectives.

In Brent, meanwhile, the strikers had been put into the Hythe Road branch of APEX, a branch which included the members at the Mulliner Park Wards and Hythe factories of Rolls-Royce and the General Electrical Company (GEC) factory of Associated Automation. With the addition of the Grunwick strikers, the membership of the branch swelled to over 600.

The APEX official responsible for the branch was Len Gristey, the Senior Area Organiser of the London and Home Counties Area of the union. Apart from a short period after a motor accident, when he was replaced by a younger organiser, Chris Ball, Len was the official responsible on the ground throughout the dispute. He was a hearty individual who was later to come over very well on television and before the Court of Inquiry. He set about the enormous task of organising members who were, in the words of a senior AUEW steward at the nearby strikebound TRICO plant, 'as green as cooking apples'. It was Gristey who first met management when, in the week of the walkout, he talked with Stacey and Ken Pearson on the pavement outside Grunwick. He was never invited inside – then or later – but the discussion led to his 27 August letter to the company, in which he formally requested a meeting. Subsequently, the company was to claim that Gristey had threatened them with an Indian march from Southall if they did not give in, a suggestion symptomatic of Grunwick's attitudes. The National Association for Freedom was later to label Brent as that 'fevered centre of left-wing activity between Kilburn and Neasden' – a description that upset the good trade unionists of Wembley who were omitted – but it was not really the North-West Frontier.

On 8 September, it was Gristey who tried yet again to open up negotiations. He offered the personal intervention of Roy Grantham but Grunwick rejected it. Gristey too now faced up to the prospects of a long hard battle. An eternal optimist, he would have made the best out of the sinking of the *Titanic* by saying that at least the iceberg was still afloat. The strikers were to become disenchanted with his weekly reports to them which were basically 'if I'm smiling, you should be smiling'. Through the long hard winter that was to follow, he would regularly say that he had tricks up his sleeve that Ward had never heard of. Some strikers nicknamed him 'elbows' Gristey, because that was all there was up his sleeve. Nor was his strong point, at the beginning, his ability to communicate with people of different races and cultures. Kalaben Patel asked at a mass meeting in November of 1976 if the strikers had any hope of victory. Len raised himself to his full height and, to an audience which was almost entirely Asian, he said: 'I promise you that no power in Christendom will defeat you'. To his credit, Gristey changed enormously as a result of the strike and, in the bitter atmosphere of betrayal one year later, he was one of the few APEX officers who could command any respect from the strikers.

From the start, the strikers came into contact with another trade-union body, the Brent Trades Council, the local representative of the TUC in Brent. On the second day of the dispute, the Council's Trades and Labour Hall was handed over to the strikers for use as headquarters. Its location was ideal, halfway between the two Willesden factories of Grunwick. By 3 September, the Trades Council had circularised all affiliated branches, calling upon them to send in donations, to black all Grunwick supplies and to march through Willesden with the strikers on 10 September.

With Len Gristey, who sought its help on the third day of the dispute, the Trades Council helped the strikers to organise. A Strike Committee was elected and a regular strike bulletin began. Sunil Desai, the only student on it, was elected as the first Secretary, and his mother Jayaben as Treasurer. Noorali Valliani became Chairman (he was later succeeded by Kamlesh Gandhi). When Sunil left to pursue his studies, he was replaced by Mahmood Ahmad. The Strike Committee, comprising fifteen strikers, with Gristey and the Secretary of the Trades Council as non-voting members, was to be highly effective in the first months of the dispute. Such was its enthusiasm and that of the strikers as a whole that daily mass and committee meetings took place for the first six weeks in the Trades Hall.

The Brent Trades Council, one of 450 in Britain, was formed in 1965 from the merger of the Willesden and Wembley Trades Councils. As well as coordinating the trade-union bodies in Brent on behalf of the TUC, the Trades Council is a democratic organisation with delegates elected from the local trade-union branches, capable of devising its own policies for the area. By 1977, the Trades Council had 21,000 members in seventy-four affiliated branches, 130 delegates and an Executive Committee of twenty-three. It had a long and honourable record of firm links with the immigrant community in Brent: in the 1960s, the Willesden International Friendship Club, sponsored by the Trades Council, had pioneered Community Relations Councils; part of the Council's premises housed the West Indian community's 'Apollo Club'; and the previous Secretary of the Trades Council had been black.

The Trades Council was hated by George Ward. In particular, he denounced Jack Dromey, Secretary of the Trades Council since 1974; he accused him of 'fabricating' the strike out of thin air. In Ward's scenario, the virgin strikers knew nothing about trade unions until the demon Dromey poisoned their minds. The following summer, Ward was to tell radio listeners that the strike was like a divorce and that he could no more take back Jayaben Desai and her friends than a divorcer could take a divorcee back into bed. Jayaben Desai had gone off with Jack Dromey, so no reinstatement was possible. That winter, Ward complained to the *Willesden and Brent Chronicle* that Dromey was 'just trying to use his position to get a political platform'. Ward boasted to the reporter: 'I'll make him a political eunuch before I'm finished'.

Jack Dromey was born and brought up in the area, the son of Irish immigrants. After leaving school he first became involved in the trade-union movement while working in the print industry. Aged twenty-eight when the strike began, he had also been active in the community for ten years, mainly in the tenants' movement. In 1969, he began to study law on an external basis but continued to work to support himself. In 1970, he brought a group of young lawyers and law students together with the local Trades Council and Federation of Tenants' and Residents' Associations to found the Brent Community Law Centre, a free legal service for working people in Brent. He gave up his studies to devote his spare time energy to the development of what was then the second such scheme in the country and one which was run by the representatives of the local tenants' and trade-union movement. In 1972 the Centre obtained an Urban Aid grant to set up full time. Dromey had worked with and knew intimately the network of local groups. Apart from working-class organising, he had also been deeply involved in the struggle for democratic rights through the

National Council for Civil Liberties, of which he was Chairman in 1975-6. Six years earlier, in 1970, he had helped to organise a demonstration in Wembley against a visit by Enoch Powell to speak in a multi-racial school. Some of the pupils that Dromey was trying then to defend were now Grunwick strikers.

The other leading figure in the Brent Trades Council is its Chairman, Tom Durkin, a building worker and a member of UCATT, famous in Brent for a deep Irish voice that needs no megaphone. He is equally well known for his letters to local newspapers on trade-union matters in which he denounces right-wing social democrats, 'the moderates' so praised throughout the media. In a letter to the *Willesden and Brent Chronicle,* for example, he wrote characteristically:

'Moderates' are those who back pay restraint, meekly accept the sack, oppose any strike action or activity for nationalisation, socialism and radical change ... cur unions have made impressive gains for working people from the time when women worked in coal mines and children of six and under toiled in 'dark satanic mills'. Shorter hours, holidays with pay, protection at work – it was not the 'moderates', the timid, docile status quo supporters but the bold, courageous, self-sacrificing revolutionaries who made the major contribution.

It was perhaps because of public sentiments like these that Ward felt justified in accusing the Trades Council of political motivation. John Gorst, Ward's Conservative MP and later his closest adviser, described by the *Guardian* as the 'effortlessly unpleasant MP for Hendon North', insinuated that there were Communist connections with the strikers. He once pointed out that Jayaben Desai had spoken at the People's Jubilee of the Communist Party in the summer of 1977 and had received a cheque for nearly £300 from a collection taken.

Ward and Gorst were simply displaying their ignorance of the labour movement. First, although socialists may vote Labour to keep the Conservatives out of power, the role of the Communists is highly valued by many trade unionists and, even if some of the Grunwick strikers had been Communist, this would not necessarily have undermined support for them inside the movement. Other recent historic struggles had been led by Communists, for example, the Upper Clyde Shipbuilders and the Briant Colour Printing work-in. Second, the red-baiters in the company camp were unable to grasp that trade unions, unlike management, are democratic. APEX is controlled democratically by its members, the Strike Committee was run democratically and the Trades Council has its policy decided by its delegates, whether its officers are Conservative, Liberal, Labour or Communist.

The frantic search for reds under beds is something that trade unionists have come to expect during industrial disputes. Sometimes those searching come unstuck. The summer of 1977 saw a prolonged strike of Air Traffic Controllers at Heathrow Airport. Dark accusations were made by some against the Civil and Public Services Association (CPSA) members involved. Were there not leading Communists on the National Executive Committee of the Union? The McCarthyism stopped when it was revealed that the leader of the strike was a card-carrying member of the Conservative Party. The movement waited with baited breath. Would Gerard Kemp of the *Sunday Express,* a man obsessed by the fear that he was drowning in a sea of those dedicated to destroying society as he and his editor knew it, take up his Parker, and point out that the initials of the Conservative and Communist Parties are the same?

In 1976, the Trades Council was indeed politically to the left of APEX. It opposed the Social Contract, but there were only five Communists, including Tom Durkin, on the Executive Committee of twenty-three. The rest, apart from one International Socialist, who came off the Executive in the annual elections in February 1977, were either Labour Party members or non-aligned trade unionists. One was a firm supporter of the Liberal Party. Dromey described himself as someone subscribing to the Marxist analysis of history whose only affiliation was to the Labour Party. In political terms, he supported the 'Tribune' Group in Parliament and in industrial terms he, like the Trades Council as a whole, was part of the 'broad left', that is the major grouping in left politics in Britain, whose main components are the Communist Party and the left of the Labour Party. However, in practical terms the left-wing Labour politics of the Trades Council had no more, and probably less, chance of influencing the strikers than did the right-wing Labour politics of APEX. Besides, the strikers took all decisions collectively in committee, and even then such decisions were subject to ratification by mass meetings.

The Grunwick Strike increasingly consumed the energies of the Trades Council which, that autumn, was simultaneously fighting hard against cuts in the National Health Service in Brent and cuts in education. It was also, with the Hounslow Trades Council, responsible for the coordination of the trade-union movement's efforts in London in support of the long-running strike for equal pay at the TRICO-Folberth factory in Brentford, which involved twenty-four hour picketing. Nonetheless, factory tours were organised to win support for the Grunwick Strike. The strikers took their case into major workplaces, many of them household names like Heinz, Guinness, British Leyland (Park Royal Vehicles), United Biscuits, Glacier Metals, GEC and Express Dairies. The Trades Council insisted that the delegations should comprise equal numbers of men and women, and the meetings that they had with local shop stewards were an education for the strikers. They met the cream of the trade-union movement in Brent, noted the fine facilities won for convenors and shop stewards, including spacious offices and phones, and were everywhere received warmly with promises of assistance and not even a suspicion of racial discrimination. At Glaciers, for example, they were invited into a warm conference room on a cold day and offered tea while George Hawkins, a member of the AUEW Southall District Committee (which was later to play a major role in support of the strikers), read out Glacier's rates for sweeping the floor – 50 per cent higher than the rates at Grunwick.

It was not all easy going. In November, at a meeting of local convenors organised by the Trades Council, some had to admit that the race of many of the strikers had caused problems with backward elements in their factories. The strikers too began by being sensitive about race. The Strike Committee objected to Jack Dromey's mentioning in a letter from the Trades Council to the local factories and branches that all bar one were black and Asian. But eventually it was recognised that the problem of prejudice had to be faced and that it could only be overcome by working hard to take the strike into the movement and to face up to the fact that prejudice existed and had to be fought.

However, the response of the trade-union movement in Brent was first rate. One of the early bulletins records a flow of donations, including £50 from Mulliner Park Wards/Rolls-Royce Works Committee, £20 from Express Dairies, £17 from Associated Automation (GEC), £30 from 01/524 TGWU, £27 from the UPW Cricklewood Sorting Office Branch and £10 from a Miners' Lodge in South Wales. The last two, dated September 1976, it must be remembered, were to acquire greater significance when some newspapers were later to accuse the

Brent Trades Council of importing 'thuggish' miners and 'mindless militants' of postal sorters into the dispute. In fact, the miners and postal workers from the start saw Grunwick as an issue of trade-union principle and responded accordingly.

As part of the effort to spread support for the strike, the Trades Council invoked the help of the Greater London Association of Trades Councils, the coordinating body of the thirty-six Trades Councils in Greater London. The Trades Council also printed a weekly bulletin on behalf of the Strike Committee. The first authors were Paul Vig and Sunil Desai who, in their enthusiasm, made two mistakes; they exaggerated the numbers of those on strike and spoke of several previous attempts to organise at Grunwick. It was true that, over the past four years, some had talked of joining a union, but the only record of a serious attempt to organise was that of 1973. Nevertheless, the bulletins were highly effective and within weeks were going all over the country. In this respect, the help of the Liaison Committee for the Defence of Trades Unions and its Chairman, Kevin Halpin, was invaluable in providing contacts. The bulletins were a very sore point with the company, and its counsel at the Court of Inquiry was to press Dromey hard on their authorship. Scarman found that the Trades Council helped with their reproduction and English language only.

The Strike Committee and the Trades Council organised jointly a number of events, including regular socials and 'straight-from-work' meetings in the Trades Hall for local stewards and convenors. Marches ending in public meetings were arranged every month or so, starting on 10 September. Even on that first march, over three hundred local trade unionists turned out and marched via the two factories to the Trades Hall. As the march passed the Chapter Road factory, Ward and some directors stood laughing and jeering just inside the gate, while other directors filmed and photographed the marchers from upstairs windows. The meeting was addressed by Tom Durkin, Jack Dromey, Sunil Desai, Brian Eagles, the Mulliner Park Ward/Rolls-Royce Convenor, and Len Gristey.

On 1 October, nearly 400 people marched from Cobbold Road to Chapter Road, and the final meeting was addressed by Durkin, Dromey, Gristey, Mahood Ahmad, who had by now taken over as Secretary of the Strike Committee, and Abdul Wagu, the convenor of Associated Automation. In an article entitled 'Sari Power' by Graham

Taylor in the *Morning Star,* the first feature in a national daily on the Grunwick strike, the march was described as follows:

> As workers munched sandwiches outside the factory gates of Willesden, the High Road suddenly exploded into a blaze of colour. Down the road, banners flying, swept hundreds of demonstrators, led by Indian workers. In the vanguard, saris swirling, were the Indian women. Not submissive housebound women but Grunwick strikers – fists raised in anger. Not the inarticulate immigrant women we are often told about. Hardly. For at every building they passed, they shouted their one resounding slogan: 'Union! Union! We want Union!'

But if there was one major innovation by the Trades Council and strikers, and one that deserves to be copied elsewhere, it was the organisation of a meeting for the husbands and other relatives of the Asian women strikers. The idea came from Jayaben Desai and Jack Dromey, when some of the women complained that their families did not like them picketing or going out on delegations. For three hours one Sunday, forty of the husbands fired questions at Jack Dromey, Adrian Askew, an APEX official, and the officers of the Strike Committee, while some of the younger male strikers made tea and Indian food in the kitchen of the Trades Hall. The meeting made a decisive contribution towards helping the women play a full part in the strike and brought into the dispute the families of those on strike. Often, the media creates differences between men on strike and their wives and elevates to the order of merit those who are prepared to demonstrate their hostility to the union. In the Grunwick strike, no such division was allowed to be created.

So it was that, in September and early October 1976, APEX, the Strike Committee and the Trades Council all pulled together to bring pressure to bear on the company. Their aim was simple: to get Grunwick to sit down around the negotiating table and conclude a peace settlement. The pressure on Grunwick and those still at work was great; the Trades Council and the Strike Committee had involved the organisations of the Indian community and they asked fellow Indians to join the strike. The local MPs and Brent Council were also brought in. Dromey arranged for a delegation of strikers to meet Phil Hartley, the leader of Brent Council, and Hartley made tireless efforts to open up negotiations. APEX meanwhile contacted their sponsored MPs in the House of Commons, while the Trades Council asked for the help of Laurie Pavitt and Reg Freeson, the MPs for Brent South and Brent East respectively. They too wrote to the company offering their services to break the deadlock.

Inside Grunwick those still at work were complaining. Their confidence bolstered by the walkout, the minutes of Grunwick's Works Committee records that they pressed the company for improvements in pay and conditions and complained about lack of promotion prospects for immigrants. Collections were taken for the strikers. The work of the company was hard hit. The extent of the walkout, particularly in the Mail-Order Department, severely disrupted the organisation of labour. Further, the blacking at Kodak and elsewhere created shortages. The barons were in disarray. Their serfs outside the gate were cock-a-hoop. The stage was set for a speedy settlement.

6

The Struggle Begins

Any hopes of a quick settlement were soon dashed. The replies from the company to Freeson, Pavitt and Hartley were less than encouraging. Ward was contemptuous of the strikers of whom, he wrote to Phil Hartley, there were only thirty left. As October wore on, the company began to find ways round the blacking.

The response of Grunwick to the refusal of the postal workers to cross the picket lines was simply to collect the mail from the sorting office itself. As for the blacking of the continental mail-order work at the airport and docks in the UK and in Belgium, the Netherlands and West Germany, the company played cat and mouse with the unions for weeks, by changing from one port of entry to another. Eventually, when the noose became too tight, the company bought a plane, hired its own pilot and flew the work in to various small airfields. As for chemicals and photographic paper, all the main suppliers blacked the company but Grunwick responded by sending out its managers to purchase small quantities here, there and everywhere, which could easily be transported through the picket lines in the boots of managers' cars.

On the picket lines, directors and managers baited the strikers and used loudspeakers to threaten them with blacklisting. Management cars were driven aggressively at the women on the picket lines. A director's car passed over Jayaben Desai's foot and she was taken to hospital for treatment. A pregnant woman was knocked over. During the meeting for the relatives of the strikers, two directors sat menacingly outside the Trades Hall in a car, hoping to spot APEX members still working at Grunwick. The marches continued to be filmed and photographed. On 14 September, Ward read out the school record of a Strike Committee member over a megaphone from a file supposed to be confidential. Later, even Roy Grantham was to be subjected to this process of intimidation. He bumped into Ward after the House of Commons debate in November on the Union of Post Office Workers' blacking. He introduced himself, hoping to break the ice. Ward tersely replied: 'I've had you checked out, Grantham'.

To those who experienced the constant taunts and harassment on the picket line and, on one occasion, outside their own homes, management's claims that the 'loyal' workers were subject to harassment were grotesque and laughable. The evidence produced by the company was that Azadi Patel, a young mother who stayed at work, had been the victim of a campaign of hatred against her. She claimed that she had had threatening phone calls, been followed in the street, visited and harassed at her home, had her young son threatened with being kidnapped and the word 'scab' daubed on her front door.

Azadi had a very fertile imagination. Certainly she had been visited at home, but it was by representatives of the Indian Workers' Association and leading figures in the local Indian community. She discussed coming out on strike with them at length, made them tea and expressed sympathy with the strikers. As for the daubing of her door, the Strike Committee immediately condemned the action. It was not in its interest in any case, because its relations with those inside were still very good. Many strikers had lifelong friends still at work and such actions could only damage their chances of persuading them to join the strike. But feelings within the local Indian community were running high: those still at work were disowned by many members of their own community, who stood full square with the strikers.

The intimidation of the strikers, on the other hand, was carried out not only with the full knowledge of the company, but by leading figures in it. So obvious had the aggressiveness of the management been that, as early as 26 August, when Len Gristey went to knock on the company's door, he was stopped by a police constable who told him that, if he did, 'he would not answer for my safety, which is something I have never experienced in this country before'.

Why did the management react so violently to the strike? Why did it reject out of hand all offers of mediation? Why did it prolong the strike through September and October? As far as its intimidation was concerned, Jayaben Desai believes that its attitude was not hard to understand. Intimidation was built into Grunwick's style of supervision.

The reason for its rejection of mediation and for the prolonging of the strike was equally simple; the Grunwick directors were and are strongly anti-union. They are a type of enterprising, self-made men who cannot bear any challenge to their divine right to rule. There is no doubt from the company accounts that Grunwick was so prosperous that it could have easily 'bought' industrial peace; the extraordinary increases subsequently paid to the 'loyal' workers proved that. But the directors chose not to. There is also no doubt that the Grunwick Strike would not have attracted such major national fame but for the totally intransigent attitude of management. Thousands of supporters flocked to support the strikers in 1977 for one reason above all others; Grunwick was an anti-union firm that challenged all that had been fought for over two centuries.

As early as 1973, it had become obvious that the company was anti-union. Two workers who were seeking to organise the workforce into the TGWU were suddenly made redundant. Twenty others walked out in protest. The TGWU claimed recognition for those on strike and for its members still inside. After at first appearing to hesitate, the company sacked those on strike and refused to talk to anyone. For seven weeks, the sacked workers, a third of the then workforce and their union, backed by the Trades Council, did battle with the company.

The TGWU took the dismissals to an industrial tribunal but ran into difficulties because it was not registered under the Heath Government's Industrial Relations Act. The Tribunal ruled that all but one of the cases were outside its jurisdiction because the workers involved had not been continuously employed for 104 weeks. The remaining worker, a Ms Mulvey, had her case rejected on the grounds that Ward and Alden could not have known that she was a union member because, when asked, she had lied, out of fear, and told them she was not.

Grunwick was not, however, completely let off the hook. The Tribunal felt obliged to state in its findings that, although the sacking was technically within the letter of the law, 'the manner of dismissal left much to be desired' and did not accord with the Code of Practice. Later, Ward was to claim the Tribunal had ruled that the sackings were fair. It had done nothing of the kind.

On 15 March 1973, the then-Secretary of State, Robin Chichester-Clark wrote to Laurie Pavitt, MP, stating that the company had refused to meet either with the union concerned or with the Conciliation Officers of the Department of Employment to try and settle the dispute. As Stephen Sedley, counsel for the Brent Trades Council, told the Court of Inquiry: 'The 1973 dispute left a bitter reaction throughout the trade-union movement in north-west London. Grunwick came to be regarded as an aggressively anti-union employer.' The employees of the company always knew that it was anti-union. Kevin Slattery, one of the drivers, who also acted as Ward's chauffeur, told the Court of Inquiry that Fanning, the transport director and Ward's brother-in-law, had warned him that the company would close down if ever a union was established. Slattery also alleged that Fanning told the drivers, who in 1976 were thinking of joining a union, the story of a man called Conal who had been sacked in 1973 for giving out union forms. When three men secretly joined the TGWU in the spring of 1977, during the APEX strike, Fanning told the other drivers, including Slattery, that the three would be sacked as soon as the APEX strike was defeated. According to the drivers who came out on strike in July, Fanning pulled into his office drivers whom he saw chatting to the three marked men and warned them not to speak to them in the future, thus effectively sending them to Coventry. As the editorial of the *Observer* commented on 26 July 1977: the superficial reasons for the prolonged strike are various but 'the basic cause goes deeper: to the anti-union attitudes of Mr George Ward'.

Ward's attitude towards unions is not simply an irrational prejudice but seems to have a profound class basis. As he told *The Times* in June 1977: 'I am my own man and that is what I am fighting for'. In other words, he is committed to being an employer and, as an intelligent man, he knows that not everyone can become an employer. He could only become an employer by turning others into employees who would never be given a share in the decision-making process within Grunwick. He always denies, however, being anti-union; he stoutly maintains that his company is not 'anti-union' but 'non-union'. This pedantic distinction is typical of the smokescreens that he and his backers were so adept at throwing over the hardness of attitude that would have certainly lost him public sympathy if it had been explicitly stated.

It was in this respect that the cross-examination of Ward by Stuart Shields, counsel for APEX, was such a highlight of the Court of Inquiry. Shields patiently tried to establish whether or not Ward was opposed to a trade union at Grunwick:

Shields: In 1973 when there was the previous dispute over recognition with the TGWU, your company dismissed, was it some 30 people?

Ward: I think your mathematics is somewhat inaccurate.

Shields: You tell me the correct figure.

Ward: We did not dismiss anyone; we made two people redundant. Other people walked out. I believe that the maximum number of people was between ten and fifteen but traditionally, I believe trade unions always double figures, so I have been told.

Shields was not satisfied with the reply that Ward 'did not dismiss anyone'. He returned to it later: did Ward sack anyone or did he not?

Ward: I have indicated to you that we sacked no one at the time. We made two people redundant – the rest walked out.

Shields: And you then sacked them.

Ward: We sacked them for walking out.

It took Shields many more questions to pin Ward down. Finally, he cornered him:

Shields: What I want to know is whether what you have just stated, that there is no room for collective bargaining in a small, well-run factory such as yours, has not been your attitude right from the start?

Ward: That has been my attitude right from the start.

At last! A straight answer – but what exactly did it mean? It seems that Ward's view on trade unions amounted to this: putting it at its most charitable, he was prepared to tolerate *individual* membership of a trade union. (Ward boasted to the Court that there was a member of Equity, the actors' union, working in the company; Scarman asked if he was 'resting'.) But Ward was not prepared to tolerate any right of his workers to bargain *collectively* with him. He told Scarman that he never objected to his employees being members of a union provided that they did not try to 'force' other people to join. Scarman concluded: 'It was the desire of the directors and top management of the company, while professing to accept the right of individual employees to join a trade union, not to recognise a union for collective bargaining purposes'.

Ward also thought that, while trade unions were necessary in the nineteenth century, they were not now – a novel version of anti-trade unionism. According to the *Daily Telegraph* of 23 August 1977, Ward said: 'Power rests today not with Parliament but with the trade unions ... The poor chap who's being exploited today is the man who's trying to run his own business'. One striker expressed sympathy: 'I suppose it must be tough nowadays for racehorse owners'.

Of APEX, Ward was totally dismissive. He did not even accept that it was an appropriate union for workers in the film-processing industry, a view Scarman disagreed with. To the *Daily Mail* of 23 June, Ward said: 'APEX, APEX, what the hell is it? Some kind of new contraceptive?'

He did not even accept that there was any demand for union recognition from his workforce because he had sacked the 137 on strike, and they were, as far as he was concerned, no longer his workers. On London Weekend Television's 'London Programme', he produced another variation on the theme. Consistently, over many months, he said, 260 workers had disagreed with Jayaben Desai and Mahmood Ahmad. He thought it was 'immoral' to 'force' these 'loyal' workers to join a union: 'This would be a loss of liberty ... and I think the state has already taken enough liberties off them'. This was the bogus ghost of the closed shop, a ghost that was not to be laid until the company conceded before the Court of Inquiry that the closed shop had never been an issue at Grunwick. APEX wanted recognition only for the workers who joined the union and for those who wished to belong. It was made absolutely clear from the start that those who did not want to belong would not be forced to do so. But that was not enough for Ward and his backers. John Gouriet was later to say that resistance to recognition was legitimate because recognition was the first step on the road to the closed shop.

Ward's figures of 260 loyal workers were unreliable in any case. The APEX claim was in respect of the weekly paid staff only, and many of the 'loyal' workers were later to join the strike. Besides, even if a worker does not want to join a union, it by no means follows that he or she objects to fellow workers joining. Visitors to the picket lines throughout the autumn of 1976 were amazed at the friendliness between the pickets and those still at work. Some supporters were critical, saying that the strikers did not put enough pressure upon them. Recruitment went on inside the company, and many of those who didn't join the strike would say to the pickets that they were terrified of losing their jobs because of financial commitments, or that they would leave the company as soon as they got another job. Many chose the latter, easier course.

APEX lost patience with Ward's intransigence at the beginning of October. Roy Grantham wrote to Albert Booth, the Secretary of State for Employment, demanding a Court of Inquiry. On 15 October, Grantham led a march of his members to the House of Commons. A petition was handed in to the Prime Minister at 10 Downing Street asking for his intervention. 6000 residents of Brent had signed it in four days. A delegation of strikers led by Grantham had hoped to meet Booth to press the demand for a Court of Inquiry. Booth sent a message instead in which he refused the demand. There was, he said, a perfectly satisfactory machinery for the resolution of such disputes laid down in the Employment Protection Act. He urged APEX to make a reference to the Advisory, Conciliation and Arbitration Service (ACAS), under Section 11 of the Act, which allows ACAS to investigate the claim of a union for recognition.

The idea of ACAS had its roots in the Report of the Royal Commission on the Trade Unions, the Donovan Report. The Service had actually been constituted under the Conservative Government of 1970-4 but its terms of reference were greatly enlarged by the new Labour Government of 1974. As the framework of legal sanctions and NIRC, the National Industrial Relations Court, was dismantled, the Government sought a consensus approach to the resolution of those problems that could not be resolved through the normal machinery of collective bargaining. That approach was embodied in ACAS, whose governing Council comprises three representatives of the Trades Union Congress, three representatives of the Confederation of British Industries and three academics. ACAS is independent of government and is charged with the duty 'of encouraging the extension of collective bargaining'. This principle is notionally public policy, since its enunciation by Donovan, and it is, in theory, supported by both main political parties.

ACAS has no powers to enforce its decisions. Such was the desire of both sides of industry in the aftermath of the disaster of the Industrial Relations Act. The idea was that a union would make a reference to ACAS under Section 11 of the Employment Protection Act. If ACAS could not persuade the employer to meet the union, it would proceed with obtaining the opinions of the workers in any one of a number of ways, normally by use of a ballot or questionnaire. Jim Mortimer, the Chairman of ACAS and a former leading official of AUEW/TASS, prefers questionnaires and confidential interviews with employees, because workers are often unclear about what is at issue, or are afraid to vote for a union for fear of losing their jobs.

ACAS, having carried out its investigation, then considers each situation in full Council before making a recommendation. Its recommendations are not legally binding, and the employer has two further months to reconsider their position if the recommendation is favourable to the union. After those two months, the union can take the recommendation to the Central Arbitration Committee (CAC), a new creation of the present Labour Government. Again, the CAC cannot compel the employer to recognise the union but it can adjudicate on a claim by the union for better pay and conditions. Its decisions on such matters are deemed to be included in the contract of employment and, if the employer remains intransigent, those decisions are legally enforceable by a civil action in the High Court for breach of contract.

The procedure is convoluted and, from start to finish, takes at least a year, and quite conceivably could take two or even three years if the employer did everything possible to delay. At the end of it, the issue of recognition might still remain unresolved, with the union having to go back to the CAC at regular intervals to make further claims in respect of wages and conditions. And none of this resolved the issue of reinstatement, which could not legally be compelled. However, when the Act was passed, it was thought highly unlikely that a union would have to go through the entire procedure in any but the most exceptional of cases. The tripartite approach of Government, the TUC and the CBI was to persuade and not to compel. It was expected that both sides would act reasonably.

Grantham was reluctant to make the reference to ACAS. It had already tried and failed to bring the two sides together, on the request of APEX, as part of its general brief to break the ice in such situations. With his experience, he rightly sensed that this was possibly an exceptional situation. Further, it would not be easy for ACAS to carry out its functions in a dispute, and his members might have to wait months for its report. Grantham was not reassured by Booth's statement that he would ask ACAS to report as quickly as possible, but he felt that he had no choice. Besides, ACAS would not be the only string to his bow.

He was determined to pursue what his members had been asking for, official action by the UPW.

Grantham went, at the head of the delegation of strikers, to see Jim Mortimer. Grunwick will be our number one priority, said Mortimer. Three days later, Grunwick was officially notified of the reference under Section 11. Ward was still not falling over himself to be cooperative. John Gorst was later to explain that Grunwick regarded ACAS as necessarily biased because of the phrase in the Employment Protection Act about it 'encouraging' collective bargaining. Ward was his usual pedantic self: ACAS was not biased, he said, but its 'function' was.

The union did not sit back and sift the latest theological hair-splittings from Ward. In Brent, the delegates to the Trades Council from the Cricklewood Sorting Office branch of the UPW, Dave Dodd and Archie Sinclair, had reported back favourably to their members on Grunwick. The mail should be blacked completely, they said: it is useless not to cross picket lines but allow the company to pick up its mail. The sorting office should refuse to hand it over to the company. Such a move would cripple a company, the main bulk of whose work was mail order. The branch agreed.

Thus APEX soon wrote to the Executive Committee of the UPW, asking for the total blacking of the Grunwick mail. One week before the Executive was due to consider the request, Len Gristey and Mahmood Ahmad addressed the full London District Council of the UPW on 21 October. Unanimously, the Council agreed to call upon its Executive to support APEX'S request. APEX argued that there would be no resolution to the dispute unless such pressure was applied and, on Friday 28 October, the Executive Committee of the UPW agreed. An instruction went out to all branches throughout the country – black the Grunwick mail from the morning of Monday 1 November.

A triumphant Archie Sinclair read out the instruction to a cheering crowd of strikers, their families and supporters the following day, Saturday, at a Strike Committee social in the Abbey Hotel on the North Circular Road. To the strikers, victory was imminent. The company was panic-stricken. Ward was to describe the blacking as cutting 'the jugular vein of the company'. On 25 October, hearing that the UPW intended to meet Len Murray to ask if its action would command the support of the entire movement (a question to which the answer was 'yes'), Ward approached Gorst for advice. The following day, the 26th, he agreed for the first time to meet ACAS. He told Harry Bainbridge, an ACAS official, that sustained UPW action would quickly force the company into liquidation. The company lawyers told Ward that there was little that he could do in legal terms. He was trapped. The unthinkable stared him in the face – a union at Grunwick.

7

'NAFF v. The Unions – Who Wins?'

G runwick was saved from almost certain defeat by the intervention of an unashamedly right-wing organisation called the National Association for Freedom (NAFF). Right-wing forces had started to rally to Ward's support as soon as the UPW decision became known. No sooner had the postal blacking started on Monday 1 November, than Conservative MPs led by John Gorst organised parliamentary action. On the Tuesday, rallying over a hundred Conservative MPs in support, Gorst secured a debate on Grunwick in the House of Commons for the Thursday. Simultaneously, the NAFF announced through John Gouriet, its Administrative Director, that it was contemplating legal action against the postal workers for violating the Post Office Act of 1953. In one week NAFF had elevated Grunwick from a local trade-union dispute into a national political issue.

The debate in Parliament on 4 November hardly got under way before Albert Booth, Minister of Employment, rose to make an announcement. He told the House that the UPW had agreed to suspend its blacking on receiving an assurance from Grunwick that it would cooperate with ACAS. For the general public, that seemed to settle the overnight sensation of the Grunwick Strike. The following Tuesday, the seal was set on the apparent compromise, by the withdrawal of Ward's NAFF-backed action against the UPW, after it promised the High Court it would not interfere with the company's mail.

Back in Willesden these swift developments inaugurated a new phase in the strike. There opened up a gap in the labour movement for the first time, between the left who immediately recognised Booth's 'compromise' as, in effect, a defeat, and the right wing of the trade-union movement who welcomed the 'compromise' apparently without reservation, although Grantham was still uneasy about the adequacy of the Employment Protection Act procedures. Experienced militants, such as Tom Durkin, had learnt from past dealings with employers that what is promised under coercion is not performed once the weapon of coercion is removed. The Brent Trades Council was sceptical but naturally had temporarily to accept the assurances of Tom Jackson and Albert Booth that Grunwick had turned over a new leaf. The strikers hoped for the best.

From this point on in the Grunwick Strike, the left-wing viewpoint time and again clashed with the more right-wing opinions that were predominant, on the whole, in APEX and the TUC. As long as the issue remained mainly a trade-union one, these differences were of little importance, but once NAFF had dragged the Grunwick Strike into the political arena, it became an all-out class battle. The right wing on the union side, hoping to avoid such a political confrontation, relied extensively on official procedures and the processes of law. The left, on the contrary, seeing defeat as a demoralising blow for the working class, wished to mobilise the power of the trade-union movement to defeat Grunwick by the time-honoured working-class weapons of blacking, picketing and demonstrating.

By allying with the NAFF, Ward had placed his cards on the table. By shirking the challenge that Ward increasingly threw down to the movement, APEX and the TUC set off on a course that was to end in a prolonged strike and unnecessary violence. To Grunwick, as its counsel, Stuart McKinnon, told the Court of Inquiry, the situation was crystal clear: 'The company put nothing in writing and, as far as the company was concerned, was asked to put nothing in writing. The company did not understand it was giving any understanding, let alone an understanding to the UPW.'

Whether it was Tom Jackson, Roy Grantham or Albert Booth who first gave the impression that Grunwick had promised to cooperate with ACAS is not clear. Perhaps it was one of Ward's pedantic turns of phrase that deceived Tom Jackson. Certainly, hardly anyone on the Executive Committee of the Trades Council believed, from what they knew of Grunwick and of NAFF, that there had been a genuine deal. It did not make sense. With those inside still so friendly with the pickets, how could Ward possibly risk a ballot? Why should he accept a ballot that he would definitely lose? The left saw that the only way to win the strike was for the TUC to back the postal workers' right to boycott Grunwick, whatever the legal obstacles. The alternative was to send out an invitation to all employers to sack workers on strike and to encourage the NAFF in its crusade.

Those who founded the NAFF were drawn from a network of individuals and organisations on the right of British politics, which included an organisation called 'Self-help'. This was run by Ross McWhirter in conjunction with Lady Birdwood, who has frequently shown an interest in the National Front. Ross McWhirter, one of the McWhirter twins, famous for producing the *Guinness Book of Records,* was full of ideas for 'saving Britain', by which he meant saving British employers. He planned a newspaper to run in the event of a General Strike. He offered to supply blacklegs to strikebound employers. He was especially fond of using legal niceties in the courts against left-wing policies. In 1967, McWhirter had taken legal action against the introduction of state comprehensive schools in Enfield and, again, in 1970 against a Labour Party political broadcast. He built up a reputation for himself amongst the right for these, and many other, legal forays. In November 1975 he put up a £50,000 reward for information leading to the conviction of IRA bombers responsible for explosions in London. The Provisionals, lacking the left's commitment to mass action as opposed to individual terrorism, shot McWhirter dead at the door of his house in London.

McWhirter's friends vowed to continue his work and within a week of the murder the National Association for Freedom was launched. With the involvement of right-wing intellectuals such as Robert Moss, the NAFF certainly registered an improvement over 'Self-help'. It sought to establish non-fascist and even democratic credentials, although Moss and other members were prepared to defend fascist governments, as in Chile, if the alternative was Marxist.

The use of the word 'freedom' was certainly intelligent. There is no one in Britain – Conservative, Labour, Liberal or Communist – who will oppose 'freedom'. The catch was of course that in practice the NAFF's 'freedom' was 'freedom for the few'.

The kinds of freedoms that the NAFF campaigned for were in the main those only the rich could afford; and yet, at the same time, it claimed its 'freedom' was for everybody. For example, the NAFF favours 'freedom of choice' in education so that workers can be 'free' to send their children to Eton and Harrow public schools at £2000 per annum. The NAFF also favours 'freedom' in the health service so that workers can 'choose' to be ill in private clinics costing £200 per week. In industrial relations it is the same theme: enterprising workers should not be held back by trade unionism from spending the thousands they have accumulated as a consequence of starting up their own businesses.

The NAFF soon attracted to its ranks many captains of industry and well-heeled journalists and its ruling council became like a roll call of the right wing in Britain. In 1976-7, its members included: Sir Paul Chambers, former head of ICI; Hugh Astor, a director of Hambros Bank; Frank Taylor of Taylor Woodrow, the building company; Lord Brookes, life-president of Guest, Keen and Nettlefold, the giant engineering company; Peregrine Worsthorne, assistant editor of the *Sunday Telegraph;* Alec Bedser, the cricketer who opposed the West Indians playing in Britain; John Braine, novelist and right-wing campaigner; Rhodes Boyson, the Conservative Party's deputy spokesman on education (and Jayaben Desai's MP); Winston Churchill junior, grandson of the Prime Minister who bitterly opposed Indian independence and ridiculed Gandhi; Jill Knight, Conservative MP, a pro-hanging zealot and vociferous opponent of women's liberation; John Gorst, Conservative MP, supporter of Margaret Thatcher against Ted Heath in 1974. Margaret Thatcher herself has shown her sympathy for the NAFF by attending its inaugural dinner and subsequent functions.

The NAFF's domestic policies in Britain had aroused the anger of the left long before Grunwick. It ran a fortnightly newspaper, *Free Nation,* which laid great stress on the sanctity of private property and the reduction of income tax. In the summer of 1976, the NAFF had paid £8000 legal costs for the Manchester Tameside parents' campaign against comprehensive state schools. In economics, the *Free Nation* championed the views of American economist Milton Friedman, in opposition to the economics of both Karl Marx and Maynard Keynes.

Typical of the NAFF's policies were its recommendations for the government budget of 1976: scrapping aid to poorer countries; ending all food and housing subsidies for the poor; ending grants to help the unemployed in the regions; stopping subsidies for children's school meals; and the cutting of social services such as health and education. How did the NAFF plan to use the money thus 'saved'? First, to abolish taxation on company profits; second, to abolish capital gains tax, which falls mainly on speculators; and third, to expand military spending.

The *Free Nation* interspersed these policies with relentless attacks on Tony Benn, Michael Foot, and – in 1977 – Jack ('Jackboot') Dromey, of the Brent Trades Council, their favourite target in the Grunwick

Strike. Their adoption of 'Jackboot' for Dromey is not casual. The NAFF always takes great care to distance itself from fascism and the National Front, admittedly with some degree of justification. It utterly opposes the state as, it seems, all good old-fashioned Tories should. It opposes 'government' and 'bureaucracy' with all the righteous indignation of rich people subject to heavy income tax. The NAFF also distinguishes itself from fascism, which, it claims, is rooted in 'socialism'. Hitler called himself a 'socialist', the NAFF and Thatcher are fond of pointing out. In the *Free Nation* of 5-18 August 1977, there was a picture of Hitler and Wedgwood Benn headlined: 'Who are the fascists?' The article points out that Oswald Mosley, founder of the British fascists in the 1930s, was a Labour Cabinet Minister, like Booth or Denis Healey now. Dismissing the National Front lightly as a low-grade evil', the article claims insistently that the NAFF is 'Britain's only real anti-fascist group'. The 'Tribune' Group, like the National Front, says the NAFF, favours state power, nationalisation and import controls, all typically socialist measures. Yet the NAFF fails to mention the enormous difference between the socialist politics of the 'Tribune' Group, and the fascist elitism of the National Front. It fails to mention that *Tribune* wants state powers for socialism while the fascists want state power to maintain the status quo.

NAFF spokesmen are terrified by the rising tide of socialism in Zimbabwe, Angola and Mozambique. The donations that the NAFF receives from the South African-based company, Consolidated Gold Fields, proves that the Grunwick strikers' poster, 'Grunwick-Soweto: ONE STRUGGLE!' was not far off the mark.

Free Nation, as usual, has a theory to explain the intervention of Britain and the USA in the Third World. According to this theory, there has been no exploitation in Africa, Asia and South America by British and American imperialism. On the contrary, according to the NAFF, Europe and the USA brought Western technology to those impoverished regions of the world. No one can deny there is some truth in this. What it omits to mention is that these benefits were brought incidentally. The aim of imperialism and colonisation was exploitation and, if they ultimately failed, it was not for want of trying. The British colonisers and imperialists did not run the slave trade to 'civilise' the slaves. Nor did they jail Nehru and Gandhi to raise India's cultural level. It was not to impress Indians with Western technology that they shot down a thousand Indians at Amritsar.

A corollary to the NAFF's pro-imperialism is its anti-communism. The NAFF recognises that its chief opponent in Africa, Asia and Latin America is Marxism, just as its chief opponent in British trade unionism is Marxism. This link is the explanation of John Gouriet's statement to Robert Taylor of the *Observer* that the Grunwick Strike is part of 'an international conspiracy'.

The NAFF even opposes a detente between the USA and the USSR. It opposes disarmament and all other moves towards peace. Robert Moss, the leading director of the NAFF, drafted Margaret Thatcher's infamous 'Iron Maiden' speech in which she opposed disarmament and attacked the Soviet Union.

Communist influence in the world attracts the NAFF like honey attracts bees. One of its members, Sir Robert Thompson, advised President Nixon on the Vietnam War, while another, Brian Crozier, wrote a book about Communist influence in South-East Asia. Another NAFF member, Sir Gerald Templar, is renowned for his campaign against the Communists in Malaya. In June 1977, *Free Nation* launched a bitter attack on the BBC for showing an interview with Fidel Castro. South America especially interests the NAFF. Robert Moss, for example, went to Chile as a representative of the *Economist* magazine. There he wrote an article in *SEPA,* a Chilean magazine read by Chilean military officers, which appeared on 20 March 1973, only a few months before the military coup in which President Allende and thousands of socialists were murdered. Moss's article was entitled: 'An English Recipe For Chile – Military Control'. Brian Crozier later underlined the NAFF view on Chile in the *Daily Telegraph* of 3 May 1976 when he opined that in Chile and Uruguay the military 'saved the people from a fate infinitely worse than anything that is now happening' (what was then happening was the arrest, execution and torture of thousands of socialists and trade unionists). Naturally, the NAFF backed the extension of the same trends to neighbouring Argentina in 1976. While Roy Grantham was denouncing Grunwick at the TUC, Moss was giving a speech of encouragement to the Argentinian military at its Air Force Headquarters.

On Grunwick, the NAFF has always insisted that it intervened ɔ uphold 'individual freedom'. Moss claimed that Grunwick had never denied its workers the individual right to join a union. Strictly speaking, of course, this may have been true. But the whole essence of trade unionism is not just the right for individuals to join but the right to organise, to recruit and to bargain collectively with the employer. The NAFF has never once championed a case of the freedom of a trade union to organise against an employer.

Many might consider the NAFF as just another crank organisation. To do so would be seriously to underrate what is the most sophisticated organisation of the ultra-right in Britain since the war, and one which has learnt from all the mistakes made by its predecessors. Its two pronged strategy poses a considerable threat to the trade union movement and the left: first, it seeks to galvanise all the small and medium anti-union employers into a vigorous 'third force' in British industry, one that is utterly opposed to the TUC but which also opposes the adherence to consensus politics in the industrial relations of the CBI and liberal Tories like James Prior.

Its second objective is to work as a pressure group within the Conservative Party, seeking to promote the politics of confrontation with the trade union movement, and a return to the policies of the fundamentalist Tory right. In this, it has had some considerable success. By January of 1978, Barney Hayhoe, Jim Prior's deputy as Conservative spokesman on employment, was saying in Parliament that collective bargaining was not necessarily synonymous with good industrial relations. Other Tory MPs complained of workers being 'overprotected' by legislation, and championed the cause of employers who they said were thereby unable to sack anyone or take on extra labour. Neither was the NAFF averse to helping out the right wing in the Labour Party. Alex Lyon, MP, a former Minister in the Home Office, revealed in February of 1978 that the NAFF had assisted the right wing 'entrists' in Newham North-East Labour Party. Three months later, in May, the NAFF again was accused by William Van Straubenzee, MP, a Minister in the Heath Government, of practising extreme right-wing entrism into the Conservative Party.

By 1978, the NAFF's effective use of the courts and manipulation of the media had done much to popularise the cause of the Tory right and to give it an ideological respectability at a time when the left was in retreat.

8

NAFF Wins

There is no doubt in the minds of the strikers that, following the defeat of the postal workers' blacking, the outmanoeuvring of APEX in the winter of 1976-7 was largely due to the influence of the NAFF. The first victim of the sea-lawyers at the NAFF was ACAS itself, which was optimistically operating on the assumption that it would soon be permitted to assess workers' opinions at the company.

As early as Friday 12 November, APEX (after hearing about an entirely fruitless meeting between ACAS and Grunwick on the Wednesday) was expressing concern to ACAS that the company was going to delay the procedure. All three parties, of course, realised that delays benefited the employer. It was not the directors who were standing in the rain, for strike pay of £12 per week.

ACAS therefore pressed the company by sending a copy of its proposed questionnaire and, at the same time, asking for the names and addresses of employees. Nothing happened. On Friday 19 November, ACAS sent a representative to Grunwick but he was not able to expedite matters. On the following Monday, ACAS phoned George Ward, who explained that the company was objecting to the questionnaire for reasons set out in a letter that was 'in the post', and that there could be no further meeting with ACAS until ACAS had replied to this letter.

On the Thursday, Grunwick announced it was increasing wages by 15 per cent, but ACAS had still not received a letter. Although ACAS rang up, and even offered to send a representative to collect the mysterious letter, it seems that it was not until the Saturday that it was posted. ACAS did not receive it until Tuesday 30 November, and immediately despatched a reply, delivered by hand on the same day.

The basis of Grunwick's objection was that those on strike should not be included in the survey by ACAS because 'they no longer work for us'. Grunwick claimed that the strikers were not, in the words of the law, workers 'to whom the issue relates'. It claimed, however, that it was not obstructing ACAS.

In the first week of December, ACAS tried to contact Grunwick by telephone but was at first unable to do so. Eventually, Ward spoke to ACAS and agreed to a meeting on 10 December. ACAS even allowed itself to believe that Grunwick was about to accept the idea of a survey or ballot. At the meeting, however, a new objection emerged: Grunwick would not have the name 'APEX' on the questionnaire, thus making it rather difficult for ACAS to frame the central question of its investigation. It is true that Ward did not ask for all workers supporting union recognition to be excluded from the ballot – but perhaps that was the one objection that did not occur to him!

The Conservative Party now intervened, following a report in the press that the UPW would renew the postal blacking unless there was progress in the Grunwick–ACAS talks. After the fall of the Heath Government in 1974, the Conservatives had adopted a new policy of entering the trade unions and fighting from within. On this basis James Prior, the Conservative spokesperson for employment, had become an APEX member. On 14 December, he wrote to Grunwick urging the company to cooperate with ACAS which, because it had as many employers on it as trade unionists, the Conservative Party had accepted as a neutral body.

George Ward did not, however, agree with the Conservatives that ACAS was neutral because, as he told the local paper, the purpose of 'ACAS, as constituted under the Employment Protection Act, is to encourage collective bargaining. That means trade unions.' Ward also reverted to the question of whether APEX was really the best union for his workers. He gave the impression of spending many a sleepless night worrying whether his workers would not be better off in the TGWU, or even Equity.

Ward also expressed anxiety about the translation of the ballot questions into Gujarati. In particular, he felt that the initials 'APEX' would prove too tricky to translate. He suddenly discovered a need for accurate translation into the Gujarati language that had previously escaped his managers when presenting new workers with their contracts. Ward's sense of democracy was also sharpened up by the ACAS proposals: he felt it was only fair that directors, managers, drivers and warehousemen should also be allowed to participate in the vote for APEX, even though they were not eligible to join!

ACAS spent the rest of December phoning Grunwick and offering dates for the next meeting. By Christmas, ACAS had had enough. Confessing defeat, it sent out 110 questionnaires on 29 December to all the addresses in its possession from a list supplied by the only party that would cooperate, APEX. Not surprisingly, the ninety-three questionnaires returned all registered a vote in favour of trade union recognition at Grunwick.

In February 1977, to counter the result of the ACAS ballot, Grunwick ran a ballot of its own. An independent organisation was brought in: MORI, the Market Opinion Research Institute. The result of the ballot seemed highly satisfactory for Grunwick. Of the weekly-paid staff 153 voted against having a trade union and twenty-one voted for.

The union's response to this was that, quite apart from the voting not including the 137 who walked out, the vote did not even reflect the true position inside the company because many workers were frightened to vote 'yes' for fear of losing their jobs. When more workers came out on strike in the June and July of 1977, this position seemed to be vindicated, for many of them testified that they had voted 'no' to the union in February out of fear. They alleged that Grunwick had pressurised the workers in the days immediately preceding the ballot. According to Delcie Claire, of the Preparation Department, Ward told the workers he wanted a 'big no' against the union. Ward, she alleged, also declared that those who voted 'yes' would be classed as 'political revolutionaries' who were 'not fit to work for him'. Joyce Pitter, of the re-order department, backed up Delcie Claire's evidence at the Court of Inquiry, recalling in particular a meeting at Cobbold Road two days before the ballot, at which Ward had demanded a 'big no'.

APEX also accused Ward of 'bribing' the workforce to support him. It pointed out that on top of a 15 per cent pay increase given on 19 November, when Grunwick was first confronted with the possibility of an ACAS ballot, Grunwick had also announced increases in holiday entitlement and sickness benefit in February, just before running its own ballot. Ward, APEX claimed, was expertly combining the carrot and the stick to produce the right result.

Later, before the Scarman Court of Inquiry, Malcolm Alden, in response to the question from Stuart Shields, QC, counsel for APEX, 'Are you really suggesting that the wage increase in November, a week before it was anticipated that there would be an ACAS ballot, and this mini-budget a week before the MORI ballot, were completely coincidental?', stated: 'Yes, because you are associating unrelated events'. Scarman had to ask those present not to laugh. 'It is not fair to the witness', he said.

Roy Grantham was, in any case, unimpressed by Ward's arrangements. If Ward wanted a ballot, why did he not accept an ACAS ballot? Perhaps what Ward feared was ACAS's habit of using questionnaires backed by confidential interviews? This aimed to overcome workers' fears by asking a variety of questions, not only on the respective union but on representation by a union generally, in a situation where they could personally be reassured of confidentiality. Perhaps, for Grunwick, that was too likely to ascertain the truth?

There were also more general criticisms. The *Guardian* editorial of 15 June, commenting on the MORI ballot, compared Grunwick's action unfavourably to other employers, such as IBM, who had recently cooperated with an ACAS survey, which had gone on to confirm that the majority of IBM employees did not want a union. Some trade unionists also pointed out that MORI's apparent objectivity did conceal an assumption, which is a potential danger to democracy. The assumption – often made in opinion polls and postal ballots – is that the voters are fully and fairly informed, have heard both sides, and are not subject to any pressure. That is why trade unions fight to have important meetings in working hours and to have the right to distribute information around factories. Needless to say, APEX was not offered these facilities at Grunwick.

Ward believed that the MORI ballot vindicated his stand and denied calling for a 'big no'. As he and Gorst were fond of pointing out, MORI was a reputable company that had carried out work for the Labour Party. The number on the ballot paper did not enable identification of the voter, because the same number – it was a batch number – appeared on *all* the ballot papers. As for voting by department, that was no trick. ACAS itself followed that procedure. It was necessary to have a departmental breakdown to prove that APEX did not have a majority in any section. Ward's defence was strengthened by the head of MORI itself, Robert Worcester, who told the *Observer* newspaper that the MORI questions were more objective than the ACAS questions which, in his opinion, were weighted towards obtaining trade-union recognition.

Grunwick also denied 'bribing' the voters. John Gorst described the 15 per cent rise in the November and the 10 per cent rise in the spring as 'inflation adjustment' payments, similar to an increase of 16 per cent that had been given in 1974 (at a time of 30 per cent settlement generally). Ward's version, as usual, was rather more sophisticated than that of his camp followers. He explained that after the strikers left, productivity rose enormously, so he naturally gave out the extra profit to the workforce rather than put it in his own pocket.

ACAS was not impressed by this new image of George Ward as the just employer. It decided in exasperation that, regardless of the fact that Grunwick would not hand over the addresses needed, it would produce a preliminary report on 9 February – to go to APEX and Grunwick for their comments – and a full report one month later. The strikers looked forward expectantly to the reports. They recalled Booth's statement in Parliament on 4 November, when he had quoted the UPW leader, Tom Jackson: 'Since Monday, however, the firm has now agreed to provide facilities for ACAS to undertake a Section 11 canvass. It has also agreed to bind itself to the result of that inquiry. It is likely, therefore, that the recognition question can be settled by the end of next week.' Now, three months later, they hoped the reports would publicly pillory Grunwick for its obduracy and thus, if the firm failed to accept the ACAS report, justify the TUC in deploying powerful solidarity that would swiftly bring the company to its knees.

February and March 1977 did not bring the strikers their victory but, instead, a further series of setbacks and defeats that drove them to the edge of despair. Firmly enmeshed in procedural devices and legal quibbles, the strike lost all momentum. The APEX officials tried to bolster the strikers' faith in the law, but any faith that they had was soon eroded by the weakness of the Employment Protection Act. The strikers were not experienced trade unionists; they had to learn about the class prejudice lurking behind the apparent impartiality of the law. As Michael Foot told the UPW conference in 1977: 'If the freedom of the people of this country, especially the rights of trade unionists, if these precious things in the past had been left to the good sense and fair-mindedness of the judges, we would have few freedoms in this country at all'.

This inexperience was only just teaching the strikers what Anatole France once described with such sarcasm: 'The law, in its majestic equality, forbids the rich as well as the poor, to sleep under bridges, to beg in the streets, to steal bread ...'

For NAFF, the spring of 1977 was a victory for its anti-union strategy. It now dealt the UPW yet another knockout blow. In 1976, the TUC backed the call by the international trade-union movement for a week of action against South Africa, as retaliation for the imprisonment of black trade unionists, some of whom had disappeared without trace, 'fallen out of high windows' or 'committed suicide' in their cells. As their contribution to the cause, the UPW decided to black South African mail for one week. Ever vigilant, the NAFF stepped in with yet another legal action against the UPW. An injunction preventing the blacking was obtained in the High Court and upheld on appeal.

The effectiveness of the NAFF's strategy lay not so much in whether it won or lost its causes but in the degrees of deflection it achieved from the *political* issues involved. Most people in Britain believe that there should be a democratic right to strike. Most people, therefore, would have some sympathy for the Grunwick strikers and for the postal workers. NAFF diverted the public away from this democratic sympathy, into arguments about technicalities of the law. Perhaps postal workers should have the right to take sympathetic strike action, some people said, but they shouldn't break the law. People forgot that nearly all democratic rights had been won after violation of the law by courageous idealists, from John Hampden, through the first illegal trade unions, to the suffragettes.

The industrial tribunal that APEX appealed to on 23 March turned out to be yet another legal cul-de-sac. There, fifty-nine of the strikers intended to obtain a ruling of 'unfair dismissal' against Grunwick. There were only fifty-nine because, of the original 137, the students had left the strike, others had found new jobs, while there were also many whose service qualification was not long enough for their case to be considered. However, it was all to no avail. The tribunal found 'no case'. It found their dismissal neither 'fair' nor 'unfair'. APEX had to show that the company had taken back at least one of the strikers but not the rest.

The APEX case fell because the worker, Solankey, whom APEX claimed had been on strike and was then taken back could not be proved, in the end, to have ever been on strike even though he had left the Grunwick premises. He could not be strictly compared to the other fifty-nine, and there was therefore no case to answer. The company later tried to make propaganda out of this negative victory but, as Tudor Thomas, Deputy General Secretary of APEX, pointed out in a letter to the *Guardian* on 7 July, the verdict of the industrial tribunal failed, not because Grunwick were vindicated, but because of 'lack of jurisdiction'.

The decision of the industrial tribunal, although it was only technical, was yet another victory for the NAFF and a defeat for trade unionism. As Stephen Sedley, counsel for Brent Trades Council, was to point out to the Court of Inquiry, the dismissal of the 137 strikers obscured the merits of the strike itself to the law. From then on the law could examine only the merits of the dismissals. The conclusion Sedley drew from this was the existence of a dire threat to democratic rights in Britain: 'Undoubtedly, as the law stands, an employer can insure himself against proceedings by dismissing every striker in a strike situation', he said.

On paper, of course, the publication of ACAS's final report, received by the strikers on 10 March, was a setback for the NAFF and Grunwick. ACAS, while criticising the strikers for some personal attacks on George Ward in their bulletins, came down firmly in favour of recognising APEX. The report said:

> In the light of our findings and conclusions we therefore recommended that the employers, Grunwick Film Processing Laboratories Limited, Cooper and Pearson Limited and Cobbold Computer Centre Limited, should recognise the union, the Association of Professional, Executive, Clerical and Computer Staff (APEX), generally for the purpose of collective bargaining in respect of weekly-paid staff, including despatch staff, computer staff, laboratory processing staff, mail order clerks; finishing, preparation splicing, film- and negative-processing staff, employed by the employers at their Chapter Road and Cobbold Road, Willesden, establishments.

This recommendation was reinforced by support from an unlikely quarter. Jim Prior, Conservative Party Shadow Minister for Employment, a new member of APEX, now urged Grunwick in a public statement on 30 March to accept the ACAS report, and recognise APEX.

The strikers' victory, however, soon proved to be only a paper one. The NAFF had no intention of accepting advice from Prior. It took a dim view of the Macmillan-Heath 'left wing' of the Conservative Party, to which Prior had attached himself. To the NAFF, these Conservative 'liberals' were too weak-kneed and flabby for the rigours of the new class war: trade unionism was there to be fought, not appeased. As *Free Nation* put it: 'It is not confrontation, after all, which would be the ultimate tragedy. The ultimate tragedy would be to have a confrontation and lose.'

The NAFF's response was hard and, as always, very legal. On 19 April, Grunwick, after consulting its 'advisers', served a high court writ on ACAS. Grunwick asked that the ACAS report be declared void on the grounds that it was based on the opinion only of Grunwick's 'former employees' – the strikers. The trade-union movement stood amazed at the NAFF's insolence. Grunwick was taking ACAS to court for not carrying out a survey which Grunwick itself had refused to allow.

9

'Company Police'

In the summer of 1977, British trade unionists descended on Grunwick in their thousands. One of the chants that could clearly be heard from the crowd was: 'Company police! Company police!' To television viewers, this may have appeared as a gratuitous insult to police officers. The truth, however, was not so simple. The British public were never told that throughout the winter months of 1976-7 the Grunwick pickets had been continuously harassed by police, who behaved time and again in a manner that was partial to the employer. This was not just the opinion of the strikers, but also the judgement of the courts. One court, in finding arrested pickets innocent on appeal against conviction in Willesden Magistrates' Court, vigorously condemned the behaviour of the Willesden police. Another court acquitted Jack Dromey, when he was charged with calling the local force 'company police'.

Yet not a word was heard from most of the press. If one of its functions in a democratic society is to act as a safety valve, then, over Grunwick, the press failed. And that failure was a contributory factor to the explosion in June, because yet another channel for the airing of grievances proved to be shut off to the trade-union movement. Only the *Morning Star* gave consistent coverage to the extraordinary behaviour of the police in the first ten months of the dispute. The *Guardian, The Times* and *Financial Times* trailed well behind; the popular dailies were nowhere to be seen.

The local police, from Willesden Green police station, had intensified their activities around Grunwick from September. The strikers, like many immigrants new to Britain, held the British police in high esteem. An unarmed British copper who stops and chats in the street does, indeed, compare favourably with police in other parts of the world. The British trade-union movement has however learnt from bitter experience that, even if the British police are comparatively civilised, in industrial relations they are still an arm of a social order that defines most employers' activities as legal but most activities by workers against employers as illegal. In a lock out, for example, it is legal for an employer physically to stop workers going into work, but it is illegal for pickets to stop blacklegs in a strike.

In Brent, there seemed to be a 'special relationship' between Grunwick and the police, dating back some years. Perhaps it was to do with Woollett, the Personnel Manager before and after Stacey, who used to be a local police officer. There was also a rumour that Grunwick processed film for Scotland Yard. The strikers first realised that something was wrong when the police lectured them on the picket line about how impartial they were, and then disappeared into the Grunwick canteen for cups of tea. The police could also be seen chatting amicably to the management, with whom some were on first name terms. One day, a company van bumped into a picket, who complained to the police nearby and described the driver. 'Oh, that's only Arthur', said the officer, intimately, 'just a little accident, I'm sure'.

At the end of October 1976, as the blacking spread, the police suddenly decided to try and limit, without cause, the pickets at the gate to a maximum of six people. No sooner was the news out than the Brent trade-union movement bristled. The police ruling was wrong in law and totally unreasonable, particularly at the Chapter Road entrance, which was almost twenty metres wide and for most of the day not at all busy. Moreover, restrictions by the police on picketing are always regarded as menacing by the movement, because so often in the past, trade unions have won legal rights by Act of Parliament, only to find them systematically whittled away by the judges.

The climax came on the first Monday of November 1976, the first day of the UPW blacking: an entire picket line was arrested in Chapter Road. Among the nine arrests were five members of the Brent East Constituency Labour Party, including the Chairman, Councillor Cyril Shaw. This set a pattern of punitive arrests. Whenever the strikers won a victory there was police harassment.

To the strikers, the police seemed to be at the beck and call of management. The police did nothing against the dangerous driving of company vans and cars, even when pickets were knocked down. Managers would even threaten pickets with their fists in front of police, and nothing would be done. By Christmas 1976 not one striker retained her or his original respect for the British police. In three months, the police converted a group of people who started out convinced that the police were neutral, into a group convinced that the police were servants of the Grunwick directors.

At first, it looked as if the courts would always back up the police. The strikers were bewildered when six of the pickets arrested on 1 November were found guilty on 24 February of obstructing the highway. How could they have obstructed such a quiet road as Chapter Road? It made no sense to the Strike Committee. Roy Grantham was also disturbed. He denounced the court's decision as 'a threat to the fundamental right to picket peacefully', and declared APEX's intention to appeal to a higher court as quickly as possible.

February 1977 was one of the most depressing months for the strikers on a number of counts, and this was when the strike most resembled a war of attrition. With the official movement bogged down in procedure, in an appeal for unfair dismissal to the Industrial Tribunal, in the ACAS struggles, and in the various court actions over picketing, attendance by strikers on the four picket lines visibly dwindled. The burden fell upon local workers, led by the Trades Council, to sustain the morale of the strikers.

That winter, the picket lines were often buttressed by these local supporters, either trade-union delegations invited by the Trades Council or groups organised by the Brent East Labour Party, led by Cyril Shaw, Brent East Young Socialists, led by Paul Franklin, or Brent Communist Party, led by Les Burt. On some days, special pickets were mounted. On Monday 14 February, for example, there was a picket in Chapter Road by Brent Labour Councillors, and the local press carried pictures of Councillors Botfish, Lebor, Goudie, Wall, Hussein and Roxburgh standing in the bitter cold with Jitendra ('Johnny') Patel and Manji Varsani.

Some new life was temporarily injected into the picketing when the Strike Committee and the Trades Council decided to extend it to all shops dealing with Grunwick. Months before, chemists using Grunwick Processing had been sent two, sometimes three, letters asking them to desist. On 29 January, they were to be asked one last time on threat of a picket line outside their door. In Brent, this picketing was very effective. Of sixteen shops discovered still to be using Grunwick, ten agreed to stop, four refused and two pondered. With the help of trade unionists all over London, coordinated through the

Greater London Association of Trades Councils, most of Grunwick's four hundred outlets in the area received a visit. The biggest store in Oxford Street, Selfridges, chose to ponder at first but quickly abandoned Grunwick when Jack Dromey rang up to say that thirty pickets would be arriving the following Saturday. The NAFF was furious; it was not long before it sought the assistance of the law to defend the free enterprise of the chemists from the free enterprise of the pickets.

When the Executive Committee of the Trades Council met on 9 March, the very evening the ACAS report was to be published, the legal onslaught of NAFF and the intimidation by the police was reaching new heights. Letters had arrived from Grunwick's solicitors threatening Mahmood Ahmad, Jack Dromey, Ron Anderson (Secretary of Brent East Labour Party) and Cyril Shaw (Chairman) with legal action if the picketing of chemist shops continued. As the chemist shop front had been the one battle zone where progress had been tangible, this was depressing news. When Jack Dromey told the meeting, 'We'll go ahead, but it looks as if NAFF has found a law preventing the picketing of chemists' shops', so low was morale on the legal issues that one delegate immediately groaned resignedly: 'There *had* to be one'.

The Trades Council was also very concerned with the apparent unison between the company and the police. There had been another four arrests that very afternoon. It was noted that police action seemed to coincide with crises for the company and seemed to be intended as a sort of retaliation. There had been arrests at the time of the postal blacking, now, there were new arrests just before the publication of the ACAS report which, everyone knew, would be unfavourable to Grunwick. The police had been particularly brazen that week. One day, they had ushered five women pickets into Dollis Hill Station, saying emphatically: 'The picketing is over'. The pickets were not, of course, surprised. With the ACAS report due out that week, they had been warned by the Strike Committee to expect police harassment.

On that March day, the Trades Council EC was just discussing what, if anything, could be done about the police, when the door opened and one of the strikers led in a tall young man who had not been seen before among them. This was Raschid Muhammed. He was not a Gujarati, he came from Mauritius. He was nervous but indignant. The striker explained that Raschid Muhammed had been crossing the picket line every morning at Grunwick where he had a good job (earning, it was learnt later, over £4200 per year) as the company's Assistant Accountant. No wonder he was nervous: from scabbing to appearing before the EC of Brent Trades Council was quite a step for one evening.

Jack Dromey called Raschid to the front of the meeting, and sat him down on a chair as if he were the prodigal son. A joke or two was exchanged about the furniture and conditions of the Trades Hall being worse than Grunwick – though the supervision was better: it was possible to go to the toilet without written permission in triplicate from Tom Durkin. Raschid, however, did not smile very much, for he had taken a serious decision. He had come to tell the EC that he was prepared to give evidence against the police and the Grunwick management. The Council was astounded. What had caused such a sudden conversion?

It was not the strikers' propaganda, but the evidence of his own eyes that had convinced him. He had witnessed the latest police swoop on the picket line. From his office overlooking the main gate he had seen the police arrive, the men dragged away and the women pushed to one side, apparently with no reasons given: 'I could not believe my eyes. I could not believe the British police would act in that way. I was brought up in Mauritius to believe that the British police were just. But what I saw was not justice.'

Raschid Muhammed ran down to the yard from his office and told the women that he was appalled by the actions of the police and would testify against them. Ward later said that Raschid then complained to him bitterly that 'the arrests are bloody racialist and bloody unfair'. Raschid was then demoted from being an accounts' clerk to a junior clerk. Two days later, he left, complaining that he had been 'constructively dismissed'. Before the Industrial Tribunal, Ward denied that he had tried to humiliate Raschid. He could no longer trust him, he said. Besides, he was a man who had 'a chip on both shoulders when it comes to racial matters'. Ward went on to say that he knew that Raschid had relatives in Mauritius with Communist sympathies – Raschid's father was in fact a Cabinet Minister, and his uncle had been knighted by the Queen at Buckingham Palace – but, Ward said, 'I do not discharge people for their political beliefs'.

Raschid was to lose his case before the Tribunal. He should, the Tribunal said, have resolved his dispute with Ward through the established works' machinery, the very machinery that was later condemned as ineffective by the Scarman Report.

That same Friday, 11 March, the strike did score an important victory, very cheering amid so many defeats. Grunwick's attempt to obtain a High Court injunction preventing the picketing of chemists' shops met with failure. The Grunwick directors were now provoked by this one legal setback into direct action where the law had failed. Ward led a group of managers to the chemists' shops that weekend and there harassed and abused the pickets. He transferred the intimidation by management on the Grunwick picket lines onto the chemists' picket lines. Confident of its general position now that the postal blacking had been lifted by the NAFF, but incensed at the failure of the courts, for once, to suit its purposes, the Grunwick management was obviously in an aggressive mood.

The Strike Committee should have read into these danger signs the need for increased vigilance, but morale had slumped further after the publication of the ACAS report led to no immediate change in the situation. Despite the Strike Committee, the picket lines sagged and, on occasion, were non-existent. It should also be remembered, before condemning the strikers too harshly for the temporary lapse of discipline, that the police attacks had been very effective. Some pickets were genuinely scared. In the case of the younger ones, heavy pressure was often put on them by their parents to stay away from the picket lines and so avoid 'getting into trouble with the police'.

This was not hysteria, but a combination of natural, parental protectiveness and the reputation built up by the police in the area for the harassment of immigrants. So bad was the relationship between the police and the immigrant community that the Brent Community Relations Council had just suspended all its formal links with the police.

On the Tuesday, what was in retrospect inevitable, actually occurred. A young striker called Kantilal Patel was left alone on the picket line during a change of duty. When his comrades returned, they found him beaten up, bleeding from the lip and cheek, his face badly bruised. The strikers escorted him to the Trades Hall, called a doctor and phoned Len Gristey. His face was photographed for the purpose of evidence at a later time. In the event, APEX was advised that the case could never be brought to court with any hope of success. There were no witnesses. The photos proved that he sustained injuries, but they did not prove who inflicted them. If picket line discipline had been maintained, the incident would probably never have happened.

The incident had a sequel. Jack Dromey rushed down to the picket line, to find that the Willesden Green police had been called. Although less than a mile away, they did not hurry. One large police officer towered over Kanti and told him that he deserved what he got. Jack insisted that the police officer leave Kanti alone and deal with Jack directly. 'Fuck off', the police officer replied. 'You're nothing but a company force', Jack retorted. The police officer then arrested him for insulting words. Later the police added the charge of 'insulting behaviour and obstruction of a police officer in the course of his duty'. By the time they had finished, Jack said, 'I thought they would accuse me of complicity in the disappearance of the crew of the "Marie Celeste"'. Although Jack was later acquitted on all charges, the strikers were very upset that the police had taken wrongful action against him.

An emergency Strike Bulletin, No. 31, responded to the spate of physical attacks and harassment. The bulletin called for reinforcements to defend the four picket lines, at Cooper Road, Beaconsfield Road, Cobbold Road and, most of all, at Chapter Road, on Friday 18 March at 7.30 a.m. The Strike Committee wrote: 'Help us mount a mass protest picket to show George Ward, our Managing Director, that this is London – not Chicago, Soweto or Chile'. So great was the feeling in the locality against the police that with only twenty-four hours' notice, over 200 people turned up at Chapter Road. Len Gristey, by no means an extremist ready to damn the police out of hand, summed up everyone's feelings when he explained to the crowd: 'The position quite plainly is that for the fourth time police have swooped on the picket line and, regardless of the provocations offered by the company, the police only take action against the pickets'. The police surrounding him looked straight ahead.

Of course, Malcolm Alden and his sidekicks were particularly happy in this period of victory. They jeered at the pickets from the yard and dared them to trespass on company property. They would put up their fists and shout: 'Come over here and say that'. Sometimes, if there were not many pickets, they would fetch cameras, come up to the pavement and take close-up photographs: 'Come on, give us a nice pose'.

Visitors to the picket line, enraged by the arrogance of the management on the one hand, and amazed by the continuing friendliness between pickets and blacklegs on the other, exhorted the strikers to be tougher. 'Why don't you occupy the factory? Why don't you give those scabs a harder time?' It was still most unusual for a striker even to use the word 'scab'. The strikers still had many friends among the 'loyal workers', some of whom were secret APEX members.

The tide did eventually turn in the strikers' favour, on 2 May, when the Middlesex Crown Court upheld an appeal against the conviction of the six pickets arrested in November. Of the original nine seized on the day the postal blacking began, the Labour Councillor, Cyril Shaw and two others were acquitted, and six found guilty. Now, to the joy of the strikers, the appeal produced the ruling that in certain circumstances, people could obstruct the pavement if they were peacefully picketing. The six convictions were quashed. Nor was that all. The court severely reprimanded the police for using the pretext that more than six pickets were an obstruction, and took the extremely unusual step of awarding costs of £3500 against the police.

Of course, this belated vindication of the pickets could never wipe away the deep resentment at the police's behaviour but – in the midst of so many Grunwick victories – it was sensational news for the local movement. No one could think of a previous case in Brent in which the police had been financially penalised for molesting pickets. Jack Dromey commented to the local press: 'This unprecedented action more than justifies all the criticism that we have made of the police action against us'.

APEX, the Trades Council and a number of MPs now renewed their pressure upon the Home Secretary for action to be taken to stop the harassment. Within days of the court decision, the strikers were delighted to hear that Chief Inspector Robert Johnson of Willesden Green police station had retired. Meanwhile, Woollett, a former local police officer, was appointed Personnel Manager – Stacey had emigrated to Australia. Nonetheless, the court's reprimand of the police, the liaison between police and management and the presence of Woollett had the result of destroying any remaining faith in the Brent police as far as the strikers, the Brent labour movement and the Brent immigrant community were concerned. At its next meeting, Brent Community Relations Council confirmed the decision to break off all formal relations with the police.

The effect of the court's judgement and Johnson's departure on the behaviour of the police was magical. Many police assured the strikers that things would now change because 'we are under new management'.

Their presence on the picket line was reduced and throughout May there was not a single arrest. The management of Grunwick became much less talkative and there was little provocation. The suspension of hostilities lasted until 1 June when Jayaben Desai was arrested.

She was detained at the Chapter Road entrance after exchanges with George Ward and Malcolm Alden. The directors announced their intention to bring a private summons for assault against Mrs Desai, who is four feet ten inches tall. Later, Jayaben too was to win her case, although only after an appeal. The incident marked the end of a period when the local police, under their new Chief Inspector, Robert Hay, tried very hard to rebuild relations with the strikers. He stopped the regular visits of management to Willesden Green Police Station, and even attended the picket line in plain clothes to try and observe Malcolm Alden's actions. However, Hay arrived too late. In May, the strikers, now convinced that they would never get justice from police, procedure or tribunals, issued the call for the mass picket. The court decision had not even been reported by the popular press. Joe Rogaly does not mention it in his book (*Grunwick,* 1977), which completely underestimates the effect of the 1976-7 winter events. Yet an understanding of that verdict and all the police behaviour behind it, is absolutely essential to understanding why the strikers called upon the trade-union movement to take to the streets in the summer of 1977.

10

'Honey on Your Elbow'

The ACAS recommendation in March and the court's ruling against the Willesden police in May were both moral victories for the strikers. They had hoped that, after Grunwick flouted the ACAS report, the trade-union movement would swing into action behind them and help bring the dispute to a speedy and victorious end. They had struggled hard, despite intimidation by management and police. The NAFF had dealt them a body-blow but they had not broken. As Tom Durkin told the Brent Trades Council at its February meeting: 'There has been no struggle in Brent more glorious, none more courageous, than that of the Grunwick strikers since the General Strike of 1926. The trade-union movement cannot afford their defeat.'

The labour movement in the locality had certainly shown its solidarity throughout those months of hardship. There were often local 'mass pickets' by London trade unionists, the most successful of which was probably that called by the North London AUEW on 11 February, when 150 engineers turned up. When the Strike Committee organised another march on 10 December there was once again a turnout of several hundred people.

The strikers successfully raised money for the strike fund by socials and other fundraising events. APEX tried to counter the low morale of the strikers – and the wage increases paid by Grunwick to the blacklegs – by increasing strike pay. In January, it was raised to £18, in March to £20 and in May to its peak of £30, after Grunwick had awarded its workers a 10 per cent pay increase from 1 April. This money was, of course, tax-free and, supplemented with 'hardship money' of up to £6 from the strike fund, meant that some of the strikers were in 1977 earning more on strike than they had been at work in 1976. This was at once a revealing comment on the low wage levels at Grunwick before the strike, and a tribute to the generosity of APEX.

It was in the arena of blacking, however, that solidarity mattered most. There was a good response from trade unions at Britain's airports and docks. Grunwick supplies and products were hunted down and turned back. To continue its very large European trade – mainly from West Germany, Belgium and the Netherlands – the company was eventually forced to buy a six-seater plane, knock out the back four seats and hire a pilot to fly the work to Rotterdam. International solidarity was equally determined; trade unionists from Belgium and the Netherlands came to Willesden to see the situation for themselves. At Christmas the strikers were touched to receive a Christmas card from the Northern Region of the CGT, the powerful French trade-union organisation.

Solidarity with the strikers was also expressed inside Parliament, initiated by two Labour MPs: Laurie Pavitt and Ted Fletcher. So strong was the strikers' case, that a motion calling on Grunwick to implement the ACAS report and recognise APEX was signed not only by the two Labour MPs but also by two Conservative MPs, one Liberal and one Welsh Nationalist. The motion called on the company to accept 'the rule of law as embodied in the Employment Protection Act of 1975'. The NAFF, unfortunately, had no intention either of accepting the rule of law or a majority in Parliament.

The best show of solidarity came on 27 April in a demonstration organised by the No. 8 District of the Confederation of Shipbuilding and Engineering Unions, the South-East Regional Council of the TUC and the Greater London Association of Trades Councils. Because it was called in working hours for twelve noon on a Wednesday in Willesden, no great crowd was expected. In the event, over 1400 workers marched past the Grunwick gates to demonstrate their admiration for the ninety strikers and their contempt for the company.

There was an interesting sequel. Encouraged by the atmosphere of trade-union solidarity, three government ministers – Fred Mulley, Denis Howell and Shirley Williams, all APEX members and all belonging to the right wing of the Labour Party – put in an unexpected appearance on the picket line on 19 May. Their action provoked a classic example of the anti-union bias of the press. For, although the three stayed on the line for less than an hour, and although the press had passed over in silence the most outrageous behaviour by management and police, there was an immediate uproar over the MPs' 'controversial' behaviour. Grunwick zoomed back onto the front pages for the first time since the postal blacking of November.

With few exceptions, the press condemned the behaviour of Mulley, Howell and Williams, even though they represented a parliamentary majority, and even though the very papers that were most indignant had found nothing strange in the intervention of the NAFF MPs in November. In terms of newsworthiness, there had been plenty of incident to report, including considerable violence in which several pickets had received medical attention, without a single police officer being hurt. There had been the newsworthiness of the company's defiance of ACAS. Out of over 800 references to ACAS, only Grunwick had at that stage refused to accept its recommendations. Wasn't that newsworthy? Apparently not, for it did not receive one-hundredth of the coverage to which the unfortunate Labour ministers were now subjected.

Grunwick took advantage of the press campaign to claim contempt of court in respect of its writ against ACAS. The ministers' action, it alleged, could be construed as favourable publicity for one side of the case. The company said it was considering legal action. Such arrogance would not have been possible without the press intervention.

This was the solidarity with the Grunwick strikers in these difficult months, and this was the hostility they encountered from the company, the NAFF, the police and the press. From every side, they were under fire. It seemed to some that all of the institutions of British society were hostile and conspiring against them. They were hostile, but there was no formal conspiracy. Such is the nature of the structure of modern society in Western Europe, that the Government scarcely intervened in the first eight months of the Grunwick Strike, yet the strikers had to confront this extraordinary concert of opposition. To their credit, they did not take it lying down but hit back, likewise on a very broad front. Thus it was in this period that the Grunwick strikers joined in the campaign against racism. On 21 November, the Strike Committee had supported an anti-racist demonstration in London called by the TUC and the Labour Party by sending a large delegation which included Kamlesh Gandhi, Jayaben Desai, Yasu Patel, Urmila Patel, Susan Moroney, Vipin Magdani, Noorali Valliani and Mahmood Ahmad. However, the highlight of the anti-racist campaign for the Grunwick strikers was the weekend of 19-20 March, when a delegation of four women and four men, led by Mahmood Ahmad and Jayaben Desai, attended an anti-racist conference organised by 'Liberation' at Friends' House, Euston. Maurice Styles, representing the UPW, told the conference: 'The Grunwick management, typical of many employers, are seeking to develop their business by using our black brothers and sisters as cheap labour. Mahmood and Mrs Desai – and their fine colleagues – have got to win.' The packed audience gave the strikers a standing ovation.

There were some fine speeches also from speakers not normally associated with the labour movement, one of the best from Pauline Webb of the British Council of Churches, who told the meeting:

> Racialism is a blatant denial of the Christian faith. It denies our conviction that all people are created equal in the image of God. It is, of course, associated with the most appalling exploitation. And it relies for its appeal on pernicious lies. The whole presentation of a white Jesus is a blasphemy.

The next day, the strikers attended a rally organised by the newly-formed Brent Campaign Against Racialism, an organisation set up by the Brent Labour Parties and Brent Trades Council. It was held in Alperton High School, Wembley, and attended by over three hundred delegates. The main speech was a fiery one from Tony Benn, but it was Grunwick that dominated the proceedings.

The strikers' second major broad front activity in this period was the Strike Committee's decision to support the struggle for women's rights. In February, it supported the rally on women's rights at Alexandra Palace. This solidarity was, of course, a two-way process. Support from women in the movement was especially useful to the strikers; to have confidence in a male-dominated world, women on strike need the support of other women. There was to be a more long-term repercussion: the strikers did not realise it at the time, but their involvement with the women's movement was to have a curious outcome, of great benefit to their cause, in the violent days of June.

Thirdly, the strikers contributed to the movement at this time by announcing in January a new venture: tours of Britain. In a letter to the strikers signed by Kamlesh Gandhi, the Strike Committee made clear that their prime objective was, of course, to win support. However, the tours helped the fight against racism inside the trade-union movement by introducing shop stewards all over Britain – from engineers in Glasgow to miners in Kent – to immigrant workers, and in particular to traditional Asian women whose courage and trade-union principle won the shop stewards' respect. The tours, on which there were always two women and two men, also helped to develop the confidence of the women strikers. The equality redressed the balance of the Strike Committee membership in which, despite the majority of women amongst the strikers and amongst the activists on the picket line, there were in the winter of 1976-7 only two women, Jayaben Desai and Kalaben Patel. However, the major impact of the fifteen tours was to make Grunwick a household name within the organised trade-union movement.

The key to solidarity for the strike, however, lay not in the campaign against racism or in the movement for women's rights or even amongst the local factories, but in the policy of the TUC, which coordinates all the major union organisations in Britain. It was clear that if the TUC could be moved on the Grunwick Strike for basic democratic rights, it would open up all sorts of possibilities for the strikers.

It was because the TUC was so crucial that on 7 December, Jack Dromey had led a delegation to visit Len Murray, General Secretary of the TUC, at Congress House. The delegation was extremely impressive. The engineers in Southall – an area heavily populated by Indian immigrants – were represented by Roger Butler, the AUEW District Secretary. The North London AUEW was represented by Vic Swift, its District Secretary, and Bill Thomas, UCATT by one of its officials, John Flavin. There were also local representatives of important factories such as Brian Eagles from Rolls-Royce, Pat Reilly from Express Dairies, and Tom Horan from British Leyland. They met Len Murray for forty-five minutes and were very satisfied with the response. Murray promised full support for the strike, financial aid to Brent Trades Council and, above all, promised to speak at a public meeting on Grunwick fixed for Sunday 12 December, in the Brent Trades Hall.

The Sunday meeting was a spectacular success if attendance is any criterion. It looked as if the entire labour movement had been won to the side of the strikers. Not only did Len Murray, Roy Grantham and Maurice Styles accept invitations, but the National Executive Committee of the Labour Party was represented by Lena Jeger, MP. Her presence had the useful effect that on 15 December, Labour's NEC backed the strike.

The Brent Labour Party was well represented by Reg Freeson, MP, plus Councillors Philip Hartley, Cyril Shaw, Karamat Hussein and others. From the rank-and-file came excellent contributions. Dave Dodd and Archie Sinclair described their efforts to persuade the UPW to black the Grunwick mail. Abdul Wagu, of GEC's Association Automation, in a fine outburst, challenged the platform speakers to outline their practical proposals for backing the postal workers.

When Maurice Styles rose to speak on behalf of the UPW, there was an expectant hush. In the event, his speech gave the strikers hope that the UPW might still find some way to reimpose its blacking. The UPW would reconsider its undertaking to the court, Styles claimed, if Ward broke his promise of cooperating fully with ACAS. In fact, said Styles, turning towards Grantham, if Roy Grantham was to request UPW intervention in a letter tomorrow, it would be most seriously considered at its very next meeting. Grantham smiled and nodded to tumultuous applause.

Roger Butler dealt with the racist angle. He recalled how an Indian youth had been knifed to death by white aggressors the previous summer in Southall, and how Kingsley Read, a racist politician, had made his outrageous speech: 'One down, one million to go'. Grunwick, said Roger Butler, was another symptom of the same disease.

The speech everyone was waiting for, of course, was that of Len Murray, a small, alert, business-like man with sharp features and an authoritative tone, hailed patronisingly by the mass media as the first 'educated' General Secretary of the TUC. Murray started off by telling the meeting of well over 200 people that he was very proud to be there. If any MI5 (British secret police) were present, he told them to record his name clearly. Yet, he added, it was sad that such a meeting was necessary in the twentieth century.

Murray then turned to the theme that laws could not replace trade-union action. It was the function of trade unions to operate in the delicate area of industrial relations where rigid laws are inappropriate. In this way, he defended the Labour Government's Employment Protection Act, which Grunwick had demonstrated was totally inadequate. He attacked Margaret Thatcher for not, on behalf of the Conservative Party, condemning Grunwick's initial refusal to cooperate with ACAS. Murray challenged Thatcher – and the Shadow Employment Minister, Prior – to 'declare themselves' in favour of conciliation. He ended powerfully by turning to Jayaben and Mahmood and promising that the TUC 'are not just behind you. We are right alongside you!'

Murray's speech, judging from the applause, went down very well. The television cameras broadcast an excerpt from it on the news – the first time in history that a meeting of Brent Trades Council, perhaps of any Trades Council, had been filmed for television. It was also possibly the first time that a Trades Council had succeeded in eliciting on-the-spot intervention from a General Secretary of the TUC in a local dispute. Philip Hartley, leader of the Brent Labour Party, Laurie Pavitt, Labour MP for Brent South, and Reg Freeson, Labour MP for Brent East, all sent letters of congratulations to the Trades Council on this excellent meeting. The Strike Committee, who mattered most, were delighted with what they had heard.

Its euphoria, however, was grounded to some extent in inexperience. Older hands had heard such speeches many times before. Militant activists have grown accustomed to looking through rhetoric for precise formulations and concrete proposals. Here, they found no concrete commitment to support the postal workers, no promise to indemnify any fines imposed on the UPW, no guarantee to campaign for the release of those who might be imprisoned as a result of the proposed action.

Nor did the emphasis of Murray's speech against Thatcher and the Conservatives, although unifying for the meeting itself, cut much ice. Many delegates were unhappy that this anti-Conservative point scoring was accompanied by other Labour speakers appealing to the audience to join the Labour Party. They felt it would have been better to allow the strikers to address the meeting. Combined with the lack of support for the postal workers, they feared that Murray's appearance at a local Trades Council may have had more to do with making political capital out of the strike for the Labour Party, than it had to do with helping the strikers. In this respect the universal presence of the television cameras was felt by some not as an asset but as a drawback, perhaps a pre-planned drawback: the Grunwick workers had been denied the right to strike, the postal workers had then been denied the right to support the strike: the very basis of trade-union power was under attack, but Murray's speech appeared on television merely as another swipe at Margaret Thatcher.

Such a harsh, immediate reaction was almost certainly too hard but it was fuelled by disappointment at the outcome of the meeting in concrete terms. In fact, Murray's intervention had further isolated the Grunwick management, and it gave the strikers' morale a tremendous boost. As Jack Dromey was to point out at the next Trades Council meeting, it was also true that it was neither Len Murray nor the Labour Party that had introduced party politics into the dispute but the Conservatives, led by John Gorst, who had forced the debate on Grunwick in Parliament on 4 November. Murray's challenge to Thatcher was not so much an attack as a defence against the Conservatives' tactic of concentrating public attention on the legality issue. Murray was trying to swing attention onto the Conservatives' dishonest position on industrial relations. Nonetheless, despite these points in Murray's favour, there remained a gut feeling that while this high-level chess game was in progress, determined young Indian women like Bina Shah, Dharmishtha Patel and Vibha Voralia were freezing on the picket line.

Nothing more was heard from the TUC until after the ACAS report was published in March. Roy Grantham told a meeting on the eve of the ACAS report's publication:

> Within a fortnight, APEX will ask the whole of the trade-union movement to bring this dispute to a speedy and victorious end. The General Council of the TUC meets on 23 March. We will approach the TUC between now and then. If the company continues to defy the movement and, now, ACAS, APEX will ask for all services to the company to be cut off, including the water, gas and electricity ...

This is what the strikers and the Trades Council had asked for. Sure enough, the General Council meeting was lobbied. Resolutions from trade unions all over Britain poured in. The TUC admitted that in March 1977 it received more resolutions on Grunwick than on any other dispute in Britain – including the miners' strikes – for fifteen years. Local trade unionists recalled Len Murray's promise in December: 'We are not just behind you. We are right alongside you!'

Yet the outcome was that the TUC did nothing to mobilise the movement in the light of Murray's pledge and the company's snub of ACAS. The TUC pointed out that it could not instruct its member unions, only advise them, and, as for the severance of water, gas and electricity, that – like the post – was hedged by too many legal obstacles. The General Council sent out a 'call' embodied in a circular, asking all trade unions to help APEX. Nobody took much notice of it, for it contained, once again, rhetoric as a substitute for activity. But action on the key question of essential services was effectively dodged. Everyone knew that, as the TUC had not backed up the postal workers, there was no reason why it should back up electricians, gasmen or anyone else.

There was an underlying political motive for the diffidence of the TUC. The majority on the General Council belonged to the right wing of the Labour Party, which, although content to see the TUC defy the law in 1972-4 and bring down a Conservative government, was not now prepared for it to support actions that may have been illegal, on behalf of the right to strike, in case such action embarrassed a Labour government.

It was not long before the strikers' hopes, temporarily raised by the promises of Grantham and Murray, plunged to an even lower level. As the early days of April turned into weeks, the picket lines grew thinner, until even the most optimistic recognised that all the 'calls' of the TUC were so much hot air.

When Mahmood Ahmad addressed nearly 2000 trade unionists at the British Leyland conveners' conference in Birmingham Town Hall on 3 April, he spoke, for the first time, not in the confident tones of the early days, but with a resignation that verged on bitterness. Mahmood told the meeting what was on everybody's mind: the TUC had made promises, but these promises had not been translated into effective action. 'The TUC should be coming to us to ask us how they can help. Instead we have to keep going to them.' He spelt out the harsh truth in simple words: 'If the British trade-union movement wants to recruit Asian workers, then it has to do better than this'. Mahmood was the only speaker that day to receive a standing ovation.

Unfamiliar with politics, most strikers were simply confused by the TUC's inaction. Most had started the strike with no perspective of democratic rights or anti-racism. Many were on strike only because they hated Ward, Alden or Chapman, or because their friends had struck. They only wanted to win the strike, they had not set out to change the world. Jayaben Desai had her own interpretation, and she explained to a journalist one day how she analysed the demoralisation:

> I do not feel any hatred for Ward, or even Mr Alden. They are not really to blame. It is the workers who are so divided. If the workers cared enough for each other to act as one, then all the Wards and

Aldens would be helpless. Love holds the world together. That is what I believe.

APEX made one last desperate effort to enforce the blacking. It launched a twenty-four hour picket on 12 April. It hoped to list all vehicles entering Grunwick so that union pressure could be applied to the companies they came from. To house the pickets through the night, it hired a white mini-bus which was parked outside the gates. The idea was good, but its practical effect was disastrous. The twenty-four hour picket bit deeply into the strikers' energy. After a couple of weeks, they could see no point in it. They knew most of the registration numbers by heart and their patience was strained to breaking point: 'The TUC does nothing; so we have to stay up all night.' That was their bitter mood.

At a meeting Jayaben Desai summed up their frustration about the ambivalence of the TUC General Council: 'Official action from the TUC', she said, 'is like honey on your elbow: you can smell it, you can see it, but you can never taste it'.

11

The Road to The Mass Picket

It was the street battles of the mass picket that brought the Grunwick Strike to the television screens of the world. It was the mass picket that transformed the strike from the depression of April 1977 to the intensity of June. It was the arrival in Willesden of thousands of trade unionists from all over Britain, which was to reassure the strikers that they were not, after all, alone, and that besides the right-wing section of the labour movement there was also a left-wing, a radical and a militant section which responded with class feeling to the call of all workers in struggle, whether male or female, manual or clerical, black or white.

The idea of a mass picket was not new. It is a product of modern transport and modern militancy, which dates back at least until the Roberts-Arundel dispute in Stockport in 1967. Then, in response to the strong-arm tactics of local police and management, the Roberts-Arundel picketing had been reinforced by trade unionists from all over Lancashire. During the miners' strike of 1972, mobile mass pickets groups, assigned to cars and vans who reinforced any picket line under strain, became a 'controversy' in the press, which dubbed them 'flying pickets'. Both the workers at Roberts-Arundel and the miners won their strike, so, in the summer of 1972, the striking building workers used the mass picket in response to the blacklegging of self-employed 'lump' workers in North Wales and Yorkshire. This led to the rounding up of 800 trade unionists by the police, and to serious charges being brought against the 'Shrewsbury 24', one of whom, Des Warren, was sent to prison for three years on a nebulous charge of 'conspiracy'.

As the building workers also won most of their demands, the powers that be soon became hysterical about 'mass pickets'. The conspiracy charge at Shrewsbury was a product of that hysteria, as was the revealing comment by a judge that a blacklegging lorry driver who killed a miner was carrying out his patriotic duty. The employers were haunted in particular by a nightmare called the 'Battle of Saltley Gates', in which engineering workers in Birmingham closed down the Saltley Coke Depot by a mass picket in support of the miners in 1972. Apart from Russian tanks and sex education, there was nothing in the 1970s which frightened the right more than the dreaded 'mass picket'.

It was not just the right, however, who were astonished in June 1977 by the sight of a mass picket called by the ultra-moderate Roy Grantham outside the Grunwick gates. Readers of the *Daily Telegraph* might have been forgiven for believing that the red revolution was nigh. There certainly was an irony in APEX's launching a mass picket in the footsteps of the miners, the engineers and the builders, particularly as some APEX members had, in 1972, earned the contempt of the movement by crossing a miners' picket line.

There is an explanation for APEX's apparently out-of-character use of a mass picket, hitherto regarded as a weapon only of the most militant. First, this was a period in which white-collar unions such as APEX, the teachers' unions and even civil servants were becoming more and more militant, usually exceeding the militancy of the manual workers. Secondly, Roy Grantham himself, however right-wing his politics, was unquestionably a principled trade unionist, who felt that the mass picket was the only way to avoid the defeat of his members. Thirdly, Grunwick was an exceptional case. As Grantham told the Court of Inquiry:

> In my experience as a serving trade-union official and indeed throughout my working life as a trade unionist, I have never come across a company which has been so averse to the normal procedures of conciliation and negotiation as Grunwick Processing Laboratories.

As for the Strike Committee and Brent Trades Council, they had pressed for such action, but their approach to the mass picket was a mixed one. Although the tactic came with a splendid pedigree, experience seemed to show that the mass picket could easily lead to confrontation with the police and to the involvement of people who were not as interested in democratic rights as they were in punch-ups. The mass picket was therefore a risky weapon unless good discipline was maintained. It was also felt that calling a mass picket was not something to be lightly undertaken, because at Grunwick it was an admission of failure. The mass picket was seen as a weapon of last resort in a strike, just as a strike is itself the weapon of last resort in a negotiation. The justification in the case of the Grunwick Strike was this: all the procedures laid down by the law had been exhausted, the strike was of historical importance, and the alternative was total defeat.

The importance of the strike had been recognised very widely by June 1977. Politically, there was a general consensus, embodied in Laurie Pavitt's motion in Parliament, that Grunwick was wrong not to accept ACAS. From the trade unions' point of view, the issues were excellently summarised in the May bulletins of the Strike Committee:

IF THIS STRIKE IS LOST

1. The right to organise will have been made a mockery of.
2. ACAS will have been discredited – and the Employment Protection Act.
3. Millions of unorganised workers at other Grunwicks will be discouraged from joining a union.
4. The confidence of Asian and West Indian workers in our movement will be severely affected.
5. 'Sweat Shop' employers up and down the country will take heart.

There was also a less rational reason why APEX and the strikers felt the mass picket was necessary. This was that each legal coup by the NAFF, every 'smart' trick pulled out of the hat by Gouriet and Moss, had led to a kickback of revulsion in the heart of the working-class movement. To every class-conscious worker, the issue was plain: Grunwick was an anti-union company that had victimised 137 strikers after they joined a union. Every time the union applied the ordinary, trade-union pressures of blacking and picketing, some upper-class twit appeared on the television screen with a court writ in his hand. The NAFF was breaking the ground rules for industrial relations, disturbing the balance of power, not 'playing cricket'. There was a growing feeling amongst militants in the late spring of 1977 that if one side was not 'playing cricket', it was time the other side stopped playing it as well.

There was a similar 'gut reaction' amongst the strikers. The sight of the police, declared to be 'neutral' by the press, merrily strolling in and out of the Grunwick canteen, chatting happily with management, made them despair of the law. Grunwick's legal action against ACAS, which could mean another year on the picket line, had set the seal on that despair. The rich, it seemed, could postpone the law's operation indefinitely. That is why Jayaben Desai told the press in June: 'I have no faith in the legal position. I believe only in the power of the trade-union movement'.

There was also an important tactical consideration for the strikers. About two-thirds of Grunwick's business was carried out in one-third of the year, from June to September. If Grunwick were allowed to operate without hindrance in those months, it would be able to coast through the winter months once again into 1978. To hurt the company badly, the strikers had to disrupt its lucrative summer trade.

Naturally, the main aims of the mass picket were stated in its publicity. The *Morning Star* announcement was in the form of a simple and mild statement: 'APEX are calling for mass picketing next week to persuade those still working there not to break the strike'. This was true, but it was far from the whole story. Getting blacklegs to join the strike was very important and, even after ten months, still quite possible, as events proved. Jayaben Desai was particularly confident on this score. When asked by a reporter she replied: 'There is good in everyone as well as bad'. She added mischievously: 'Look at Mr Ward. He never said "hello" to any of his workers before the strike. Now he says "hello, good morning" to everybody.' She seemed to believe that if the mass picket could improve the manners of George Ward it was capable of anything.

The Trades Council called for a 'ring of steel' to be thrown around Grunwick in the vital summer months. The emphasis here was in blockading Grunwick and enforcing the blacking, in particular by encouraging unions or union members at local level such as the UPW (post), the EEPTU (electricity), and the GMWU (water and gas) to carry out the TUC appeal. The Strike Committee varied its emphasis from week to week. The most controversial formulation came in bulletin No. 37 of Saturday 28 May, which said: 'In the week beginning Monday 13 June, there will be mass pickets at the Grunwick factories to try and stop those still going to work from doing so'. Right wingers pounced upon the phrase, 'stop those still going to work' – did it not imply physical restraint? That was not 'peaceful picketing'.

There were certainly some trade unionists who believed that physical obstruction of the entrance was the way to end the dispute. That was how the engineers helped the miners at Saltley Gates, it was said: the police were simply outnumbered and the blacklegs could not get through the crowd. Some on the left argue that such physical confrontation is justified, because the employer inside the factory is permitted by law to intimidate workers with loss of their livelihood. Similarly, the police outside intimidate pickets quite legally, but do not intimidate blacklegs stealing the jobs of strikers who may morally and legally be completely in the right. It was therefore argued that it is justified – as law is class-biased – to intimidate blacklegs with abuse or physical obstruction, and that this merely balances the intimidation of the employer.

Whatever the merits of this argument, when the decision was taken at Grunwick, mass picketing by intimidating blacklegs was never justified by APEX, the Strike Committee, Brent Trades Council or the *Morning Star* – the only daily paper that supported the mass picket. On the contrary, the stress was on winning over blacklegs to leave Grunwick and join the strike. As for obstruction of the entrance, that was more ambiguous; there was a suggestion of that in the Strike Committee's bulletin quoted above, and it was acknowledged that there would be obstruction, particularly if the police construed the law rigidly.

The original and main purpose of the mass picket was, however, to attract attention to the Grunwick strike and focus trade-union sympathy on the plight of the strikers. It was felt that, in terms of justice, the strikers had an overwhelming case. The mass picket, intended to last a week, was meant to put on the spot those in the trade-union movement who had not backed the strikers. The idea was that 200 people would be at the two main gates daily throughout the week, from Monday 13 June, in a show of strength to demand action, particularly on essential services.

One thing is absolutely certain. Neither the Strike Committee, the Trades Council nor APEX in any way expected the size of the escalation that occurred. As the Court of Inquiry put it: 'The union, we are satisfied, had no intention of provoking violence and disorder by calling for the mass picket'. No one expected the extraordinary reaction of the police on Monday 13 June, a reaction that could have been decided only at the highest levels. No one set out to create what the Court of Inquiry was to call 'the scenes of violence which have shocked the nation'.

12

The Battle for Chapter Road

Monday 13 June, the first day of the mass picket, had been ear-marked as the women's picket. The Communist Party Women's Group had taken the initiative at a meeting of women's organisations in calling on women to demonstrate their support on that day. Jayaben Desai, speaking to the meeting, had called on women to support the struggle for 'trade-union recognition and respect – to be looked upon as human beings, not animals'. The Strike Committee was pleased at the arrangement; its members considered that the presence of a large number of women would emphasise the peaceful intention of the picket, and have a restraining influence on the police.

At 6 a.m., the pickets began to gather at Chapter Road. By 6.30, there were about sixty. The Chapter Road gate became the most important. It was here that the strike had broken out and Dollis Hill tube station, whose back entrance was in Chapter Road, twenty yards from the factory, was also the main disembarkation point for the pickets. About thirty pickets stood across the factory gate. The rest stood to either side of the gate or opposite, on the forecourt of a sweet shop whose owner was very friendly to the strikers. About a hundred police were present, most of whom stayed initially in police buses fifty yards up the road, towards Dudden Hill Lane. The police were under the leadership of Commander Sadler, the head of Q Division. Under his direction, the police kept the pickets off the road and ensured that a way was cleared along the footpath for pedestrians. George Ward peeped expectantly through the net curtains of his office window, which overlooked the gate. The pickets were tense but good-humoured. Three hours later, eighty-four out of the 200 who turned up had been arrested without a single police officer sustaining any injury. 13 June was to prove a monumental blunder by the police.

The trouble began shortly before 7 a.m. Most of the 'loyal' workers were expected between 8 and 9.30 a.m. A few, however, arrived early, mainly cleaners. Those passing through the gates were shouted at and called 'scabs', but they got into work with relative ease. A film shot at that time clearly showed this. Later, George Ward was to claim that a Nigerian cleaner called Sam had been assaulted. In fact, according to the police on the spot, he stumbled after he had passed through the picket line. No picket was arrested for assault on a 'scab'. In any case, these exchanges were not the cause of the extraordinary police action.

Sadler determined that he would assert his authority right from the start. He suddenly demanded that the picket should be restricted to six people, and six only. The rest would have to stand on the other side of the road. The strikers argued with him. 'This is a return', they said, 'to "Johnson's law" – your ruling has no basis in law unless you have good reason to believe that there will be trouble. Besides, the last time you tried this on, all those arrested were cleared on appeal, the police were rebuked by the Appeal Court judge and you had costs awarded against you of £3500.' They could not believe that police would once again flout their rights quite so flagrantly. Sadler refused to give grounds as to why he thought that the picket should be limited. Neither did he observe what is good police practice of seeking to negotiate with the picket marshalls a limitation in the size of the picket. He was boss and that was that.

It is beyond doubt that the intention of Sadler and the other senior officers from the start was to interpret the law rigidly and arrest *en masse* those who did not instantly obey their dictates, however unlawful. A hard line, they felt, would deter others from coming later in the week. Subsequently, another senior officer who took control of the picket on most days after the Sadler debacle, told the APEX Officers that, if he had been in charge, the whole thing would never have happened.

Forty pickets were arrested within minutes, as the police emptied out of their coaches and were ordered to pile into the pickets, hem them in either side of the factory gate, and arrest anyone who stepped off the pavement. Mahmood Ahmad and Councillor Karamat Hussein, the mildest men on either side of the local authority, were amongst the first to go. There was no resistance from the pickets. More police joined in. The film shows them whiplashing into the pickets on the pavement in a 'snake', arms linked. Mahmood went limp and dropped to the ground. He had to be carried away. Others followed his example. It was then that the police used a degree of force which shocked those

Jayaben Desai: 'The strike is not so much about pay, it is about human dignity'. This image has come to personify the strike. Years later, Jayaben Desai told Andrew Wiard, the photographer who captured the moment, that the police officer she was confronting had just stamped down, hard, on her foot. (*Andrew Wiard*)

Working life inside the Grunwick Processing plant. The glass office from which management observed their employees is, for once, empty but still clearly visible at the back of the shop floor. (*Andrew Wiard*)

Who's watching you? Management photographing strikers and pickets from Chapter Road. (*Andrew Wiard/ TUC Library Collection*)

GRUNWICK STRIKE COMM
APEX
NOTHING HILL

BREN
TRADE

Kanti Patel, one of the strikers, having experienced rough treatment at the hands of those opposed to the dispute, 15 March 1977. (*Andrew Wiard/ TUC Library Collection*)

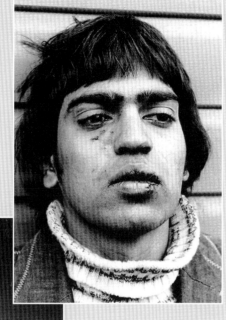

A tense meeting at the Brent Trades Council, 2 September 1976. From left to right: Noorali Valliani (Strike Committee Chair), Sunil Desai (Strike Committee Secretary), Mahmood Ahmed (Grunwick striker), Jack Dromey (Secretary of Brent Trades Council), & Len Gristey (Apex Senior Organiser). (*Andrew Wiard/TUC Library Collection*)

Tom Durkin, Communist, trade unionist and anti-fascist, addresses the strikers at Brent Trades Hall, 1 October 1976. The audience includes Kamla Ram (front row, right, nearest to Tom Durkin), Jayaben Desai (second row, centre) and Urmilaben Patel (second row, furthest left). (*Andrew Wiard/TUC Library Collection*)

Official pickets from the APEX Union preparing for a mass demonstration outside Grunwick, June 1977. (*Andrew Wiard/TUC Library Collection*)

Summer 1977: police struggling to hold pickets back, as the daily bus drives those still working towards the factory. (*Andrew Wiard*)

Metropolitan Police Commissioner David McNee (after 1978 Sir David McNee) inspecting the picket line, accompanied by his entourage of senior Met officers. (*Andrew Wiard*)

The police presence at Grunwick, 27 June 1977. (*Andrew Wiard/ TUC Library Collection*)

Jayaben Desai and her colleagues on the picket line, June 1977. Dwarfed by the policemen, the women's banners not only reference their union, but draw parallels between the injustices that they had

suffered at Grunwick, under George Ward, and those that had recently driven them from East Africa, and been perpetrated by tyrants like Idi Amin. (*Andrew Wiard/TUC Library Collection*)

Left & below: The first day of mass picketing – and mass arrests: 13 June 1977. (*Andrew Wiard*)

Above: Faces of Solidarity: on 11 July 1977, thousands of trade unionists, led by Arthur Scargill and the Yorkshire Miners, arrive at the gates of Grunwick. *Opposite:* Blockade runners, June 1977. (*Andrew Wiard*)

In 2007, Jayaben Desai returned to her union's congress to be honoured by the GMB with its highest award – a Gold Badge – for her bravery and services to trades unionism. (*Andrew Wiard*)

present and led Roy Grantham to seek an urgent meeting with the Home Secretary.

At first, the police had pulled those who resisted passively along the ground. Now, under pressure from a red-faced Sadler, they prodded their victims on with kicks and punches, irrespective of age or sex. As Len Gristey described it: 'I saw boys being dragged by their hair across the road. I saw girls dragged away screaming.' Gristey did not blame individual police officers. He heard Sadler reprimand two junior officers: 'You're not here to push them, you're here to arrest them and I don't want any pickets left'. One police officer got hold of Jayaben Desai by the hair and dragged her across the road. Chris Wright, an official of the National Union of Bank Employees and a leading lay member of APEX, protested that he and several others saw her repeatedly kicked. Another of the Asian women stood in the gutter and talked to Grantham and Dromey forty yards from the entrance. 'On the pavement', a police officer said brusquely. She turned and said, 'I'm not obstructing anyone'. 'You're nicked', he said, and she was dragged away. This time, the police were not so successful. Half a dozen of the sari-clad Grunwick women descended upon the police officer. Two of his colleagues came to his rescue. But the three of them stood in amazement as they were berated in Gujarati and pidgin English by fiery souls half their size. They released the woman. But the ugly face of racism surfaced; Chris Ball, another official of APEX, saw Jitendra ('Johnny') Patel repeatedly hit by a police officer yelling 'you Paki bastard!' (Later a friendly copper told a picket that 90 per cent of the Wembley police supported the National Front.)

Lawyer John Bowden saw two police officers grip a youth by the collar and ram his head against the side of a police van. A BBC cameraman, Chris Marlow, attempted to film the brutality and was himself arrested. His equipment was knocked to the ground. Roy Grantham complained bitterly to Sadler, but in vain. He said afterwards: 'The police used excessive violence ... We saw policemen kicking and punching pickets who were stretched out on the roadway.' The *Evening Standard* reflected the shock felt by its reporter: 'Police were being accused on all sides of being excessively violent. One demonstrator was dragged to a police van by his hair and several others were clearly punched during the arrests.'

Ward, of course, saw it differently. He told the press that there were over 600 pickets outside of the gate, even though the official police figures produced by Merlyn Rees claimed that there were not more than 700 pickets at all four gates. According to Ward, the police had no choice but to act because of the menace to his loyal employees. The police are a 'neutral' force, Ward claimed: 'The police do not arrest peaceful pickets.'

At Cobbold Road, meanwhile, the same number of pickets as at Chapter Road had been allowed to communicate with those going into work. Six of them joined the strike, and the signs were that more would follow their example the following day. But it was the events at Chapter Road that guaranteed the success of the mass picket. The first of the objectives of the mass picket – to get the waverers to join the strike – was already being met. Now, the second objective, to focus public and trade-union attention on the plight of the strikers, was being realised beyond the wildest dreams of APEX, but at terrible cost. It had never been the intention of the union or the strikers to create mayhem to gain column inches. Their goals had been much more modest. But the sledgehammer tactics of the police had turned the dispute into a national issue. Trade unionists up and down the country were shocked. Emergency meetings were held in hundreds of workplaces and trade-union organisations. Help was on the way to the beleaguered strikers. The press was confused and muted in its criticism of the pickets. Even the most partisan hacks could not substantially alter the evidence of their own eyes. The *Economist,* to which Robert Moss was a regular contributor, made the understatement of the summer: 'The police overdid their initial show of strength'.

The Bus

More surprises were to come. Ward knew that 'the rot' was once again setting in amongst his 'loyal' workers. He had to prevent the pickets from communicating with them. Thus, on the Tuesday, the blacklegs were driven to work in a bus, having been picked up at prearranged points near their homes. No choice was given to them about how they should come to work. Bussing meant that no communication was possible, and therefore no question of 'peaceful persuasion' could arise even though this was a right thought to be guaranteed by the law. The bus was driven, either by Ken Pearson or Malcolm Alden, through the picket line, often at speed – on the Wednesday it crashed into a car. The police deviated from normal practice by refusing to stop it to allow representatives of the Strike Committee to address those inside, or at least to ask them if they wished to be communicated with. The intention of the law was thereby thwarted. But the law was weak. In 1974, the Home Office and the then Commissioner of the Metropolitan Police, Robert Mark, had fought a successful rearguard action. Their action prevented the new Labour Government from using the Trade Union and Labour Relations Bill to give pickets a statutory right to stop vehicles or individuals, for a reasonable period of time, for the purpose of peaceful communication. But the Act, for all its weaknesses, had at least restored rights to trade unionists that the judges had taken away from them in the 1950s and 1960s. Now, with the developments at Grunwick, those rights were not worth the paper they were written on.

The Special Patrol Group

The other innovation was the introduction of the Special Patrol Group (SPG) onto a picket line, for the first time in British labour relations history. The SPG are unashamedly a 'heavy squad' of officers who serve in it on a rota. They are specially trained, heavily armed, and the group was formed for use against terrorists in London. They operate in highly mobile squads, in blue Ford Transit vans, each containing a dozen men. From the Tuesday onwards, they flanked the 'workers' bus' and were positioned at strategic points around the area. Many could not believe that such an operation, involving the purchase of a bus, and close and effective liaison between the police and the company, was thought up overnight. Monday's operation, they said, was an excuse for the innovations of Tuesday. Neither did the police learn any lessons from Monday. The introduction of the SPG was bound to increase the temperature of a situation that was already developing its own momentum. Their presence hardened feelings on the picket line. 'We're not bloody terrorists', said one local engineering convenor.

The Postal Workers

However the most important consequence of Monday was taking place two miles away at the Cricklewood sorting office. On the Monday afternoon, Colin Maloney and Jack Dromey met on the picket line at Chapter Road. Maloney, the Chairman of the Cricklewood sorters, was furious. A striking looking Southern Irishman, he was very much a man of action. 'It's now or never', Dromey said. 'We move and fuck the consequences', Maloney replied. The following morning he arranged for the officers of the London District Council of the UPW, led by the two organisers, John Taylor and Derek Walsh, to come to Chapter Road. Maloney knew that Cricklewood would need the help of the London District Council of the Union to get the mail blacked throughout London, and to prevent the blacked mail being diverted to other sorting offices.

John Taylor took Jack Dromey to one side. Taylor, whose power base in London was the Eastern District Office where he had worked as a sorter from the age of sixteen, was a tough and determined individual. Very much a militant within the UPW, he was a brilliant speaker and a rising star in the union, having just been elected to their National Executive Committee. Derek Walsh, a milder but equally determined individual, was active in the organisation of commuters from the Kent area where he lived. He described himself to Dromey as being considered a right winger within the LDC. But he was a trade unionist of firm principle. It was Taylor and Walsh who took the bull by the horns.

That afternoon, they met the officers of the Strike Committee. Mahmood Ahmad gave them an official written request for their support, and they sped back to their Central London office. Within an hour, a circular had been dispatched, with the support of their Committee, to their branches in London. The unofficial circular said that the LDC advised them to black Grunwick mail. The intention was that the blacking should come into effect on the Thursday morning, following meetings on the Wednesday at the key sorting offices, the most important of which were Cricklewood and West Central.

Maloney and Dave Dodd, the Cricklewood Secretary, were delighted; they could not move quickly enough. On Tuesday afternoon, their committee met and was unanimous in their decision to recommend to the branch the blacking of the Grunwick mail. The committee put it on the line to their members. The risks are appalling, they said. You will be taking on the law, the Post Office and maybe even your own union, they went on. But, said Colin Maloney, the question is simply this: is what we're doing right? Dave Dodd triumphantly announced the response of his men: sixty-four for the committee, forty-three against. Jack Dromey told the pickets at Chapter Road. A mighty roar went up. Grunwick's outgoing mail would now be bottled up and no other sorting office would handle any diverted items under the 1967 agreement with the Post Office.

The action by the Cricklewood sorters, an action that could have led to legal proceedings and the sack, was a splendid, unselfish and courageous act of solidarity. In November 1976, they had only reluctantly submitted to the decision of their Executive to call off the blacking. Even then, they had felt that by taking unofficial action, they could draw the legal fire onto themselves, protecting Tom Jackson from prosecution and the union's funds from confiscation. To Gorst and Gouriet, they said: 'You can't prosecute our union because we alone are blacking Grunwick mail, not the UPW nationally. If you wish to imprison us, then try it. We have had enough.'

The other branches in north-west London followed suit and, at West Central, the committee voted by twenty-three to one to recommend their 800 members to black as well.

Solidarity poured in. A number of TGWU drivers, working on contract for the police, refused to drive them to Chapter Road. Even the London members of the National Union of Bank Employees, a union not known for militant solidarity action with others, moved to try to black the handling of the Grunwick accounts. More of the 'loyal' workers came out on strike. Ward was desperate, the NAFF helpless. APEX, the Strike Committee and the Trades Council piled blow upon blow and were coming out top in the propaganda war. The NAFF was, however, to turn the propaganda tide by luring Grantham into a well-prepared trap.

The Trap

On Wednesday 15 June, John Gouriet started to talk openly of a possible exchange of views between Grunwick and Grantham. It seems that some on the APEX side, including Grantham himself, normally the sharpest of operators, were dizzy with the success of its offensive, and they let drop their guard at the expectation of Ward collapsing and coming to the negotiating table.

On Thursday 16 June, Grantham agreed he would visit Grunwick in the afternoon and 'exchange views' with George Ward.

Instead of meeting Ward as he had been led to believe, Grantham was kept waiting for a considerable time, and then asked into a room full of Grunwick employees. At the front of this gathering were the most rabid anti-unionists and a clutch of managers, who proceeded to shower Grantham with abuse. Instead of immediately walking out, Grantham tried to reason. That was his second mistake. He was howled down by the blacklegs, while the whole performance was being filmed.

The television that night carried shots which convinced even trade unionists that the remaining Grunwick workforce was solidly anti-union. The company exploited this later to argue that reinstatement was impossible, whatever the merits of the strike, because of the bitterness between strikers and workers. In fact, as was shown in June and July when another twenty workers joined the strike, the NAFF had created a false picture. This was dramatically portrayed in October by the 'Tonight' programme, when one of Grunwick's 'loyal workers' pleaded for union recognition, but only on condition that his face was kept in silhouette and his words were read by an actor, so there was no way Grunwick could identify him.

Ward was delighted with Gouriet's little trick. He told the *Daily Telegraph:* 'Grantham was called a scab, scum. There were shouts of "out, out". It was lovely.'

Antonio Jimenez, a cleaner who came out on strike after that meeting, described to the Scarman Inquiry how Grantham had been 'set up'. Ward went round to his employees beforehand and instructed them to abuse Grantham. 'Let's go and give it to him!' he told staff in front of Jimenez. According to Kevin Slattery who went on strike in July, Ward also brought in alcoholic drinks at lunchtime to help along the mood of the more extreme anti-unionists. It remained only to deceive Roy Grantham for the trap to be sprung.

The Picket Grows

The British trade-union movement delivered its awaited reply to the police brutality against the pickets with a huge turnout on the morning of Friday 17 June. A mass picket of about 1500 gathered around the Chapter Road premises. The Strike Committee announced to the crowd, which for the first time seriously outnumbered the 700 police, that instead of ending the mass picket that day – as had been originally intended – it had voted to extend it into a second week so that the trade-union movement could make its protest against the police tactics, and support the action of the post workers. A roar of approval greeted this announcement made by Jack Dromey over a megaphone in Chapter Road.

The strikers were very excited. Jayaben Desai, despite black bruises left on her legs by the gallant bobbies of Q Division, was overjoyed by the sight of hundreds of workers bearing on their shoulders beautiful trade-union banners of gold, red, yellow and green up Chapter Road. Her eyes sparkled as marching detachments of building workers and engineers strode up the middle of the road in the early hours of the morning. She was amused at the glum consternation of the police who had pushed and bullied the Indian women in the winter months, but now looked increasingly sheepish. 'I was sad before', she told the press, 'but now I am happy. When they talked of the power of the trade-union movement I listened but I didn't really believe. Now I see that power.'

More green police coaches drove up with reinforcements, but the trade unionists kept pouring in. One diehard police officer tried to usher away Yasu Patel, a young Indian woman, from the line at the gate, mumbling something about 'no more than six'. Two burly engineers turned on him: 'Don't start that shit again, that was on Monday. What do you want, a replay?' The copper looked at the determined features of the workers and shrugged his shoulders. 'It's not just women and young lads that's here today', a building worker shouted from the adjacent pavement. Jayaben Desai's face lit up at the discomfiture of the police. She whispered excitedly to Tom Durkin: 'So, after ten months, we have found out about the trade-union movement in this country ... that power you talked about, it is here'.

Each morning, the police had kept the pickets guessing about whether the bus would try to enter at the front entrance in Chapter Road or at the rear entrance in Cooper Road. The latter seemed less plausible for Grunwick, because the bus could not actually pass through the narrow gate. Instead the bus would drive up to the gate and the blacklegs would jump off and run the two or three yards into the gateway. But the police usually chose Cooper Road if the pickets were numerous, because it was away from the public view and because stationed along the road, outside and inside the premises of Willesden College of Technology, were the blue vans of the SPG.

To the outsider the 200 SPG men based in London probably looked identical to the other police, apart from their vehicles. However, they can be identified close up by the letters 'CO' on their shoulders standing for 'Commissioner's Officer'. Their tactics are also different; they form into triangles in front of crowds and then charge through, like a knife through butter.

The SPG now carved a path through the Cooper Road picket, for the bus to enter. Their ferocity on this Friday sent another shock-wave through the labour movement. This was how their attack was described by Maria Duggan who was badly injured: 'Suddenly the SPG men got out of their vans and hurled themselves at us. One of them kicked me in the shin and then dragged me along the ground. The pain was so excruciating that I was vomiting.' The reason the pain was excruciating was discovered at the hospital: the SPG kick had fractured her leg and severely torn the ligaments of her left ankle. Witnesses had noticed that, as on the Monday, the police seemed to make a beeline for the women. The SPG, however, according to Maria Duggan, were even more violent: 'Women were grabbed by the breasts, and punched around the neck and face'. She watched with horror and waited her turn.

Mary Davis, a lecturer from North London, told a press conference afterwards: 'The SPG rushed us like animals. It looked as if they were picking on women and smaller men.' One of them gave Mary Davis what appeared to be – from dozens of similar incidents reported – the standard treatment; he brought his boot down hard on her foot. Normally it just caused a swelling that kept a picket hobbling around at home for a week – Mary Davis ended up in hospital with a slight fracture.

These assaults enraged the whole trade-union movement. The media did their best for the police, but in omitting mention of the SPG attack on the women that weekend, they only added fuel to the flames of outrage that they aimed to cool.

The Second Week

On the Saturday morning, 18 June, it was admitted by the authorities that bringing in the bus on Friday had cost another forty or so arrests, thus bringing the total for the week to 150. Booth cast around him for a way out. Desperately, he asked Grantham, Ward and Mortimer to meet him. Grantham and Mortimer immediately accepted. Ward of course refused. He was adamant that no compromise was either possible or desirable.

Throughout the next few days, the Government struggled to contain the situation while not appearing to back either management or strikers. On the Monday, Booth had talks with Grantham and Mortimer. Over the weekend, Callaghan, the Prime Minister, had asked Merlyn Rees, Home Secretary, to chair a Grunwick *ad hoc* Cabinet Committee, the purpose of which was to meet daily and recommend to the Prime Minister proposals for cooling the confrontation. One of its first decisions was to bring forward the hearing of Ward's case against ACAS to 4 July. It also arranged talks between Grantham and Scotland Yard, which were to develop into daily telephone chats between Grantham and McNee, Commissioner of police. It was an interesting example of how government, despite protestations to the contrary, can influence the police and the courts if it really wants to.

Booth got nowhere with Ward who, accompanied by Gorst, Hickey and a legal adviser, finally deigned to talk to the minister on Thursday. The next day, 24 June, Booth proposed an independent mediator to settle the dispute. Grantham immediately accepted the offer. Ward dismissed it. Grunwick and the NAFF won no support from the 'moderates' for their recalcitrance but, then again, it was not 'moderates' they were out to enlist for their cause. Ward represented the forces in Britain bent on destroying 'consensus' politics. As the *Observer* of 28 June commented: 'Not long ago no union leader or employer would have hesitated to see the Employment Secretary or his officials during a dispute'.

On the picket lines, war resumed on Monday 20 June, with 1200 pickets in attendance. The police tactics had doubled the numbers in one week. What was even better from the Strike Committee's point of view, was the news during the day that the miners had voted to join the picket lines later in the week. The Trades Hall, headquarters of the picketing, was busy from six o'clock every morning. Delegations would sink gratefully down on the chairs in the main hall, shedding the weight of banner poles and sipping coffee served by the strikers. Although the hall itself was rather dilapidated, delegates had plenty of decorations to study while they were waiting for their mates. At one end was an enormous NUR banner of the Neasden No. 1 Branch, in red, green and gold, dating back to the days when unions were friendly societies: 'We succour widows and orphans', it read, above a picture of a poor Victorian family. Next to it were posters in red, showing Jayaben

Desai and the original leaders of the strike. Its slogan read: 'Defend Workers' Rights to Organise'. Then there were huge blown up photos of Kanti Patel's face, showing the weals, swellings and cuts. In addition, there were pictures of Boyson, Crozier, Moss and Gorst with the captions: 'The Outsiders at Grunwick'. Placards on and off poles lay scattered about the room: 'Soweto – Grunwick: ONE STRUGGLE' and, to be held up at the windows of the bus if possible, 'Your Rise is Paid For By Our Blood!' There was also by the door an enormous photo of Len Murray shaking hands warmly with Jayaben Desai. Across his smiling face a blue biro had scrawled: 'Traitor!'

After a quiet start to the week, there was a new eruption of violence on Tuesday 21 June. This was witnessed by a group of 'Tribune' MPs led by Ian Mikardo, who were conducting an on-the-spot investigation. What they saw was, in the words of Jack Dromey to the press conference later that morning, the 'most violent scenes on the picket line so far'.

The police decided to bring the bus in through the Chapter Road gate, perhaps because the majority of pickets had concentrated in Cooper Road. The bus got in and came out again shortly afterwards. An incident developed between a police officer and a picket. The picket wrestled free from the police officer's grasp, who then instead laid his hands on a young black man called Mike Otui. Mikardo, who was nearby, swore that Otui was behaving no differently from the others: 'Perhaps it was because he was coloured and easily identifiable that he was picked out'. Perhaps he had shouted something provocative. Whatever the reason for the arrest – and Otui was subsequently acquitted – the method was, once again, inexcusable. Otui was seized by three police officers and punched viciously. Friends raced into rescue Otui and suddenly a raging battle developed as more police waded in.

Mikardo was aghast. There was genuine anger in his voice that evening when he told television news: 'At no time during the course of the morning did we [the MPs] see anybody offer violence to the police of any sort. Nor did we see anything that could be called provocation other than vocal provocation.' He compared it to the battle of Cable Street in the 1930s, when left-wing demonstrators fought with police attempting to escort Mosley's fascists through the East End of London. Even one of Mikardo's colleagues was arrested, MP Audrey Wise. She fell afoul of the police when she watched a police officer dragging along a woman picket by the hair. Unable to stand in silence she upbraided the police officer for his barbaric behaviour. 'You'll do instead', he replied and yanked Wise into the nearest police coach.

The MPs also expressed concern about the manner in which the bus was driven. According to Mikardo, the bus was used as a projectile to slice through the picket line. An elderly trade unionist, Bob Doyle, was knocked down as the bus swung at high speed through the gateway and he spent some time in hospital recovering from his injuries. The MPs asked the police to prosecute the driver for dangerous driving but they did nothing.

On Wednesday, two leading Communists addressed the crowd in Chapter Road through megaphones. Gordon McLennan, General Secretary of the Communist Party, presented a cheque for £288 to Jayaben Desai, money collected at a Communist rally in Alexandra Palace on the previous Sunday. Despite being hissed by a Trotskyist section of the crowd, McLennan spoke a few words about the significance of the strike.

Mick McGahey, the Communist leader of the Scottish miners, received a more enthusiastic welcome. He was there to represent the NUM not the Party and the British labour movement respects no union more than the NUM. McGahey delivered a powerful speech to the smallest crowd of the week, which was nonetheless still slightly larger than that on the first day. His theme was that, if necessary, Grunwick would have to be closed down, for there was a certain level of misbehaviour by an employer that the trade-union movement could not tolerate. 'We must stop that industrial hooligan Ward, in his tracks', he shouted, just a few feet below Ward's half open window. He told the strikers: 'You will win as night follows day ... the whole of the Scottish miners will come here if necessary'. McGahey ended, however, with an appeal for action from organisations a little closer than Scotland: 'I want to see marching down Chapter Road the General Council of the TUC. Behind them I want to see marching the National Executive Committee of the Labour Party. And behind them, the Parliamentary Labour Party led by the Prime Minister.' The pickets applauded ecstatically. Callaghan near a picket line! An incongruous thought. McGahey's political thrust, of course, lay in the order of the march he envisaged.

The Thursday and Friday were the high water mark of the June picketing outside Grunwick. There were over 2000 pickets on both days, with official police figures counting 2200 on the Friday, as compared to 1521 police. Thursday 23 June, was the most bitter day so far, the day of fifty-three arrests (the second highest tally in June). This was the day that Arthur Scargill led the Yorkshire miners into Cooper Road.

Enter the Miners

The miners are the toughest and most militant section of the British working class. Overwhelmed by the solidarity they received in the great strikes of 1972 and 1974, they reciprocated by sending a delegation to Grunwick. What they expected was probably a repeat of the picketing of 1972 – pushing, shoving and a few kicks. Times had changed; the reception given them by the SPG took them utterly by surprise. As one miner told Capital Radio: 'I have never seen police like this. This is not traditional British policemen we have here. These here are thugs in uniform.' Another was asked to compare Grunwick with the battle of Saltley Gates in Birmingham in 1972. 'There's no comparison', he replied, 'I was at Saltley Gates and it was a children's Sunday picnic by the side of this'.

If the police had blundered politically on the first day, by misjudging trade-union reaction, they now committed a similar blunder by arresting Arthur Scargill and his colleagues. Once again, it was the SPG who rammed into the pickets in Cooper Road. Scargill was whisked off to Wembley police station with others, and charged with obstructing the highway and obstructing the police. Later, a court found him innocent on both charges, thanks to photographic evidence of his arrest produced by Pat Mantle of the *Morning Star.* Other pickets were not so fortunate; if it is just the word of a picket against the word of a police officer the court has little choice but to accept the police officer's case.

The miners were furious; they descended on Wembley police station like a swarm of hornets. One miner, James Miller, told reporters outside: 'I'll tell you this; if they are going to jail Mr Scargill for supporting APEX, they had better devise better methods for getting coal out of pits than miners'. Scargill and the others, including Maurice Jones, editor of the journal, *Yorkshire Miner*, were released on bail later in the day. Scargill was flushed, angry and eloquent; Jones was white, trembling and silent. As a result of police threats that Jones alleged were by Special Branch men inside Wembley police station, he was soon to generate a new controversy by fleeing the country with his wife and child, and seeking political asylum in East Germany.

According to Jones, the Special Branch suggested he should tone down his articles in the *Yorkshire Miner,* perhaps by getting some left-wing Labour MPs to write them instead! They had a file on his Finnish-born wife, and mentioned that, as she had worked illegally for a hairdresser in 1970, she might be liable to deportation. It was their final remark, however, which frightened Jones most. This was, he alleged: 'You have a delightful little girl, Mr Jones. The roads become very busy at this time of the year.' Determined to divulge the conversation but scared by what he took to be a threat to his daughter's life, Jones flew with his family to the GDR.

PC Wilson and the Right-Wing Backlash

The history of 23 June was, however, by no means exhausted by the arrest of Scargill. There was, unfortunately, a tragic follow-up later on in the morning, while most of the miners were in Wembley and most of the other pickets had gone off to work. The double-decker had got in at about ten o'clock, and the few remaining pickets were walking to the Eighty-Seven Café in Dudden Hill Lane. A fight broke out between them and the hated SPG. Punches were thrown and, at the end of the struggle, an SPG officer, struck by a bottle, lay on the road with blood pouring from his head.

According to the *Guardian:*

A Special Patrol Group van drove down from the back gates [Cooper Road] and, as it moved into Dudden Hill Lane seven pickets banged on the side. One shouted 'scab'. One of the policemen jumped out of the back and grabbed a woman. Others came out to help him. There was a lot of punching.

The *Daily Telegraph* was melodramatic and somewhat inaccurate. Its headline was: 'Worst day at Grunwick : Shouts of "kill" as PC is Hurt'. The story claimed that demonstrators chanted 'kill him, kill him' as they tried to kick a police officer who was lying injured in the street after being hit around the head with a bottle. The report was clearly not from an eyewitness because it stated that the incident occurred 'outside the besieged factory', whereas in fact it was not even in Cooper Road. The *Daily Telegraph* did, however, agree with the *Guardian* that the incident started when verbal provocation by the pickets was met by physical attack from the SPG. This is how the *Daily Telegraph* described it: 'They banged on the sides of the blue van chanting "scabs" and "animals". Suddenly the back doors opened and one police officer leaped out and grabbed one of the demonstrators.'

Ironically enough, the police officer who was hurt was not the one who leaped out and launched the attack. The one hurt, PC Wilson, jumped out of the van to help the first police officer, who had bitten off more than he could chew. Wilson was left in the road for several minutes, some say a quarter of an hour – with blood streaming from his wound while he was being extensively filmed and photographed. The police immediately recognised the publicity value of what had happened and made the most of it. There was no immediate arrest of the person who had thrown the bottle. Later on, however, a West Indian worker from the Smith's Cricklewood factory was charged with assaulting a police officer, occasioning him grievous bodily harm. He was twenty-two, an England junior triple-jump champion, and a member of ASTMS, the white-collar union for higher grades of clerical staff. His name was Richard Maull and he denied the charge.

The Strike Committee immediately expressed its sympathy for PC Wilson and condemned all acts of violence by both sides. Chris Wright and Jayaben Desai were sent to visit Wilson in hospital. A miner told a radio reporter that miners disapproved of provoking the police in the way this group had. It was clear, he said, that those involved knew little of the self-discipline of trade unionism. As for PC Wilson himself, he and his pregnant wife received massive media coverage. According to the *Daily Telegraph,* he stated that it was not 'the ordinary decent pickets' who had baited his unit, and he accepted the sympathy of Chris Wright and Jayaben Desai in a televised hospital interview.

The Trades Council equally deplored the incident and condemned the use of offensive weapons. It was also, however, very critical of the one-sided media coverage. Bob Doyle claimed that he was in hospital just as long as PC Wilson but there were no television cameras there for him. Nor did Ward and Gorst come to his bedside and apologise. The MPs' request for the bus driver to be arrested had been ignored, whereas in the Wilson case they had arrested someone the next day. Trades Council delegates also pointed out that in the cases of Mary

Davis and Maria Duggan, severe injuries had had scarce coverage in the press and on the television. As for the *Daily Telegraph* headlines, eyewitnesses – including a local shopkeeper – denied them completely. A *Morning Star* reporter, Sheila Grey, said for example: 'The report of pickets surrounding PC Wilson shouting "kill him" and kicking him when he was on the ground are just not true'.

The Wilson incident set off a whole chain of hysteria in the media and some people regard it as a turning point in the strike. Many reckon that the incident allowed the hostile sections of the media to launch an offensive which frightened the Government with the prospect of electoral disadvantage, and gave it and the TUC leaders the opportunity actively to work for the destruction of the mass picket. The evidence for this is very strong if official statements before and after the Wilson incident are compared. Roy Grantham, for example, although he stuck resolutely to his demand for a Court of Inquiry, showed signs of being under heavy pressure after 23 June. He now talked firmly of reducing the picket to less than 500 per day, an idea he had only floated vaguely the previous Sunday. He also associated himself with an idea, said to have originated with Callaghan himself, of armbands for 'official' pickets.

The strikers were scandalised by this idea. When, in the third week, APEX officials started handing out 'official picket' armbands, many refused to wear them. Tearing hers off and seizing the megaphone from an official, Jayaben Desai told the crowd to rapturous applause: 'You are our friends. We will not protect ourselves and leave you to the police.'

However, Jayaben was suffering from the same delusion as Callaghan, if she imagined that armbands would be of any protection. When, on the Friday, Len Gristey prevailed on six pickets directly on the gate to wear them, the result was instructive. Despite the fact that they wore Callaghan's armbands, four out of the six – three women and one man – were kicked from behind by police officers standing in a row between them and the gate. At least one of the pickets had to be driven home as a result of these kicks. After this nasty lesson, the fuss about armbands died away, their use being generally confined to those designated as stewards.

On 24 June, the *Daily Mail*, under the headlines of 'A Blot on Britain' and 'the ugly and unacceptable face of British trade unionism', carried a gallery of Wilson photographs. The shocking pictures were also an object lesson to the British trade-union movement, and to the political ultra-left in particular, on the need for the utmost discipline in such situations. One senseless act was now to be used to obscure the substantive issues and turn the propaganda tide. Leading right wingers jumped onto the bandwagon. Sir Keith Joseph, self-appointed leader of the Conservative Party's right wing, pronounced the Grunwick pickets to be 'red fascists'. His intervention was all the more bizarre as he seemed to be woefully uninformed about the strike and constitutionally incapable of understanding any of the basic facts. He kept telling the media, for example, that the strike was about a 'closed shop' at Grunwick, an issue which had never been raised and was never likely to be, as APEX had nowhere near 100 per cent of the workforce in membership. APEX could not even win recognition, let alone think about a 'closed shop'. In the end, Margaret Thatcher, in October, had to rescue the Conservative Party from Joseph by stating unequivocally on television: 'Grunwick was never anything to do with the issue of a closed shop'.

The extreme right in the media also raised the bogey of a too-powerful trade-union movement bullying poor, harmless little Grunwick. This was shameless audacity: if the Grunwick Strike proved anything, it was that the British trade-union movement was unable to prevent a tiny company from keeping union members on the streets, without any visible progress, for nearly a year. The only people sacked at Grunwick were trade unionists on strike. As the *Guardian* put it: Grunwick 'gives the lie to those who still claim that the unions rule'.

The right also launched a cult of George Ward, the small man fighting the big unions. A good example was an article in the *Daily Mail* that week: 'George Ward had to beat the last bars of the dawn chorus to put a wall, barbed wire and heavy steel gates between him and a mob that goes every day at 8 a.m. to bellow about union rights and justice'.

The Ward cult reached its peak around 25 June when the London *Evening News* carried the headline: 'Our family's torment, by wife of Grunwick chief'. There was an interview with Ward's wife, Loretto, and a picture of their large, detached house in Mill Hill. The article oozed concern for the poor besieged employer: 'Grunwick boss, Mr George Ward, left his North London home early today for a secret destination, suffering from exhaustion'.

It was, of course, the mass picket itself that drew the most venom from the press. By 23 June, even the moderate *Daily Mirror* was talking about 'blatant intimidation' by the pickets. The *Daily Telegraph* was scandalised by the very idea of a mass protest. One of its journalists, John O'Sullivan, for example, who also wrote in the NAFF's *Free Nation,* described the crowd in Chapter Road as 'howling mobs of blood-crazed social workers, Yorkshire Trots and International Brigade veterans'.

The Press

The onslaught by the media was not left unanswered but was carried by the trade unions into the newspapers themselves. When the NAFF placed advertisements in the press on behalf of Grunwick, and appealed for funds to fight the 'tyranny' of trade unionism, the print-workers protested and demanded that an anti-NAFF article be printed beside the NAFF advert. Both the *Sunday Telegraph* and the *Observer* lost copies because of trade-union action against the editors. The *Sun* also appeared on 2 July with a blank editorial space. When the print-workers responsible arrived on the picket lines, they received a rapturous ovation from the pickets.

The bias of the newspaper coverage only reflected what trade unionists already knew; of the nine national dailies in Britain, three were uncompromisingly right-wing: the *Daily Express,* the *Daily Mail* and the *Daily Telegraph.* Of the three, the *Telegraph,* which aspires to be a 'quality' newspaper, contained the most facts. The *Sun,* which follows a Conservative line editorially, was the next most biased against the strikers and also the least factual. The *Daily Mirror,* the *Financial Times, The Times* and the *Guardian* made the best efforts to present both sides of the case. *The Times* for example, during the hysteria of the second week of mass picketing, balanced its right-wing editorials with an article by Roy Grantham, one of the few which actually dealt with the underlying issues. The *Financial Times* and the *Guardian* were very informative. The *Guardian* articles by David Pallister contained information about events before the mass picket that were indispensable to understanding the strike. The *Morning Star,* the national daily with the smallest circulation, had of course consistently supported the strikers right from the beginning, and backed up its support with articles from a left-wing point of view. The far left also supported the strikers, but their weekly publications could not fight out day-to-day issues; of their papers, *Socialist Worker* and *Socialist Challenge* gave incisive coverage. *Tribune,* for left-Labour, gave solid support.

At the end of June there was an interesting, self-critical article in *The Times* by Brian MacArthur, the Home News Editor. He wrote: 'As usual it was not until there was violence that the BBC or ITN or most newspapers bothered to report the issue'. His analysis of the daily newspapers coincided exactly with the views of the strikers: 'Only the *Guardian* and *The Times*, [which carried twelve separate items] fleshed out the dispute and only the *Morning Star* put the case of the strikers and the pickets'.

The Trades Council paid particular attention to the press, and insisted on a full press conference in the Trades Hall on most mornings of the mass picket in June. These conferences had little or no impact on the extreme right-wing newspapers, beyond one or two sentences tucked away at the end of long reports. Good relationships were, however, struck up with reporters from the *Financial Times, The Times* and the *Guardian,* and these were fruitful both for those newspapers and for the Strike Committee. Jayaben Desai found her own way of dealing with the right-wing press. She told all pickets not to communicate with reporters from the *Mail,* the *Telegraph* or the *Express:* she censored their censorship. At Chapter Road, from June onwards, anguished news people and photographers from those papers could be seen pleading with pickets for poses and comments equivalent to those that had been given freely to the *Guardian* and the *Morning Star.*

Radio and Television

It was not just the newspapers which the strikers had to contend with, but also radio and television. The main cleavage here was between the BBC, which tended to put the establishment view, and commercial television and radio, which tended to be both more sensational and more impartial. Naturally, neither had any interest in supporting the strikers and the pickets, but the BBC produced, to our knowledge, not a single programme that could claim to be impartial. It was a BBC newsreader, Angela Rippon, who used the phrase 'trade unionists and other extremists' to describe the pickets. Those who used the excuse that it was just an oversight by the news editor had to admit that the phrase 'employers and other extremists' would have been spotted.

The best programme was undoubtedly ITV's 'London Programme'. For a start, it had reported on the strike before the mass picket began, and was therefore immune to the charge of profiting from the violence. The first of its programmes featured Dromey, Gouriet, Grantham and Ward. It was outstanding in giving as much time and attention to the union as to the management side.

The 'London Programme's' report on the mass picket – on Sunday 26 June at 11 p.m. – was eagerly anticipated by union supporters because of the relative impartiality of the first programme. However, it started off by trying to be impartial and failing: the issue it said, was – according to the unions – the right to join a union and – according to the management – the right not to join a union. In fact, of course, it was not so much the right to join a union that was at issue – many individuals at Grunwick secretly joined – but the right to *organise* a union by recruiting members. As for the right not to join a union, that was never an issue at any stage.

Len Gristey was interviewed by Angela Lambert. He stressed that the timing was intended to hit Grunwick at the peak of its business. The reason for the mass picket was simply that every other alternative had been exhausted; the mass picket was 'the only thing we hadn't tried' and 'the law had failed'.

Interestingly enough, the film showed blacklegs going into work on the first day, apparently unhindered apart from a chorus of abuse. Gristey's explanation of the escalation was that it was 'so many people taken for nothing', on 13 June, that aroused the trade-union movement. The point was made that violent scenes later did not result in so many arrests as passivity on the first day. Chris Wright was asked about 13 June: he described how just before 7 a.m. police 'charged into' 150 pickets and arrested half of them. The reporters also interviewed Richard Clutterbuck, a military expert on 'counter insurgency'. He took the line that the crowd was not a picket but a demonstration, and was therefore not entitled to the rights of picketing. He also claimed that police strategy on the Monday would certainly not have been to mass arrest. He maintained that those arrested simply did not disperse quickly enough when asked to clear the gateway by the police.

The inferiority of the BBC's coverage was demonstrated by the 'Money Programme' on Friday 24 June. Although it did probe into the main issues, it was less fair because the majority of the programme's time was given over to one side, the employer's. This is not a subjective impression: the interviews on the programme were timed. Malcolm Alden appeared on it twice and Ward had a six minute interview.

There were interviews with blacklegs on the bus. The strikers only surfaced in a studio confrontation at the end where, after a lengthy pro-employer introduction, four strikers faced four blacklegs in apparent 'balance'. Fortunately, for the strikers, this confrontation saved the day. The strikers – including Jayaben Desai, looking distinguished in an all-white sari – behaved politely and with dignity, but the blacklegs betrayed the ugliness of Grunwick's anti-unionism. One woman, Hildegaard Watte, started to shout abuse, always disastrous on television. 'APEX is one of the most Communist unions there is', she shrieked, thus revealing her ignorance of the British trade-union movement.

The strikers simply stated their grievances and ignored the frenzy. Compulsory overtime topped their list. Jayaben Desai stressed that she had been promised that she would not be required to do any compulsory overtime after moving from Wembley to Dollis Hill. That is why she had agreed to move with the company in April 1976. Poor toilets, lack of facilities for tea breaks, lack of air conditioning and low pay were also mentioned. The strikers particularly objected to division of the workforce by differing rates of pay arranged secretly with individual workers.

At the end of the programme George Ward claimed that the strikers were mainly students which, as we have seen, the figures disprove. He also asked why Jayaben Desai let Sunil Desai work at Grunwick if conditions were so bad. (According to her, Sunil worked for the money: black and Asian youths had to put up with the long hours because the alternative was no job at all.) Ward also returned to the smashing of the Cobbold Road windows on the first day of the strike, and claimed that the mass picket was based on the theory that 'might is right'. The BBC excelled itself: in a half-hour programme only about five minutes were allocated to the strikers, with Ward speaking at the beginning and end.

The Strike Committee and the Trades Council issued frequent press statements to counteract the stream of propaganda. In the first week, they were moderately successful because neither the Labour Party nor the Conservative Party supported Ward, Grunwick or the NAFF, regarding them as a threat to the remnants of consensus politics. In the second week, however, the media concentrated on the issue of law and order, and found that the police were much easier to defend than the Grunwick management. Everyone on the right felt obliged to support the police, whatever action they took. This, together with the respect for the 'good old British bobby', made criticism of the police increasingly difficult in local trade union meetings. During June, motions condemning police tactics were sometimes defeated by the very trade unionists who had previously voted unanimously to support the strikers.

Pickets and Police

The British police are rightfully praised for a number of qualities. For a start they carry no gun as a rule, and are allowed to draw their truncheons only in self defence. Their behaviour has always been compared favourably with the police forces of other countries in terms of brutality, corruption and political composition. These good features were, however, eroded in the early 1970s. More and more British police are now issued with firearms. The number of plainclothes, or secret, police and the number of political police has substantially increased. Corruption and brutality have become so widespread that scarcely a year goes by without at least one high-ranking police officer being sent to prison.

As for industrial relations, the record of the British police has never been particularly good. The police are expected to side with the employer, and they usually do. The stories about police playing football with strikers in the General Strike of 1926 reflect only the fact that many individual police officers are goodhearted and many are from working-class backgrounds. When it comes to the 'top brass', the attitude is often similar to the threat made by Superintendent Robert Edwards to Aneurin Bevan in Tredegar in 1926: 'If there's any trouble here we'll have the place running with blood'.

Perhaps the best summary of the feelings of the average picket towards the police was put together by Stuart Weir in *New Society* on 30 June. Weir described how the pickets felt the increasing tension as the bus approached. Fearing arrest, some wrote the phone number of the Brent Law Centre on their wrists. They were scared, especially of the SPG, but on the other hand were determined to hold their ground. They were convinced that workers had the right to strike without being sacked and had the right to picket without being arrested. This conviction outweighed their fear of being arrested or injured, and of possibly losing their jobs.

Weir graphically described how the bus entered Cooper Road, how the crowd massed in front of the gate, and how the bus, flanked by police, ground to a halt. He and his friend, Steve, braced themselves to stand firm as the SPG began their charges into the crowd and the first pickets were seized, kicked and dragged away. Weir: 'I felt my heart pounding and tensed myself to be hit. Steve was grabbed, thrown and punched in the face, breaking his glasses.' The pickets, jammed up against each other, unable to move, were slowly but surely 'thinned out' by the police.

Many witnesses who criticised the police were not the type to level criticism lightly. Roy Edwards, for example, Assistant General Secretary of APEX, and very much a 'moderate', told the press that the violence 'was caused by the police who waded in with their fists, knees and boots and used their helmets as truncheons'. He added: 'I have seen action on picket lines many, many times but I have never seen such brutality. It was unprovoked and I think it was planned in advance to discredit the pickets.' The point about truncheons is interesting: at no time did the police draw their truncheons at Grunwick. Regulations say that truncheons can be drawn only in self-defence and at no time did the police as a body have to defend themselves from attack.

The *Willesden and Brent Chronicle* asked local residents for their views about the fighting in the issue of 1 July. Although there was some criticism of the behaviour of some pickets, the overwhelming weight of their reaction was against the police. A Mrs M. O'Connor said:

> As far as I'm concerned, the police are causing most of it from what I've seen. The workers there are paid nothing. I went there for a job almost three years ago. I'm a qualified bookkeeper and that was what they advertised for. They offered me £15 a week. It's a joke, wages like that. The strike's justified and I'll put up with the noise and inconvenience until the workers get a fair deal.

Another resident, Mr Shakoor, told the reporter: 'If the police would just let them picket peacefully there wouldn't be this trouble'. A Mr Martin Power told the *Chronicle:* 'As far as I'm concerned I'm angry that my rates are being used to pay the police to stop people legally picketing'.

A local clergyman, the Reverend David Haslam, also voiced his concern in a letter to the *Guardian* of 30 June. He wrote:

> In my own experience on the picket line, although there is undoubtedly a small minority seeking confrontation with the authorities, the main violence has been caused by the tactics of the police and has been perpetuated by them. The activities of the Special Patrol Group have been visible to millions of television viewers; individuals are picked out completely at random, hauled and even kicked along the street, sometimes dragged by the hair – women included – and pushed or thrown into police vehicles. The majority of 'ordinary' police have not been involved in these actions; some, by their comments, are rather unhappy about them.

The Haldane Society of Socialist Lawyers criticised the police for 'the unjustified interference with the rights of pickets to peacefully communicate information, the arbitrary limitation of the number of permitted pickets, the making of unlawful arrests and the use of unnecessary force'. On 20 June, Norman Atkinson, MP, made this point in Parliament: it was the police who were breaking the law at Grunwick by preventing peaceful pickets from communicating with workers.

The police tactics at the beginning of the second week were particularly criticised because their 'sophistication' revealed a much greater element of calculation, and premeditation. It was on the Monday and Tuesday that APEX received reports of a number of incidents that had occurred among the crowd. Initially, it was fairly trivial: some pickets claimed to have been pushed from behind against police lines by unidentified men. Then a number of milk bottles were hurled from the back of the crowd at the bus bringing in the blacklegs. APEX officials could not immediately identify the throwers, whose action had no effect on the inmates of the bus – London buses have toughened windows – but had a frightening effect on pickets and police. With the help of photographs, however, the men were partially identified. As Roy Grantham told the *Guardian:*

> Union officials had photographed four men, two of whom had hurled milk bottles at the coach bringing workers to the Grunwick plant in the morning. One of our officials, Mr John Wall, interviewed the

people concerned. He elicited that they were not trade unionists. They claimed to be students but didn't appear to know which college they were at. Subsequently, one of them ran away and jumped into a police van – we don't think pickets would do that.

The Times also quoted an allegation, apparently from a different source, that the bottle throwers were plain-clothes police officers. The best journalistic coup, however, was by *Socialist Worker*. In its issue of 25 June, it had pictures of two young men dressed in rough clothes, one of whom looked unshaven. According to the reporter, the two had been challenged by pickets and accused of throwing bottles. One of them panicked and, punching a woman picket in the face, raced off down the road with his mate. The clincher was a second picture, which showed one of the two driving off with police, wearing a big smile, in a police coach. He could clearly be identified as the same man not only by his face but by a rather distinctive shirt.

There were other incidents: one day at Chapter Road, a man claiming to be a freelance journalist was allowed by uniformed police to stand right on the picket line, just before the bus was due to arrive. Usually, the police tried to thin down the pickets at that juncture. When a woman in the crowd said that she recognised the 'journalist' as a man working last winter in the police force, APEX official Chris Ball went over and challenged him. The suspect laughed at the accusation but then immediately turned away and disappeared into Dollis Hill tube station.

There were many examples of 'sophisticated' tactics. Early one morning, a burly police officer with white hair, probably in his forties, suddenly fell to the ground in Chapter Road. He had just joined a line of police pushing back the crowd. He writhed about on the ground clutching his legs, then his stomach, for about two minutes while other police on the gate looked on impassively. One of the pickets was moved to ask an inspector to go over and help him. 'Oh, he'll be all right', was the unruffled reply. It was then realised that the 'injured' police officer was directly in line with a television camera sticking out of an upstairs window of the shop opposite. Such is the residual faith in the British police, however, that even militant pickets did not accept that they were watching a police tactic until the same police officer – again with no helmet, to expose the white hair – repeated exactly the same performance in the same spot about an hour later. It duly appeared on television that night.

On 15 July, in the London *Evening Standard*, the recently retired Commissioner of the Metropolitan Police, Robert Mark, explained the philosophy behind modern police tactics: 'The real art of policing a free society or a democracy is to win by appearing to lose'. He claimed it would be disastrous to employ water cannon, tear gas, or other violent methods against demonstrators in front of television cameras. The aim should be to win the sympathy of the public. He quoted as an example a horse called Quaver, the 'Brigitte Bardot' of the Metropolitan police horses. Quaver had been trained to simulate death at a word of command in front of television cameras at demonstrations. The *Evening Standard* printed pictures showing how the beautiful horse fell, in such a way that the rider could jump clear. Robert Mark commented smugly: 'This is the way to make sure that the police image, which the British people like to have, is maintained'.

Of course, some of the rank-and-file police were sympathetic to the strikers, particularly as the Police Federation at this time was pushing for a pay increase. The best example of this came one day when a police coach drew up in Cooper Road. Pasted on the window was a poster demanding: 'More Pay For Police'. Some of the police from the bus came over to the picket line with big grins on their faces, greeting it with 'Good morning, brothers and sisters!' An inspector standing nearby looked as if he was going to be sick.

The attitude of the pickets to the police was as varied as that of police to pickets. Some expressed hatred of the police, while some went out of their way to try and convert the police to their point of view. One day, two individuals, after a chorus of 'fascist pigs' from a section of the crowd, appeared walking behind a column of police officers, in step, with pig masks and police helmets. Some police cussed under their breath, others laughed. An inspector was heard to dismiss the whole picket light-heartedly: 'You should go into the terraces at Arsenal sometimes. It makes this lot look like chicken feed.'

The megaphone speeches in the early morning reflected the dichotomy in the attitudes of trade unionists. Sometimes, visiting trade-union leaders would welcome the blue tide of police officers released from the fleet of green coaches: 'Give the coppers a clap, lads; they're fighting for a pay rise just like us and we should be backing them 100 per cent'. On another day, a West Indian speaker watched with evident bitterness as hundreds of police brought over from North London filled Chapter Road and outnumbered the pickets. 'There's one good thing', he commented acidly: 'black kids will walk the streets of North London in safety today'.

The speakers who subscribed to the 'soft' strategy of distinguishing between rank-and-file police and the top brass at Scotland Yard were the ones that seemed to worry the police chiefs most. George Smith, of Kilburn TGWU, and another speaker were warned that they could be arrested for 'creating disaffection among the police force'.

The 'hardliners' were well represented by Bill Freeman, a printer, who, on Wednesday 29 June began his speech: 'Trade unionists, comrades, human beings – I think that covers everyone here except the police'. The police on the gate muttered angrily: 'Hark at him – what a comic! What's he print, the fucking cartoons?'

Bill Freeman continued, undaunted: 'When our print delegation comes down here on Friday, if the police arrest *our* leaders, *our* General Secretaries, *our* print organisers, one thing they can be sure of – they won't *read* about it on Saturday'. The police lines bristled once again, so much so that some of the pickets started debating Bill Freeman's chances of spending the rest of the day in Wembley police station. One picket 'bet' another that Freeman would be picked out and arrested in a scuffle when the bus came in. He lost the mock wager; nothing happened that day. On the Friday, however, when the full print delegation arrived and visited the Cooper Road entrance the news came back: 'Bill Freeman has been arrested'.

In the end, Bill Freeman was lucky. There was photographic evidence of his arrest that disproved the police's story in court. He was therefore acquitted, like Scargill. His brother, Jim, was less fortunate. As he told the press, he saw Bill in a police bus and asked the police if he could speak to him:

> The sergeant said 'I'll have you'. He grabbed hold of my cobblers and pulled me onto the bus. They beat us near to death on that bus. I've had five serious heart attacks and when they got to the station I took a turn. It took them an hour and half to get me a doctor.

Jim's case never came to court: he died of a sixth heart attack later on that summer.

It is certainly not easy to evaluate accurately the role of the police.

On the one hand, the police and army act as arms of the state and are in no way neutral arbiters in conflicts between labour and capital. On the other hand, the police force consists of individuals, many of working-class origins, who may be far from sympathetic with employers like Grunwick. There is also a third factor: in Britain, which is a democracy and not a fascist country, the government of the day (rather than the state) exercises some control over the police. Most of the decisions in relation to Grunwick had to be approved, implicitly or explicitly, by Merlyn Rees, the Home Secretary. He could have vetoed, for example, the use of the SPG, which was never intended to be brought into industrial disputes. The Government also has some control over legislation: the Wilson-Callaghan Government could have put more teeth into the Trade Union and Labour Relations Act, or at least have made it more precise. The Act establishes a positive right to communicate peaceably with those passing through a picket line, but does not say how pickets are to manage this when the blacklegs are encased in several tons of metal travelling at thirty mph.

When Rees visited Willesden on Monday 27 June, he was bitterly rebuked by angry pickets who put much of the blame for the violence not on the police, but on Rees's policy. Rees replied by referring to his policies in Northern Ireland, which he seemed to imagine had been a success. He disclaimed all responsibility for what had happened at Grunwick: 'I learnt this in Northern Ireland: operational control must be in the hands of the police'. It was the predictable defence of a reformist who regards the state machine as neutral and sacrosanct. Ian Mikardo on television rephrased Rees's statement, apparently unsure people would understand it. It means, he said, that it is not Rees who tells the police what to do but the police who tell Rees what to do.

The picketing was not, however, all confrontation – that would be misleading. One day a Welsh trade-union leader tried to chat to the police on the gate. The police officer he started talking to happened to be extremely right-wing in his views. 'You support Mr Ward then?' asked the Welshman. 'Yes, I do', came the emphatic reply. The Inspector in charge looked alarmed by this outright admission. He ordered the police officer to be silent. As the Welshman had originally asked about the freedom of workers he now seized upon this: 'Ah, so you're not allowed then, not free, to talk about freedom?' No reply. Fortunately for the conversation, Jayaben Desai happened to arrive and the Welshman took her along the police line making mock introductions:

> Mrs Desai, let me introduce you to PC 187. Now 187, he's got a deep-seated longing to be a shop steward. But PC 208, over here, he's not having any of that because he's after promotion you see. And as for 169, here, he's just bored – this is the first time I've seen him laugh all day. And as for poor old 249, well he's the saddest of all. He can't talk you see – he wants to tell us all about freedom of speech but the Inspector over there won't let him.

It was these kinds of pleasant interludes between ordinary police and pickets that restored some humanity to the bitter battle for Chapter Road.

13

11 July: The Beautiful Morning

The mass picket of June brought a number of successes. It created the mobilisation needed to encourage more Grunwick workers to strike; it created the right atmosphere for the postal workers to boycott Grunwick mail; it secured a Court of Inquiry into the Grunwick dispute, which would come to support the strikers' case; and it produced the massive demonstration on 11 July, which has already entered the annals of British working-class history.

The 'super picket' of 11 July arose from the traumatic events of 23 June, when the SPG battered the miners, Scargill and Jones were arrested, and PC Wilson was later 'bottled'. So shocked were the miners that on the very next day, there was already a joint call by the Yorkshire and South Wales miners for a national day of action on 11 July. The mass turnout on that day therefore was as much a protest demonstration against the SPG as it was a picket of the Grunwick factory. Some accused the miners of diverting the issue, and of turning the picketing into a test of strength between their forces and those of the police. But theirs was not only an emotional response, it was also a political one. Trade unionism was under attack at Grunwick, and the police had lined up with those forces hostile to what the miners' own forefathers had fought for. They were determined to demonstrate that they would never surrender what the movement had won, and that they would never be cowed by aggressive police action.

Grantham, now committed to the task of placing the strike into a deep freeze, immediately criticised the day of action. He told the press: 'We want to reduce the temperature … We don't want a thousand Yorkshire miners here because they will not assist in the resolution of this dispute'.

The Strike Committee, on the other hand, was by no means opposed to a thousand Yorkshire miners lending a hand. It issued a swift reply that revealed a yawning gulf between the thinking of the strikers and their national officials:

> We were not consulted about the statement [by Grantham] and we totally reject Roy Grantham's view about the picketing. Today's violence was caused by the Special Patrol Group ... George Ward has today once again snubbed Albert Booth and confirmed his intention not to reinstate us. Unless we escalate the picketing and the blacking of vital services to the company, we will still be outside the gates, trapped in a legal wilderness, for another ten months.

The miners listened to the strikers rather than officials, and the Yorkshire Area Council soon voted, by sixty-seven to eleven, to support a day of action. In fact, but for the impending Annual Conference of the NUM, they would have held their action in the last week of June. Arthur Scargill told the press: 'We haven't fought for trade-union rights for two centuries to give them away in the back streets of Willesden'. The miners expressed their admiration for the Grunwick strikers in this gesture of solidarity. They knew that at the Saltley Gates in Birmingham in 1972 there had only been 6000 pickets, and in the whole of the miners' strike of 1972, hailed as the most important dispute since the war, there had only been 263 pickets arrested. How, then, had a hundred industrially inexperienced immigrants produced a mass struggle equal to the best of the NUM, with all its history and tradition? The miners also of course felt they had a score to settle with the SPG. As one miner was overheard to describe it: 'Well, up in Yorkshire, we say, this eleventh business, it's a hobnailed boot job'.

While the miners were preparing, the right was busy with all sorts of manoeuvres to defuse the situation. By granting the Court of Inquiry, it had swung 'public opinion' against the mass picketing (although not necessarily against the strike), and it proceeded to take full advantage of this fact. On 4 July, Grunwick took its appeal against ACAS to the High Court, and the strikers were told to 'cool it' until the legal position had been clarified. On 5 July, the Court of Inquiry opened, although it was immediately adjourned until the following Monday, 11 July.

The main offensive was directed against the postal workers. Everyone knew that their role was the key to the dispute. If they held their blacking, even though it was not complete, Grunwick would lose; if they were stopped, the strikers would lose. On 5 July, the Post Office suspended without pay the postal workers who refused to handle Grunwick mail. The Cricklewood postal workers were locked out of their own sorting office by the management. Consequently, all deliveries of mail in the London NW2 area came to a halt. Management was permitted by the law to show its solidarity, but workers were not.

The sorters now displayed a selfless courage rarely equalled in the history of the trade-union movement. Although their jobs were threatened and they had nothing to gain personally – and everything to lose – they voted to continue the blacking by a majority vote of sixty-three to forty-one. There was a fine picture of Fred Jenkins leaning out of an upstairs window after the vote was counted, giving an exultant thumbs-up sign to cheering pickets in the street below.

APEX could not secure the cancellation of 11 July. The union therefore went along with it and, with the TUC, sought to take it over. Grantham suggested a march on the same day and the TUC immediately supported him.

The reaction of the Strike Committee was hostile. But the pressure was piled on at the beginning of the week before 11 July. The Strike Committee held. The Rees Committee was told that the TUC and APEX were being very cooperative, but that Scargill and the Brent Trades Council were 'being awkward'.

With the march ploy getting nowhere, the national officials of APEX met the Strike Committee. 'Call off the mass picket and support the march', said APEX. 'No', said the Strike Committee. The APEX officials conferred with head office. Back they came to meet the Strike Committee, and to tell it that unless it agreed to send a telegram to Scargill asking him to 'support APEX policy', they and the TUC would put out a statement urging all trade unionists to stay away from the mass picket on the following Monday. A prepared text of a telegram was put on the table. The Strike Committee was confused. It was five days away from what it knew would be an enormous turnout. Some said that such a TUC/APEX statement would be divisive and disastrous. Others urged the calling of the APEX bluff. 'What will the miners do?' one asked Jack Dromey. 'They will do what the Strike Committee wants', he replied.

After an hour, Duncan Lapish, an APEX official, said they would withdraw to allow the Strike Committee to consider its position. All non-strikers were asked to leave. Twenty minutes later,

Kamlesh Gandhi went to the cafe next door to tell the APEX officials and Dromey that the Committee had agreed to send the telegram requesting Scargill's cooperation with APEX policy and to join the march later in the morning, provided that no public statement was made by APEX or the TUC calling off the mass picket. Lapish agreed. 'We know that many will turn up on the picket line anyway', Lapish said, 'but that telegram will satisfy us'.

Meanwhile, Norman Willis, Deputy General Secretary of the TUC, was in Scarborough at the NUM conference. He pleaded with Scargill and the miners from Scotland, Kent, Derbyshire and South Wales to cool it. The miners remained unbending. Scargill then received notification from APEX that its policy was for a march only and no mass picket. He stuck to his guns. 'I do what the Strike Committee tells me to do', he said. He was amazed when the telegram arrived. The strikers had been tricked. They thought that the phrase 'committee request your cooperation with APEX policy' was harmless. They were not to know what Scargill was being told APEX policy actually was. They thought that they had struck a bargain which involved them giving away very little in the trade-off with their union. Besides, they argued, we know that most of the major delegations will be leaving by 2 p.m. on the eleventh anyway. Thus, to end the mass picket for a mighty march at midday would be a rousing and disciplined end to the day's activity. Far better that than to allow the picket to dwindle slowly.

When Dromey was told about the telegram by Kamlesh Gandhi, he was surprised. 'You've put Scargill in a difficult situation. The literal reading of the telegram is that he is supposed to keep the miners away until 11 a.m.', he said. Kamlesh and Mahmood took him to one side. 'We thought of that', they said. 'What we want you to do is to ring Scargill to make it clear that our intention is that he should come to the mass picket first'.

Dromey was incredulous. 'You can't behave like that', he told them. 'You're also putting me in an impossible situation. If you want to take a view different from that of your union, you must say so publicly. You can't say one thing to APEX and another to Scargill.' Reluctantly, Dromey rang Scargill who by this time had arrived in London for a television programme. Scargill was furious and so was Dromey. Dromey told the Strike Committee: 'This is your mess; you'll have to get yourself out of it'. Thus a second telegram was sent 'clarifying' the first. The position of the Strike Committee was now clear. It supported both the picket and the march. But Scargill and Dromey, on the one hand, and APEX (who soon found out about the second telegram), on the other hand, had good cause to feel unhappy about the indecision of the Strike Committee. Fortunately for the Strike Committee, it was too late for APEX to do anything effective about its once again defying the union's will.

The NAFF was also busy behind the scenes; it came up with 'Operation Pony Express'. On the weekend of 9-10 July, it smuggled out from Chapter Road the accumulated mail that had not been posted because of the Cricklewood blacking. Supervised by Moss and Gouriet, this huge military-style escapade, involving 250 right-wing volunteers and 150 vehicles, transferred 10,000 bags of mail to a depot just outside London, where the volunteers stamped it. Then it was driven to country districts all over England where, it was felt, the UPW was so weak that a blacking such as Cricklewood's was improbable.

'Operation Pony Express' was a classic strikebreaking operation that recalled 1926, when similar teams of upper-class volunteers banded together. Here, as in 1926, it was rendered successful by the weakness and indecision of right-wing trade-union leaders. Tom Jackson was furious, and urged his Executive to declare the Cricklewood action official, a move which would have meant an instruction to other sorting offices to black diverted mail. However, he lost by two votes, thirteen to eleven, and telegrams were then sent to UPW branches telling them to sort the Grunwick mail. The decision was an abject retreat. Dozens of branches ignored it, but well over half of the mail started getting through. It was one of the decisive moments of the strike; Ward admits in *Fort Grunwick* that 'Operation Pony Express' was a huge gamble. If it had provoked a national, or even a London, postal strike it is possible that the company would have been defeated. The post was always Grunwick's Achilles' heel, but Ward had in the NAFF a more determined leadership than the strikers had in the UPW and the TUC.

For all its manoeuvres and betrayals, however, the Labour right was unable to contain the mass movement on the morning of 11 July. Over 12,000 attended the mass picket from the early hours, and the official march later mustered 20,000 demonstrators. For the whole morning, with hardly any violence and relatively few arrests, disciplined ranks of trade unionists, in huge numbers, kept out the Grunwick bus and reduced the police and even the SPG to the role of helpless spectators. It was the great victory of the mass picket. It proved what could have been done earlier with TUC support for the strikers. It showed that when the pickets completely outnumbered the police there was little violence.

As soon as the pickets realised that they outnumbered the police by three to one, the mood became almost gay, especially as 7 a.m., 8 a.m., 9 a.m. passed without a sign of the Grunwick bus. In Chapter Road, there was hearty singing and much fraternisation with police officers who looked much less menacing when lost in the crowd.

There were inevitably some tense confrontations as the police chiefs tried to achieve the impossible. At 9 a.m., forty mounted police came riding over Dudden Hill to test the pickets' resolve. They were met by a phalanx of dockers and building workers who stood their ground against the horses until they turned around and trotted back to deafening chants of 'Workers united – will never be – defeated'. At 9.30, the police tried to seal off the end of Chapter Road, which the Kent miners then occupied. The miners responded to a police line with their own line across the road, eyeball to eyeball with the police. They then literally leaned on the police and forced them back by sheer weight of numbers, step by step, like blue toothpaste squeezed from a tube. This mammoth contest went on for some time, with some arrests when tempers became frayed.

The largest number of arrests in the morning were, however, caused by a very silly police tactic. At about 10 a.m. the police sent a bus down Chapter Road that was identical to the Grunwick bus. Naturally the crowd surged forward into the road and the outnumbered police were faced with the task of arresting those now obstructing the highway. Some police said it was 'policy' on the mass picket to try and provoke some arrests, either by pushing pickets or pretending the bus was coming, so as to thin out the crowd before the Grunwick bus arrived. In this case, however, it was a totally pointless exercise, as even after a couple of dozen had been arrested by police snatch squads, the police were just as outnumbered as before and faced a more hostile crowd.

By 11 a.m., however, confusion began to set in as some pickets started to drift away to the march. The Strike Committee told the pickets that it had agreed to support the march which was beginning 'soon' at the other end of Willesden High Road. On hearing this, the vast majority abided by the decision to attend the march. Only a few hundred stayed behind to stage a confrontation when the Grunwick bus arrived at noon. This resulted in a nasty incident when the police charged a group obstructing the bus, and another two dozen arrests were made. The strikers were annoyed with the dissidents: the television was able to make it look as if the bus had got through against the wishes of the picket. In fact the mass picket of 11 July had kept the bus out for over six hours and Ward was allowed in only when the Strike Committee decided to permit it.

The march itself was spectacular, with a brilliant array of trade-union banners. At the head were strike leaders, fifteen Labour MPs and a large St Bernard dog bearing a sticker on its head: 'Support the Grunwick Strikers'. There were bands, a splendid detachment of postal workers and delegations from every trade union in Britain. The police adopted a low profile, except for one who started an argument with Tom Durkin. 'You're too near the kerb', he shouted, as Tom was hunched up trying to negotiate the Trades Council banner pole against a rather sharp breeze. While Tom was manoeuvring he rushed over. 'Move to the middle of the road! Didn't you hear? Why don't you people learn to do as you're told?' At this point Tom Durkin unfolded himself to his full height and gave the copper a history lesson, starting with how building workers had built the road, and the pavement too, and were not prepared to be ordered about on what they had built with their own honest, hard work. Durkin's words had the force of a thousand punches. The police officer looked at him completely astonished until Tom dismissed him with the advice that the next time he spoke to a building worker he should show a little more respect.

The march wound past the Grunwick premises and ended up in Roundwood Park. There was some heckling from the pavement, not from the right, but from the fraction who had stayed to block the bus against the wishes of the Strike Committee. They jeered at Arthur Scargill for his 'treachery' and lack of militancy. He replied simply that the bus never got in while the Yorkshire miners were there.

The Yorkshire miners' contingent was indeed an impressive sight. Most other delegations carried banners and placards, and straggled along chatting to their mates in groups. It was the confidence, colour and heartiness of such delegations that excused their rather desultory order of march. The Yorkshire Miners, however, registered an immediate impact on all spectators. Women with shopping baskets and local workers out for a lunchtime stroll stared in total silence as the miners' delegation approached. They marched in grey and brown working clothes, with open-necked shirts, not in groups, but in a solid line of powerful arms that stretched from pavement to pavement without a break. There were no placards, no banners, no hurry and no lingering, just a solid impenetrable mass of grim determination. They made no noise and sang no songs, but just occasionally as they rounded a bend permitted themselves a deep growling chant in thick Yorkshire accents: 'Easy! Easy!' and 'We'll be back! We'll be back!' As they marched in total unity down the narrow road that led to Roundwood Park, it was like watching the approach of a flow of lava.

Inside the Park, which few of the miners entered, there was a magnificent display of massed trade unionism. It was as well, however, that most of the miners headed for their coaches and trains, for the ensuing meeting was marred by further signs of disunity, thanks to the endless intrigues of the Labour right. Already, on the march, the APEX officials had tried to relegate Brent Trades Council to the very rear, a move defeated by the protests of Tom Durkin. Now, at the meeting, they had lined up to speak on a very abbreviated platform: Mahmood Ahmad, of course, who was enthusiastically applauded by everyone, Tudor Thomas, the Deputy-General Secretary of APEX, Laurie Pavitt, the local Labour MP, and Norman Willis for the TUC. And that was all: no UPW, no Brent Trades Council, no NUM, no Scargill, no Jayaben Desai, no Kamlesh Gandhi, no Johnny Patel, no Vipin Magdani, no Kalaben Patel; there were just two officials, a Labour MP and a token striker. Of course the four speakers spoke well, especially Tudor Thomas, but when they had finished, a musical group stepped forward to see the crowd off with a few happy tunes.

The thousands would have none of it. They shouted for postal workers, for strikers, for miners, in particular for Jayaben Desai, Jack Dromey and Tom Durkin. A genuine mood of anger surfaced, particularly directed at Willis, for many pickets would have liked to remain longer outside Grunwick and had marched to Roundwood Park only out of respect for the democratic decision of the Strike Committee. To have to listen to Willis, regarded by some as one of the pillars of the TUC's right wing, was more than they could endure.

After some stormy chanting for 'Desai, Dromey and Durkin', Jack Dromey came to the microphone. He hailed the morning's work as a great victory and regretted only that the official movement had given insufficient backing. 'We say to those who say "cool it", to those who say "wait for the Court of Inquiry", to them we say: "THE MASS PICKET MUST GO ON!'" [*enthusiastic applause*]. Of course the Court of Inquiry is all very well, Dromey said, but the leader of the Yorkshire miners was right to enunciate earlier that week what is now known as 'Scargill's Law': 'It is a strange coincidence but the stronger the mass action while a Court of Inquiry sits, the quicker and the more favourable is its report.

The media was driven to a fury the next day by the size of the turnout, the failure of Grunwick's bus to get through and, above all, by the discipline of the pickets. The *Daily Express* talked of 'the big muscle mobsters' and the *Daily Mail* bemoaned 'the drift to mob rule'. The *Sun* had got a picture of one of the few violent incidents and head-lined it: 'End of the battle for a brave PC'. The *Daily Telegraph* focused on Scargill: 'The strutting, increasingly megalomaniacal Mr Scargill paraded about …'

The BBC once again made ITV look positively left-wing. On 11 July itself, Margaret Thatcher appeared on BBC's 'Panorama' to give the Conservative Party's position: 'I have the greatest admiration for those people on the bus who have gone through the picket line day after day'. The BBC news talked of the police having 'a tough time' and referred only to the injuries suffered by the police. From the BBC, one would not have suspected that the pickets sustained injuries at least as serious. To cap it all, the BBC reporter was stationed inside Grunwick and the whole of the filming was therefore shot from the management's angle of vision.

The ITN news was much more balanced and realistic. It mentioned injuries on both sides. Unlike the BBC it credited the pickets with decent motives: 'Most had undoubtedly come with honourable inten-tions of showing solidarity'. ITV interviewed Roy Grantham and gave the view of the Government; the BBC chose to interview George Ward and the Conservative Party spokesman, William Whitelaw.

The *Morning Star* was, as always on Grunwick, excellent in its coverage. The best journalism that week came, however, from *Socialist Worker,* the weekly paper of the SWP. In its issue of 9 July, it had bril-liantly contrasted two pictures, one of Yasu Patel on the picket line and another, facing it, of a racehorse:

On the left, Kelly's Corner, bought for $65,000 in the Saratoga sales, has spent 1977 chewing grass in the Berkshire Dales. Trainer's fees: £60 per week. Owner: George Ward. On the right, Yasu Patel, hired to work in sweatshop, has spent 1977 and much of 1976 being harassed by police on picket line in North West London. Take home pay: £22 for a forty hour week. Owner: George Ward.

Vipin Magdani was particularly bitter about the press coverage after his return from hospital the next day. He had been crushed between the police and the Kent miners. When he arrived, severely bruised, at the local hospital, a doctor at first refused to treat him on discovering he was a Grunwick striker. When he was finally examined, his injuries were thought serious enough for him to be detained overnight for observation. In the next bed there was a police officer with similar injuries. All afternoon, Vipin had to watch a procession of journalists and cameramen interviewing and photographing the police officer without giving him a second glance.

The strikers were determined to give the press no excuse for not printing the facts. When seven drivers came out on strike on 11 July, great pains were taken to call a special press conference and confront all the journalists who had been writing about Grunwick's 'loyal workforce' with the real inside story.

The drivers assured the sceptical newsmen that Grunwick was indisputably an anti-union firm. They described how their boss, Fanning, had told them he was totally against trade unions and how he had kept a list of those he suspected of union membership. One driver, Bill Henwood, saw a list of drivers, marked 'OK' and 'Not OK'. Fanning also told some of them that those he knew to have joined the TGWU would be sacked as soon as the strike was defeated. Pat Collins was asked by Fanning to spy on the other drivers for union membership. He refused.

The drivers described conditions at Grunwick, and their story tallied remarkably with that of the original strikers. For a start, the money was reasonable, about £56. Before the strike began it was about £44. Their real grievance was the 'conditions'; the conditions they meant were not physical conditions, but the bullying attitude of the management. The drivers had to hand wash the managers' cars. Their boss made it clear that trade unionism would never be tolerated. Drivers who were sick were ordered in to work. Fanning used to say: 'Even if you're dying, get in here!' One driver dying of cancer used to do just that. Then there was the driver who was bleeding after a varicose vein operation and who lost two pints of blood because he was not allowed to visit hospital straightaway.

Perhaps the most damning evidence of all came from Kevin Slattery, Ward's chauffeur. He had not originally joined the trade union; on the contrary, he had been on good terms with the management. Personally, he insisted that Ward and his wife had treated him well. The turning point came, however, when he heard Ward on a Capital Radio phone-in programme saying that he was not anti-union, although from personal experience Slattery knew that Grunwick was an anti-union firm.

11 July has already become part of history. An excellent film, which captures all the warmth and power of the working class on the move, has been made of the day's events by the Newsreel Collective; it has already been shown to trade-union organisations up and down the country. Everyone who participated agreed that the morning's events were a great victory for the tactic of the mass picket. As for the more controversial aspects, 'Scargill's Law' – that judgements of courts are directly related to the mass pressure exerted upon them – was vindicated the very next day when Lord Chief Justice Widgery upheld the ACAS report in the High Court against Grunwick's challenge. Later, when the mass picket had been abandoned, the judges reversed this judgement, as expected. With regard to the adventurist attempt by a fraction of the 'ultra-left' to stop the bus, against the wishes of the Strike Committee, both the media and Ward (in his book *Fort Grunwick*) chose to portray that one incident as the main event of the day, which showed how right the strikers were to try and prevent it.

It may have been better for all the pickets to have remained outside Grunwick until the evening but, once the strikers had decided, everyone should have abided by their decision. A picket of that size could not have gone on indefinitely.

The 'left press' correctly caught the flavour of victory. So inspiring was the mass action in the morning, that the intrigues of the right and the indiscipline of a fraction of the extreme left, were temporarily forgotten. *Socialist Worker* summed it up best with some splendid photographs of the massive crowd. Their main headline was: 'Oh what a beautiful morning! The morning the rank-and-file stopped Grunwick!'

14

The Scarman Court of Inquiry

And when, at a much later stage, the union, frustrated by its inability to bring the dispute to a successful end, sought the mass picket, it was faced by a law on unfair dismissals which did not allow a claim that the strikers had been unfairly dismissed to be examined and a law on recognition which was strong in principle but slow in implementation.

Scarman Report, para. 28, page 11

When addressing the emergency conference on Grunwick on Tuesday 23 August, called by the South-East Regional Council of the TUC and TGWU Region 1, Jayaben Desai, the Strike Committee Treasurer, said that for ten months the strikers had 'drowned in sympathy but thirsted for action'; this was at a time when the company was protracting the dispute endlessly by acting, in the later words of Scarman, 'within the letter but outside the spirit of the law'.

The difficulty for the Grunwick workers was that, in the badly-organised end of the film-processing industry, their industrial muscle was weak. Thus, they required a high level of solidarity action, in respect to both picketing and essential services, if they were to have an impact upon their company, which was continuing to work, thanks to the purchased and frightened 'loyalty' of a rump of the workforce.

When the mass picketing began and, following the indiscriminate arrests of 13 June, the already immense support for the strike crystallised on the picket lines and led to the magnificent stand by the Cricklewood postal workers. Faced with a developing mass movement, the Government, which considered Grunwick to be politically embarrassing, intervened to restore order at any costs.

The Cabinet Committee that was established met once and sometimes twice a day. The Committee comprised the Home Secretary, Merlyn Rees, the Secretary of State for Employment, Albert Booth, the Attorney General, Sam Silkin, the Secretary of State for Industry, Eric Varley, and various senior civil servants. Daily reports were transmitted to Downing Street. Meetings between the Home Secretary, the Commissioner of Police and the leadership of APEX failed to cool the situation on the picket line, not least because the Strike Committee was insisting upon a genuine movement on the company's part before it would agree to relax the pressure. On 16 June, the Cricklewood postal workers refused an instruction from their General Secretary, Tom Jackson, to resume normal working and, on the same day, Sam Silkin rejected a formal appeal for him to intervene, because he feared that such an intervention would lead to an all-London and, perhaps national, postal dispute.

Also on 16 June, APEX and the Strike Committee announced that the mass picketing would continue for a further week and, on the following day, Roy Grantham repeated his call, first made in October 1976, for a Court of Inquiry. Albert Booth and the Department of Employment at first set their faces against a Court of Inquiry, which they considered to be a weapon of absolute last recourse, the currency of which would be devalued by too frequent use. They preferred mediation. There followed ten humiliating and frustrating days for the Secretary of State as, from Saturday 18 June onwards, he repeatedly tried first to bring the two sides together, then to persuade George Ward to accept mediation. Ward, obdurate as ever, said that Booth had more freedom of movement than him; in fact, Ward had no problem entering and leaving the factory at will after 11 a.m. daily. Then, Ward insisted that 'no meaningful talks can take place until the biased and totally unfounded impressions [of the working conditions in Grunwick] have been completely eradicated from the mind of you and your Cabinet colleagues'. He suggested that the Secretary of State should meet him at Grunwick and promptly published his letter before Booth had even received it.

Ward eventually met Albert Booth first on 23 June and again on 27 June. Backed by his 'political adviser', John Gorst, MP, and clearly worried by the effect of the postal boycott, Ward demanded action from Albert Booth to control the picketing and to compel the postal workers to recommence sorting Grunwick mail. But, on the substantive issues involved, recognition and reinstatement, he remained totally uncompromising. He said that under no circumstances would he ever reinstate any of the strikers.

At the second meeting, he turned down the proposal to appoint a mediator whose recommendations would be binding on both parties, a proposal APEX and the strikers had endorsed. He did so with a characteristically sexual metaphor. 'Let us suppose', he said to Albert Booth:

> that you have a pretty wife and I come up and say that I have fallen in love with her and that she's a very desirable woman. I want to share your wife with you – say Tuesdays, Thursdays and Saturdays and you can have her for the rest of the week. I am sure that you would tell me that you are not very impressed by the suggestion. So I would say to you that we have an honest disagreement of opinion concerning your wife and that we should refer the matter to a mediator. Of course, if you are any sort of husband, you will refuse point blank to have a mediator, because this type of disagreement is not susceptible to mediation. It is the same with Grunwick.

Earlier in the dispute, he had regularly hurled sexual abuse at the pickets. Now he asked the Secretary of State if the TUC's 'virility' depended on success at Grunwick, and later he described Albert Booth's despairing efforts as his 'fig leaf'.

Throughout, the pressure on Booth was mounting. The Prime Minister was demanding action to take the heat out of the dispute and, on 23 June, the Cabinet Committee heard a report from the Commissioner of Police that the force was having great difficulty in containing the picketing. The meeting with Ward on 27 June was the last straw. On 29 June, Booth reluctantly gave in and the Committee agreed that the time-honoured method of sweeping embarrassing issues under the carpet would be used: Lord Justice Scarman was appointed to chair a Court of Inquiry and its composition and terms of reference would be announced the following day.

The reaction of APEX was to welcome the establishment of the official inquiry. A meeting of the Executive Council the following day, Friday 1 July, said that APEX 'will cooperate with the Court of Inquiry and will accept its recommendations'. Predictably, Grunwick's reaction was less enthusiastic. It would 'cooperate' but not be bound by the outcome.

The reaction of the Strike Committee and the Trades Council was much more cautious than that of APEX. They had never asked for a Court of Inquiry, and feared the consequences of transferring the battle against Grunwick into the courts. In particular, a lessening of the pressure would isolate the postal workers, whose action was the most effective weapon the unions possessed. On 30 June, Jack Dromey predicted that the Court of Inquiry, appointed by the Government to get itself out of an impossible situation, would defend the basis of British industrial relations, brand the employer as 'unreasonable', rap the unions over the knuckles for calling the mass picket, and recommend recognition and reinstatement. However, in Brent it was felt that a recommendation was one thing, acceptance by Grunwick another. Dromey therefore went on to say in a press statement:

> I am confident that the inquiry will fully vindicate the position of APEX and the strikers, but I would add this word of caution. The Inquiry will not resolve the dispute unless the pressure from the trade-union movement on the company is maintained and escalated.

The Report

Eight weeks later, on 25 August, Scarman and his two colleagues, Terry Parry, the General Secretary of the Fire Brigades Union, and Pat Lowry, the Personnel Director of British Leyland, reported. Their report was a cautious and measured judicial balancing act. Particularly with the presence of Pat Lowry, who, as Director of the Engineering Employers' Federation, had strongly opposed the imposition of an American-style framework of law on industrial relations in this country, the report did what was expected; it restated belief in the traditional fabric of voluntary collective bargaining, and the need for both sides to act reasonably: 'The British tradition of compromise is implicit in the modern English law governing industrial relations'. Scarman therefore defended 'the enlightened CBI view' of employer/union relations in a liberal democracy; far better to come to terms with and incorporate the unions than to provoke a class confrontation. Scarman was different to the judiciary of the turn of the century, with their gut reactions and prejudices against unions, and whose modern heir is Lord Denning.

Scarman rejected as bogus the notion of industrial relations as founded upon the myth that employer and employee are equal in contract. His is a sterling defence of what Rogaly calls the 'New

Establishment', the Government/TUC/CBI axis that emerged in the aftermath of the disaster of the Heath Government, which was established against those who long for a return to a social order where market forces rule, where trade unions are crippled and where working people are unable to combine collectively and effectively to defend themselves.

On the facts, Scarman found predominantly in favour of the union. In Brent and Grunwick, there is a vulnerable immigrant workforce. 'They are particularly at risk', said Scarman, 'when they are employed in a fiercely competitive business where low prices and rapid service bring great rewards'.

Scarman found that there was a genuine sense of discontent and grievance, and that there was no effective machinery to deal with such grievances. Even Ward had to concede in his reply to Scarman that 'there was room for improvements in the grievance procedure'. The Works Committee, held out by the company at the Court of Inquiry as obviating the need for collective bargaining with a trade union, was nothing more than, in the words of the Strike Committee bulletin, 'a human suggestion box', the minutes of which would be 'considered' by the Board of Directors. From its inception to the time of the walkout, the minutes show that the problems of Grunwick wage reviews, holidays and sickness benefits were raised continuously but never resolved.

The procedure for raising a grievance and the representativeness of the Works Committee were exposed before the Court of Inquiry as being straight from *Alice in Wonderland*. For example, Peter Diffy, Assistant General Manager of Grunwick with special responsibility for the Mail-Order Department, said that the walkout originated there and that most of those who walked out on the first day came from that department. He said that the discontent in the department was a result of the attitudes held by its head, Malcolm Alden, towards the staff. Yet there was no representation on the Works Committee from the Mail-Order Department until Malcolm Alden took it upon himself to represent his workers. Thus Malcolm Alden, the chief butt of the Grunwick workers' frustration, was advocate, judge, jury and hangman in his own cause.

Scarman criticised the company for having acted unreasonably throughout and for thereby thwarting the legal and arbitration procedures:

The company, by dismissing all the strikers, refusing to reconsider the reinstatement of any of them, refusing to seek a negotiated settlement to the strike and rejecting ACAS offers of conciliation, has acted within the letter but outside the spirit of the law. Further, such action on the part of the company was unreasonable when judged by the norms of good industrial relations practice. The company has thus added to the bitterness of the dispute, and contributed to its development into a threat of civil disorder.

However, Scarman also attacked the mass picketing and the unofficial postal boycott, the very things that broke the deadlock created by the company's obstinate refusal even to talk to APEX. APEX and the Trades Council defended their use as weapons of last resort, which can only be used very selectively, and which were absolutely legitimate at Grunwick because the unions had exhausted all other alternatives.

In his rebuttal of Scarman, Ward said that the report 'has performed a most valuable public service by disposing of the slanders and libels about working conditions at Grunwick, which were the substance of the APEX case'. The word 'conditions' is confusing. At no stage did APEX, the Strike Committee or the Trades Council allege that the physical working conditions, particularly at Chapter Road, were bad. The only complaint had been the non-functioning air conditioning in the Mail-Order Department in August of 1976. What was meant by 'conditions' were the conditions of service under the contract of employment, matters like holiday entitlement, sickness benefits and compulsory overtime. The company used the term 'conditions of employment' in exactly the same sense before and after the beginning of the dispute, as can be seen in the minutes of the meetings of the Works' Committee. The confusion was one deliberately created by the company.

The APEX Case

APEX listed five background issues to the strike. First was low pay. Scarman recorded that, 'Prior to the strike, pay was at the lower end of the rates to be found in the by no means highly-paid industry of photofinishing'.

Ward complained after Scarman that the Court had declined to take evidence from a neutral expert, Edward Southey of the Photographic

Careers Centre, whose evidence was that rates of pay at Grunwick were average and above for the photo-finishing industry. After the publication of Scarman, *The Times* talked to Mr Southey with the intention of publishing an article on his views. They too declined when they discovered that he was a member of the NAFF!

The second issue was the long hours with compulsory overtime. Although Scarman said that the overtime was welcome to some, in particular to students employed during the peak period, he found that the length of overtime expected of the workforce during the summer, up to 10 p.m., 'could easily become burdensome, if not adminis-tered with understanding of the problems of the individual workers, many of whom were ladies with families to look after'. He went on to say that 'there was on occasion a lack of human understanding' in dealing with 'applications for relaxations on overtime working'. The strikers also alleged that, particularly in the Mail-Order Department, workers would be told only at the last minute that overtime was required. Again, Scarman found evidence that this was the case; and the evidence of the workers themselves was devastating. Indira Mistry started work at Grunwick straight from school in June of 1975. She gave evidence that she had to work from 8 a.m. until 10 p.m. from Monday to Friday and that, when she and fifteen other women refused to work on a Saturday as well, they were threatened with the sack. A company witness, Azadi Patel, a mother with a young child, proudly proclaimed that, previous to her giving evidence in the week, she had worked thirty hours overtime!

The third issue was the petty restrictions imposed upon working people. Scarman found that workers had at one time had to ask permission to go to the toilet, but that that practice had now been discontinued. He went on to conclude that the petty restrictions were 'the least of grievances' but 'part of the accumulation of discontent which led to the walkout'.

The fourth issue was the attitude towards supervision. This griev-ance arose from Malcolm Alden's manner in exercising his authority as head of the Mail-Order Department. Scarman described him as 'a tough manager, determined to maintain a high level of productivity. He believed in discipline, and believed that it was his discipline which mattered.'

The minutes of the September 1976 meeting of the Works Committee, after the walkout, record:

Mr Ward agreed that the managers may sometimes appear rude to staff. He said that they are, of course, subject to all human failings and pressure, but this in itself is no excuse. The matter would be looked into, but he stressed that the staff should make these problems known rather than suffer in silence.

Make the problems known to whom? Malcolm Alden? Interestingly enough, the 'workers' representatives' on the Works Committee at that same meeting did go on record as saying that 'there was a noticeable change in attitudes during the past few weeks'.

The fifth and final background issue was the frequent dismissals and threats of dismissals. Again, the evidence was overwhelming. Scarman concludes that, in the Mail-Order Department, where the strike began, 'the threat of dismissal must have been an anxiety for many in the workforce', and 'the annual turnover of staff in the department [was] as high as 100 per cent – a disquieting percentage'.

At the Court of Inquiry, Alden admitted that he alone had the power of dismissal. The following extract from the transcript is very revealing of the company's grasp of the dismissal procedure:

Mr Sedley: You were familiar then, I take it, with the provisions of the Code of Practice with regard to dismissals?

Mr Alden: Well, perhaps you can enlighten me.

Mr Sedley: Do you know what I am speaking about when I mention the Code of Practice?

Mr Alden: No.

Mr Sedley: You do not?

Mr Alden: No.

Mr Sedley: Have you ever heard of it before?

Mr Alden: No.

Having therefore found in APEX's favour on virtually every disputed point of fact in respect of the five background issues listed in the opening of APEX's case, Scarman then examined what the counsel for APEX called 'the one inevitable conclusion' as to 'what has prevented these grievances from being examined and resolved in the normal way'. He concluded: 'We are sure that [the company] does all that it can to persuade its employees that they are better placed without a union', and the company has sought 'to this day to maintain their non-union shop'.

Reaction to the Report

The findings of Scarman were broadly in favour of the union and were welcomed by APEX and the Strike Committee as providing the basis for a negotiated settlement.

Scarman first recommended reinstatement, and disregarded the company's argument that the hostility of those still at work would make it impossible. It is often said, during long-running and bitter disputes where the workforce is divided, that when those outside come in, those inside will walk out. In practice, it is virtually unknown for a blackleg to adopt a position of high principle, particularly when his or her job is at stake. In theory, given good will on both sides, the practical difficulties of reinstatement would not have been great, because the workforce when Scarman reported in August was less than half that of the same time in 1976.

To the compensation proposed for those not reinstated, the strikers said that they wanted full reinstatement, and that they were not interested in compensation as an alternative. They went on to insist that, while a mediator would be welcome to bring the two sides together, it would be for the two parties to negotiate the return-of-work and not for a mediator, as Scarman proposed, to decide on how many could be reinstated.

The second recommendation was on individual rights of representation, and said that the company should give effect to its declaration made before the Court that it would accept the right of individual union members within the company to be represented by their union in pursuance of any grievance. The recommendation was unobjectionable but meaningless, in a situation where union members seeking to act in this way in Grunwick had the same life expectancy as soldiers in First World War trenches. Not surprisingly, this was the only recommendation that the company was to accept.

The third recommendation was that, while concluding that union representation was necessary in Grunwick, the issue should be left to be decided through ACAS, after the House of Lords appeal by ACAS against the *Denning judgement* in the Court of Appeal. The response of the strikers was that, given that Scarman found that APEX was an appropriate union (and, in their opinion, so too was the TGWU), given that he recognised the desirability of a collective bargaining agreement in the company, and given that he recommended the reinstatement of the strikers, Grunwick should accept forthwith the principle of recognition and negotiate accordingly, and not further prolong the dispute.

The reaction of the strikers and the Trades Council to the Scarman Report – although it gave Grunwick considerable scope for manoeuvre and delay – was therefore one of cautious welcome. At a press conference on the day of publication, Mahmood Ahmad, Jayaben Desai, Kamlesh Gandhi, the newly-elected Chairman of the Strike Committee, and Jack Dromey said that they were pleased at the vindication of their stand but, in the light of Ward's position on the Court of Inquiry before the report, they were anxious to point out that the strike was far from over. They were also concerned that Scarman, in his fourth recommendation, which welcomed the review of the law on picketing by the Government, announced on 12 July, might have been assisting in laying the ground for further legal curbs on the right to picket.

They said that they wanted to see a negotiated settlement and that a hand was firmly out to the employer. 'But', said the Strike Committee statement, 'we are equally determined that there should be no further procrastination or prevarication. If the company fails to respond, then it will be for the whole movement to use its power to compel a solution. Grunwick has a week to think.' It was then announced that the Strike Committee had asked APEX and the TGWU to table an emergency motion at the TUC, beginning on 5 September, calling upon all affiliated unions to cut off essential services and supplies to the company and to indemnify any union suffering as a result. And again, said the Strike Committee, as a last resort, the strikers might eventually have no alternative but to call for the resumption of the mass picketing.

APEX was over the moon about the report. Roy Grantham had been convinced that there would now be a chorus of calls, including from the Opposition Front Bench, for the company to accept Scarman. Using phrasing straight from *Greyfriars,* Grantham said: 'Ward is a rotter. But now he will be isolated.' Ken Smith, Vice-President of APEX, had assured the strikers that a *Times* leader would urge Ward to do the right thing. An emergency meeting of the Executive Committee of the union, the following Tuesday 30 August, was to lean over so far back-wards in order to get Ward to the negotiating table that, in the words of Tom Durkin, 'they were flat on their backs'. Phased reinstatement, a promise that APEX would never seek a closed shop at Grunwick, and an agreement to take any unresolved dispute to mutually-agreed arbitration: all these were offered to the company.

In Brent, the thinking was different. 'We are firmly convinced', said the strikers, in a letter to the emergency Executive Committee meeting, 'that it would be a major mistake to lose this golden oppor-tunity and to allow Ward to think that, in our anxiety for a negotiated settlement, we might be weakening'. They advised submitting a specific emergency resolution on essential services to Congress. This motion, they said 'is a vital insurance policy and ... can be withdrawn at any time if the company responds positively'.

Their determination and caution was backed up by a letter to the Executive Committee from Jack Dromey, as Secretary of the Regional Council of the TUC. The letter was a report to Roy Grantham of the extraordinary conference that had been called on an emergency basis, the initiative for which had been taken by the South-East Regional Council and the TGWU Region No. 1.

APEX supported the conference reluctantly, and the TUC had at first tried to prevent it from going ahead. In the event, called at only two and a half weeks' notice in what is traditionally silly season for the trade-union movement, the conference took place in Friends' House on 23 August, two days before Scarman reported. It attracted 312 delegates; thirty-five regional committees of unions were represented, with twenty shop stewards committees, forty-nine trades councils and over 100 trade-union branches.

The conference was a mighty show of strength and underlined the depth of feeling in the trade-union movement over the dispute. The representatives of the highly-skilled, better-paid and highly-organised gave a standing ovation to the frail figure of Jayaben Desai. It supported the call for an emergency resolution and for the resumption, if neces-sary of mass picketing. APEX moved on the issue, agreeing that Roy Grantham and the National Officers were given the power to table a motion if Ward continued to act like a 'rotter'.

The employer and his backers were, at first, silent. On the day of the publication of the Report, Ward and Gorst met Albert Booth. Roy Grantham hung around outside the Department of Employment like an expectant father. 'The company are asking serious questions about what acceptance of the Scarman proposals would entail', he told the sceptical strikers.

Then, on Thursday 1 September, two days after the APEX Executive's olive branch, Ward published a detailed rebuttal of the Court of Inquiry, 'The "Counter-Scarman" Report', which, said George Ward, 'sums up the whole Grunwick position, as well as the corporatist philosophy that has led not only Scarman but the whole country astray'. *The Times* and *Telegraph* obliged by reprinting the whole tract in full. 'The eccentric nature of the [Scarman] Report', said Ward, 'makes the extent to which Grunwick can bind itself severely limited'. Reinstatement is out. 'The existing Grunwick workforce would never accept it', said Ward. As for the proposal of compensation, 'the Court of Inquiry does not understand the provisions of the Employment Protection Act, nor is it fully cognisant of the way industrial tribunals determine cases'. This from the company that had never heard of the Code of Practice!

The broadside of reaction opened up. The *Telegraph, Express* and *Mail*, and even *The Times*, rallied to what Jack Dromey called the 'bogus banner of freedom'. Some Fleet Street editors were clearly getting a vicarious thrill out of Ward's actions. He was doing to the trade-union movement what they would never dare do to their own printers.

Reinstatement, said *The Times,* would be to invite 'disruption' into Grunwick. Significantly *The Times,* far from being the voice of moderation hoped for by APEX, was now flying a kite for that growing section of the Conservative Party who, while not wanting to make the mistakes of the Heath era, were seeking a more aggressively anti-union stance. *The Times* sensed the climate was right; its leaders were in sharp contrast with its balanced news coverage, and some of its pundits expressed unease. George Hutchinson, on 10 December, wrote that 'Mr Ward may turn out to be an expensive ally for the Tories'. He praised the good work of Jim Prior in wooing the unions, and warned that an association with Grunwick would damage the party in the minds of innumerable trade unionists and their families.

Sir Keith Joseph entered the fray. Speaking to a full house in Hove, he preached: 'the unions are not automatically the oppressed. It is sometimes the employer, the job creator, who is oppressed. Indeed, it is sometimes the non-union members who are oppressed – by the unions.' For those who longed for the days when workers knew their place, Grunwick had become a symbol of defiance against the advance of the great unwashed. Ward was to exploit the Gordon-at-Khartoum image in his hymn to rampant middle-class individualism, *Fort Grunwick*.

Meanwhile, APEX was flabbergasted. Roy Grantham looked like a Persian Satrap who had just lost his empire. In Brent, nobody was surprised. Nevertheless, the strikers and the Trades Council were disappointed. The Court of Inquiry, said Mahmood Ahmad, 'offered the company an honourable way out'.

The strikers sought an urgent meeting with Roy Grantham. The following day, Friday 2 September, Grantham and the Deputy General Secretary, Tudor Thomas, came to the strike headquarters. There were bitter exchanges, lasting three hours. The strikers wanted a motion which made specific reference to essential services to be tabled at the TUC Conference the following week. They argued that they would never win reinstatement without such action. Grantham and Thomas, who invoked the memories of his childhood in the Welsh valleys, resisted. 'I do not understand', said Jayaben Desai. 'This trade-union movement is a great thing. We want to use it to walk. Yet you ask us to cut off our feet first.'

Then, after two hours, during which time the Strike Committee thought that they were discussing the terms of the resolution, Grantham announced that the motion had already been sent to the General Secretary of the TUC in Blackpool, where Congress was due to begin the following Monday. He didn't have a copy with him but he told the Strike Committee that it asked for unions to step up their 'financial and practical support'. No mention of essential services was made. 'Bromide', said one Strike Committee member. A leading figure on the General Council said that he couldn't understand Grantham. 'The motion is as weak as piss. He could have asked for the moon and Congress would have given it to him.' The strikers were angry and Grantham back-tracked. Everything possible would be done after Congress, he said, to ensure that essential services to the company were cut.

The Turning Point

Courts of Inquiry are not the terrain upon which trade unionists willingly fight; they have an unhappy history of being used to crucify strike leaders. Their procedures may be relatively informal compared with the mausoleum atmosphere of the High Court, but it is still difficult to convey to a judicial inquiry the flavour of a bitter struggle like that at Grunwick: what it is that keeps strikers going for ten months and what inspires tens of thousands of British trade unionists to rally to the cause of a hundred black and Asian workers in north-west London.

The task was made more difficult before Scarman because he refused to hear any evidence of the partisan police behaviour in the forty-four weeks before the mass picket, and because he labelled as 'pure politics' Jack Dromey's attempt to explain the hardening of trade-union opinion following the intervention of the NADD. Courts of inquiry are intensely political and it is not possible fully to understand the escalation of the dispute, if such key factors are excluded. Moreover, Scarman himself made several political comments during the Inquiry, including one – eagerly quoted by Ward in his book – about the impracticability of workers' cooperatives.

Scarman's finding were nevertheless remarkable in the degree to which they upheld the union case, and he was to talk later of the 'unacceptable exercise of power by the employer' at Grunwick. However he suffered from the illusion that the cautious and measured language of the report would coax Ward round to acceptance, whereas in fact it was so measured and so cautious, that it allowed the Grunwick camp the opportunity grossly to misinterpret what was a clear indictment of the company. Thus the Scarman Inquiry did not properly perform its stated function of educating public opinion in the facts of the dispute.

Scarman's view that Ward could be encouraged to play cricket was shared by some trade unionists and trade-union leaders. However, the efficacy of courts of inquiry, like that of ACAS, depends upon both sides respecting the consensus of British industrial relations, and – if they differ – in agreeing to operate within certain ground rules that do not irretrievably damage their relationship. The problem was that Ward was an unashamed critic of that consensus, stood outside it, and would accept no challenge to his divine right to rule Grunwick. Despite this, there were many in the trade-union movement, like Roy Grantham, who believed in good faith that the Court of Inquiry would resolve the situation. The sense of 'fair play' held by the right wing within the labour movement led Grantham and others to believe, mistakenly, that it was inconceivable for an employer to make industrial relations history by defying a court of inquiry.

Much more importantly than these misconceptions by, among others, Grantham and – apparently – Scarman himself, the Court of Inquiry did precisely what the Government set it up to achieve and what suited the majority of the TUC General Council: the battle was moved off the streets, the mass picketing was brought under control and the 'illegal' blacking of Grunwick's mail was ended.

In the tenth week of the dispute (in November 1976), the company had been brought to its knees by the official action of the Union of Post Office Workers. That blacking, which lasted for four days, had been lifted under threat of legal action, and in return for a promise that Grunwick would cooperate with ACAS. It had then taken thirty-four weeks for the strikers and their union to extricate themselves from the legal morass in which they became bogged down. The breakthrough came with the mass picket. It was that which led to the unofficial action, in June 1977, initiated by the London District Council of the UPW. There were gaps in the unofficial blacking but, once again, Grunwick was in turmoil during its peak workload period. This time, the postal blacking was supported by a mass movement. Grunwick and the NAFF huffed and puffed. But no one dared to enforce the Post Office Act. The law may have said one thing, but justice was being won, not in courts but by the solidarity of ordinary working people.

It was the Government and the majority of the TUC General Council who broke this second stranglehold. 'The Government might fall', Roy Grantham was told. The Government pulled Scarman out of a hat and used the TUC and the leaderships of APEX and the UPW to do what its own machinery and all the judges in the land could not do – restore 'order' and drive the postal workers back to work. When the Court of Inquiry was set up, the position of APEX was that the blacking should continue. 'We cannot allow it [Grunwick] to make full use ... of our cooperation with the Court of Inquiry while the company gives no undertakings of any kind', said the Executive on 1 July. Tom Jackson played ball. He told his members to work normally, as he had done throughout June, but stopped well short of taking any decisive immediate action against them. A nod and a wink was being given.

Just as the Strike Committee predicted, the winding down of the mass picket exposed the postal workers. A continuing show of strength was necessary to boost the confidence of any waverers at Cricklewood

– the key to the blacking operation – and to act as a warning to the powers that be that no action against the sorters would be tolerated. The Strike Committee asked for a solid turnout every day and for mass support for 11 July and subsequent 'days of action'. The nominal position of APEX was for an 'effective picket' daily. No number was publicly put on what constituted an 'effective' amount, but privately, the strikers were told that it was the intention to have only 200 on each gate. All the emphasis was put upon the Court of Inquiry. No serious effort was made by APEX, like that they had made for the week beginning Monday 13 June, to maintain the picket. The TUC assisted with a series of circulars calling attention to the 'official policy' on picketing. It could not stop 11 July going ahead but, assisted by the disarming Widgery rejection of the Grunwick challenge to ACAS on 12 July, the picketing was wound down.

At the end of July, with the momentum faltering, the Government piled on the pressure. The strikers resisted bravely. The new APEX line was that the UPW action was not really effective after all, now that Grunwick's mail had been released both from the factory and the sorting office. Then, on 'Black Friday', 29 July, came the triple disaster for the Grunwick Strike. Grantham and Ken Smith battled for two hours with the Strike Committee to get it to call off the 'day of action' it had announced for 8 August. At the same time, at another meeting in Conway Hall, the Cricklewood postal workers were battling with their Deputy General Secretary, Norman Stagg. Simultaneously, the decision on the appeal by Grunwick against the favourable High Court judgement of Lord Widgery on ACAS was being handed down.

At Conway Hall, Stagg really turned on the screws. He threatened the postal workers with expulsion from the union. This would mean: firstly, loss of pension rights; secondly, exposure to dismissal from their jobs; thirdly, no more money (£30 per week) from the UPW. There is no doubt that a threat of this kind would have tested any group of trade unionists, even if it had been fighting for its own cause. Many of the sorters had families to support. Nonetheless, the vote to call off the blacking was only forty-nine to forty-six. The forty-nine cannot be blamed. The votes of the forty-six must go down in British industrial history as a remarkable example of courage and solidarity.

Meanwhile, Grantham and Smith could not budge the Strike Committee. Not even the threat of reducing their strike pay by 60 per cent could change their minds. Then it happened. The Cricklewood

UPW branch committee returned to the Trades Hall, which was also their 'lock out' headquarters. Some of them were in tears. The news of their vote was given to the Strike Committee. It was a hammer blow. The main argument for 8 August was to protect the UPW action. Now, by twelve votes to six, the Strike Committee voted to recommend the cancellation of 8 August at the mass meeting of all the strikers.

The mass meeting was stormy. Jayaben Desai, fiery as ever, attacked the pressure that had been brought to bear. Jack Dromey supported her criticism and said that the objectives of recognition and reinstatement could only be won by trade-union action. Grantham was heard in stony silence. Then, with about twenty abstentions, the strikers voted, by a majority of only twelve, against the 'day of action'. The young Asian women who, eleven months earlier, had had to battle, in many cases, with husbands and parents to be allowed on the picket line, voted almost *en bloc* for the 'day of action', and against Grantham's recommendation.

The day was completed by the news that the Court of Appeal had found in favour of Grunwick and overturned the Widgery judgement. Many of the strikers were bitterly upset by APEX's policy. Outside the Trades Hall, Jayaben Desai wept. She was furious with the UPW and APEX officials: 'They don't know what it is to struggle', she told the *Sunday Times* reporter. 'For forty-nine weeks, rain and snow, I have been coming to the picket line every morning at six. Was it for this?' She was also angry with some of the strikers: 'Grantham was threatening to cut off our strike pay but it was only Grantham. He did not have the vote of his EC behind him. We could have called his bluff.' Jayaben had one consolation. The women she had encouraged to go picketing at the beginning of the strike were now strong enough to comfort her in the hour of disaster: 'Don't worry, Aunty, we will still win, we will continue to picket till the Doomsday if necessary. We will hold out longer than the Ward ever can.' She knew it wasn't true, but that made her cry even more.

There were also moving scenes when the UPW workers reported to the Trades Council. Colin Maloney said: 'Our union leadership has done something that George Ward, John Gorst and the NAFF failed to do. They forced us back.' Maloney, Dave Dodd and Archie Sinclair described the threats made by Stagg and others. They had been told: 'You may lose your jobs over this. You will lose your money. If you go on with this, lads, you'll lose everything.' Maloney told a hushed

Trades Council his dignified and proud reply: 'I said to them, we can't lose "everything". We can lose all our money. We can lose our jobs. But we can't lose "everything".'

On 5 August, a new Strike Committee was elected, including five of the militant Asian women. On 8 August, despite the decision of the Strike Committee against the action, over 3000 people turned up – a tribute to the continuing depth of feeling on Grunwick. The Strike Committee appealed for the strictest discipline so as not to play into the hands 'of those in the leadership of our movement' who had 'put their faith in judges'. Brent Trades Council attacked 'the sustained pressure and outright blackmail' which had forced the postal workers and the Strike Committee to retreat: 'The pressure must be built up within the trade-union movement to prevent a shabby deal'. There were many fine speeches and no arrests.

The mistakes being made were becoming all too evident by 23 August, the first anniversary of the strike. The situation contrasted sourly with the enthusiasm of those early days. Outside the Grunwick gates, Johnny Patel told the *Morning Star:* 'We aren't wishing each other many happy returns. We only want one happy return … a happy return to work.' Kamlesh Gandhi, the new Chairman, added: 'We do not want to celebrate the fact that after twelve months there is no solution … it is a day of shame for the trade-union movement'.

The Last Battle

An appeal to the parliament of our great movement – We face defeat unless our movement uses the power that it has to compel recognition and reinstatement.

So said Bulletin No. 53, handed out to the delegates to the TUC as they entered the Blackpool Opera House for the 109th Annual Congress in September 1977. Forty of the strikers had travelled up from London, together with a coachload of supporters from the local trade-union movement led, as ever, by the banner of the Rolls-Royce/ Mulliner Park Wards Works' Committee. 'Stop the NAFF – Cut Grunwick off now' read their placards.

For them, the issue was clear. There were three areas of pressure upon the company: supplies and materials, essential services and mass picketing. They said that it was not possible to defeat Grunwick merely by making the blacking of supplies and materials more effective. While they had had some success with the main suppliers – for example, Kodak, which was organised by the TGWU – what they could do was limited. This was for four reasons: first, their end of the film processing industry was an under-organised jungle; second, the company had powerful backers who had helped it in the past to break the blockade and who it could rely upon in the future; third, the company had stockpiled extensively; fourth, the company was nearing the end of its peak period and would soon need only a fraction of what it was already getting to survive the winter.

Neither could the mass picket by itself resolve the dispute. Grunwick could be shut for a day or a week only to reopen the following day or the following week. The image of a permanent siege was a convenient one for the company to conjure up; it was a nonsense in practical terms.

The key to victory was, therefore, the cutting of essential services. 'Without electricity, water and post', said the Bulletin 'the company could not survive and would have to settle'. For those who complained of the 'legal, technical and political difficulties' of such a course of action, the Strike Committee said 'no problem is insuperable if we have the necessary will'. The Strike Committee appealed for official coordinated action on essential services. As for the mass picketing, it was regarded as a weapon of last resort but, said the Bulletin, 'if our movement does not respond, what alternative would we have left?'

They had come to the 'Parliament of labour' with an air of optimism. Three days earlier, on Friday 2 September, the General Council, in a pre-Congress meeting at Blackpool, had considered Grantham's 'bromide' resolution. Len Murray, always a good barometer of Government thinking within the General Council, had also counselled caution. But a number of the big guns, led by Jack Jones and Hugh Scanlon, joined with the solid left, led by Ken Gill, to insist on a stronger statement. Bill Keys, General Secretary of SOGAT, moved for the setting up of a coordinating committee to take charge of the campaign to cut off Grunwick's trade links with the outside world and its essential services. The proposal was agreed.

The strikers had been surprised by the ferocity of the 'broadside of reaction' after Scarman. But now, other voices from outside the trade-union movement were raised against the company. David Steel attacked Margaret Thatcher for her silence over Grunwick and for her failure to disassociate herself from Joseph and John Gorst. 'Gorst', said Steel on the eve of the Congress, 'has conspired with an obdurate employer against the workers' right to join a union'. Even the *News of the World* said in its leader that 'most of us would not vote St George of Grunwick as the boss we would most like to find ourselves working for'. 'It would be suicidal', it said, 'for the Tories to adopt Mr George Ward as their new hero'.

Six of the strikers were given the 'guests of honour' places in the public gallery on the Monday afternoon. They waited eagerly for the debate, scheduled for 4 p.m. What they witnessed, instead, was the temporary humiliation of the TGWU at the hands of the National Association of Licensed House Managers, as they were expelled from the TUC, because they had not implemented the award of the TUC Disputes Committee in respect of the 'Fox and Goose' pub in Birmingham. The rest of the afternoon was taken up with rule-bending and face saving in the atmosphere of a Whitehall farce. All that was needed was for Len Murray to lose his trousers.

For the strikers it was a blow. Monday should have been their big day. Now, they would have to be content with sharing on Tuesday the headlines with the Prime Minister's address to Congress.

In the event, the debate was a low-key affair, carefully stage-managed to keep the temperature down. The motion was moved by Roy Grantham. His carefully chosen words were delivered with all the passion of someone reading from the telephone directory. In sharp contrast, Ron Todd, the Regional Secretary of the TGWU Region No. 1, seconded the motion with a lively speech calling for united action to isolate 'not reason with the rogue elephant' of Grunwick. The debate was wound up from the platform by Murray, who made specific reference to essential services as well as supplies. The motion, passed unanimously, was well short of what the strikers wanted. At one stage, they had hoped that it would be amended to include an instruction to the General Council on essential services.

However, they felt that they had made some progress: Frank Chapple was heard to mutter that cutting off the electricity would be preferable to a resumption of the mass picketing. The strikers were to underrate the ability of the General Council to play 'General Secretary's tennis'; their strike was to be volleyed from side to side for the next three months.

In the two weeks following Congress, five meetings were organised by the TUC at Congress House. Every aspect of blacking of services and supplies were examined. The service Unions – the GMWU for the water, the EEPTU for the electricity and the UPW for the post – were not anxious to rush into the breach. They pointed out the difficulties involved and, quite properly, said that they would require certain guarantees from the General Council if they were to act. Ron Todd, representing the TGWU in the discussions, pressed remorselessly for such action. He became irritated with the TUC's emphasis on what he regarded as a blind alley: relying on tightening the blockade and attempting to cut off the remaining flow of foreign work. Help was to be sought from the International Confederation of Free Trade Unions and the trade-union centres in Hong Kong and Nigeria on the latter. The Trades Council said that the reaction of the trade unionists of the not so flourishing movement in Hong Kong would be to ask what those a bit closer to home were doing.

The strikers became restless. Before the General Council on 28 September, which was due to hear a full report of the five meetings, they announced, on 19 September and 26 September, that a failure by the General Council to act on essential services would leave them no alternative but to resume mass picketing. In Brent, no one relished the prospect of returning to the streets. To do so was to risk turning public opinion against the strikers, and to expose supporters to injury and arrest. There was also concern about the impact upon the residents of the surrounding streets.

On 28 September, hundreds responded to the call of the Strike Committee for a lobby of the TUC. Within, Murray again counselled caution. But for a second time he was overruled by a majority of the General Council, led by Hugh Scanlon, Jack Jones and Ken Gill. The statement made afterwards went unusually far for the TUC. The Executive Committees of the service unions were asked 'to apply such sanctions as are open to them, with the full backing of the General Council' and to report back. The statement had the usual 'Delphic Oracle' quality. It recognised that 'both legal and practical problems are involved in preventing the provision of basic services'. But the way was now open for the individual unions to proceed. They were on the spot because they had virtually got the indemnity they had asked for.

The Strike Committee met the following day. Again, it felt that it had made progress, but it was convinced that the service unions would not move unless the pressure was stepped up. The Committee unanimously agreed that the mass picketing would be resumed on Monday 17 October. One thousand letters were sent out to all the major trade-union bodies who had supported the strike, 100,000 leaflets were printed and tours organised of the main industrial centres. 'If the service unions respond between now and then', said Kamlesh Gandhi, 'we will still go ahead but the day will be one of celebration'. The call was initially for 17 October, and for mass turnouts every Monday thereafter. The strikers also sought the strengthening of the pickets on the other weekdays.

The purpose of the mass picket was twofold: first, to put pressure on the company; second, to create a climate where action would be taken on essential services, either officially or unofficially. Simultaneously, the Strike Committee was meeting those involved in the provision of services locally and throughout London. Their reaction was good. But they wanted to be assured that, if they made a move, they would have the protection of the wider movement, and they wanted to know what their unions' Executive Committee reactions would be to the recommendation of the General Council. It would be hard to persuade their weaker elements, they said, if it appeared that official action was just around the corner.

The company, meanwhile, was digging in. It installed a generator and changed the postal address for most of its mail order work from the Chapter Road factory in NW2 to the Cobbold Road factory in NW10. Thus, most of its mail began to go through the Willesden Sorting Office. Willesden had also been blacked during the summer and its Secretary, Ashworth Elwin, had played a leading role, together with other local Labour Party activists, in the support of the 1973 strike. But there was not the same feeling at Willesden as at Cricklewood. It was one thing to refuse to handle work diverted from brother sorters involved in industrial action. It was altogether another to move into the front line yourself. The situation worsened when work was diverted to Wembley and Harrow because Willesden was unable to handle it all.

The response to the call by the strikers was good. Grunwick was a magical name in the trade-union movement. Arthur Scargill announced that he would be bringing 400 Yorkshire miners, and Mick McGahey said that the entire Executive of the Scottish NUM, plus one representative from each pit in Scotland, would be making the trip. The position of APEX was ambiguous. Roy Grantham said that he understood that his members were upset but that his Executive could not support the mass picket because it had given an undertaking that it would abide by the outcome of the Court of Inquiry, which had criticised the mass picket. Neither did APEX work against the picket, nor crack the whip over its members in the same way as it had done over 8 August. It position was difficult, because it could not hold out any judicial magic lamps for a solution. It therefore opted for a safe each way bet. Heads you lose, tails we win!

On 3 October, Arthur Scargill, Dennis Skinner and Jack Dromey joined a platform with Kamlesh Gandhi and Jayaben Desai at the Labour Party Conference in Brighton, at a side meeting organised by the Brent East Constituency Labour Party. The day before, Jayaben Desai had received a standing ovation from the thousand-strong audience at the 'Tribune' Rally. Now, 300 delegates packed into a small hall to pledge their support. The following day, the Conference pledged its continuing support for the strikers, and called for the amending of the law to compel recalcitrant employers to cooperate with ACAS. The previous week, on Thursday 29 September, the Liberal Assembly, also meeting in Brighton, had condemned Ward as a 'Victorian autocrat'. The Liberals too called for the loopholes in the law to be plugged.

On 17 October, 5000 pickets rallied to the Chapter Road factory. Although this was the second largest turnout in the entire dispute, the pickets were badly outflanked by some imaginative police work. The Met had learned many lessons from its summer experiences. The strikers were not as well-prepared, but the problem was simply one of insufficient numbers. They were also not helped by Roy Grantham's statement the weekend before, about the need for patience. He had rediscovered the ACAS case as a way out of the dispute, and it was now going to the House of Lords. Yet, only three weeks earlier, he had been saying that the ACAS case could not resolve the dispute, because it related to the question of recognition only and because, due to the weakness of the law, the prospects of success were slim.

Nevertheless, the picket showed that, even without official support, the strikers were still a potent symbol of resistance within the trade-union movement. At the end of the morning, following a press conference, they convened a meeting in the Trades Hall of over 150 of the delegation leaders. The meeting was a constructive and determined one. It was a moving experience to hear the different regional accents of those who had travelled from all over the country to defend trade unionism. The feeling was clear. The strikers could expect an even greater response to any further call, but there were limits upon how many times those from outside London could come. It was costing tens of thousands of pounds in travelling, and other expenses for those who were losing a day's pay or taking a day's holiday, in support of workers they had never even met.

The Strike Committee went into session. Two hours later, it announced that it was calling for a further 'day of Action' on Monday 7 November. A mammoth effort was to be made for a mighty show of strength on what was called 'The Day of Reckoning'. It was a risk to term it such, because a defeat on a day with that name might be fatal. But the indications were that the Strike Committee could not make calls for days of action indefinitely. With the weather changing rapidly, and Christmas approaching, it was decided to bring things to a head. 'There are two paths', said the Strike Committee 'open to the trade-union movement now at Grunwick'. One was to await the outcome of the House of Lords case. 'The Grunwick strike should have taught all trade unionists', it said, 'the foolishness of putting our faith in the "good sense" of the judiciary'. Besides, it argued, even if successful, 'recognition without reinstatement is meaningless'.

The other path was to pursue action on essential services. A mass turnout on 7 November, said the Strike Committee, could transform the situation by acting as a powerful reminder to the powers-that-be inside and outside the trade-union movement of the need for action. It would also give encouragement to those contemplating unofficial action. The strikers worked like men and women possessed. Even after fourteen months, they found the energy to visit once again every major industrial centre. 200,000 leaflets were printed, 20,000 in various languages for distribution within the Asian community. 10,000 posters were produced, with words printed over a photograph of the arrival of the Birmingham engineers at Saltley Gate. This time, the strikers put much more effort into touring other parts of London. There had been justified complaints that London had not made its contribution on 17 October.

The position of APEX was again equivocal, but the Strike Committee preferred equivocation to outright opposition. Despite the shortness of time – the Trades Council had argued that the date should have been a week later – the response of the wider trade-union movement was excellent. In London, the North London and Southall District Committees of the AUEW, the TGWU Region No. 1 Building and Construction Trade Group, and London Region UCATT all called upon their stewards to organise site and factory meetings to raise support for 7 November. In Birmingham, the Trades Council laid on four coaches to bring pickets to London. Birmingham UCATT sent one, and nine more were organised from the motor industry, including delegations from Longbridge, Tractors and Transmissions, SU Carburettors and Rovers Solihull. Effective use was made of the Newsreel Collective film of the events of 11 July. It played to packed audiences along the length and breadth of the country.

Support also came from an unusual quarter. On the morning of Friday 28 October, 140 lawyers, barristers, solicitors, law teachers and their students staged a picket at the Chapter Road entrance to the company, to focus attention upon the inadequacies of the law and the violation of its letter and spirit by Grunwick. Pinstriped advocates of workers' rights from the Societies of Labour, Liberal, Communist and Immigrant Lawyers, the Haldane Society and the TGWU Legal

Workers Branch spoke to their members through loudhailers. They complained that Grunwick had made a mockery of the laws on union recognition, unfair dismissal and racial equality. The right to picket had been frequently violated during the dispute, they said, as had the right, guaranteed under the European Convention of Human Rights, of postal workers to take industrial action. Moreover, they went on, the prerogative of the Attorney General to prosecute, or not prosecute, certain categories of offence had come under fierce attack from the NAFF who wanted to set itself up as the arbiter of the public interest. 'Such a prerogative', said one, 'should rest in the hands of a Law Officer responsive to an elected Parliament, not in the hands of an unelected judiciary or of the self-appointed defenders of the "freedom for the few"'.

On the same morning, Dan Jones, Secretary of Bethnal Green and Stepney Trades Council, and a painter, presented a picture of the summer mass picket to the Strike Committee and the Trades Council. This picture was later reproduced and sold throughout the labour movement.

In the final week before 7 November, the TGWU members on strike and the Strike Committee went to the Regional Committee of the TGWU for its quarterly meeting. The TGWU in the South East, 500,000 strong, had been exemplary in its response to the appeals of the strikers for help, long before the mass picketing ever began, and its drivers had come out on strike. It backed 7 November, and called upon its members to do likewise. It determined to renew its pressure on its four representatives on the General Council for action on essential services, and agreed to support the recall of the highly successful conference of 23 August. The call was a major breakthrough for the strikers but, with only days left before the 'Day of Reckoning', the Strike Committee was to regret ignoring the advice that the 'Day' should have been a week later.

That week saw a setback as well. It became clear that the miners were not going to come in anything like their previous numbers. A delegation from the Strike Committee made an urgent journey to the Yorkshire coalfield. The feeling about the dispute was as strong as ever, although they found that there was a certain resentment that workers closer to London had not made a matching contribution. But the major problem was that the NUM had been paralysed by the internal convulsions over the national productivity scheme ballot. A sterling victory had been won by the left. However, Grunwick had understandably taken second place during the ballot, and now there was precious little time to respond to the call of the Strike Committee.

On Friday 4 November, seven Labour MPs mounted the Chapter Road picket in support of the campaign of the Strike Committee. The seven, Neil Kinnock, Audrey Wise, Ron Thomas, Jo Richardson, Martin Flannery, Ian Mikardo and Dennis Skinner, were loyal and active friends of the strikers throughout the dispute. Later that day, Dennis Skinner, a former President of the Derbyshire Miners, did a speaking tour of factory gate meetings in North West and West London organised by the Trades Council. 'The forces behind Grunwick', he told the boilersuited engineers at CAV in Acton, 'want to inflict a defeat upon the whole working class'.

The protectors of those forces were well-prepared. Up to 4000 police would be available. 'We hear that some of your pickets might sit down and block the road', said Robert Hay, the Chief Inspector from Willesden Green Station, to Jack Dromey. Some Strike Committee members had indeed suggested such a tactic at a meeting of the Committee a week earlier. It was discounted. To sit down may have been appropriate for the Campaign for Nuclear Disarmament, but at Grunwick, it was judged to be alien to the trade-union tradition of picketing. It would also put pickets at risk from the mounted police.

At the weekend, Grantham invoked the spirit of legal procedure once again. He appealed for patience. He was now speaking about the House of Lords case with a confidence that led the strikers, for a time, to believe that APEX may have been given a nod and a wink that the ACAS appeal would be won. The case was a weak one in law, but it would not have been the first time that judges made a political decision to defend the executive. Hadn't Widgery done exactly that? 'But', Mahmood Ahmad reminded the media, 'even if we were to win, there is no legal way of getting our jobs back'.

The morning of Monday 7 November, was a mild one. The police, waking up the local residents, were in position from 3 a.m. onwards. 8000 pickets, according to the Home Secretary that afternoon, were to turn up. 'After sixty-three weeks, it is a magnificent tribute to the British trade-union movement', said the Strike Committee. By midday, 7 November had gone down in the history of that movement as one of the worst attacks upon pickets in living memory. Individual acts of aggression by police officers in such situations are understandable, although they should never be condoned. But that morning saw a police policy of organised and indiscriminate violence on a massive scale. The police were off the leash, and all ranks were behaving every bit as badly as the Special Patrol Group in the summer. Such a policy could only have been conceived at the highest levels within the police force. Clearly, 'Hammer' McNee, the Commissioner of the Metropolitan Police, had authorised giving the pickets a bit of stick. If it worked in his previous patch of Glasgow, it would work here. And a decision of that kind in an industrial dispute could not have been taken without at least the knowledge of the Home Secretary.

243 pickets were treated for injuries sustained at the hands of the police. Twelve had broken bones. 113 were arrested. The summer had been bad, but never as bad as this. 'The pickets were met', said the Strike Committee 'with a policy of unbridled savagery'. The worst incidents took place in the long approach to the Chapter Road entrance to the factory, shortly after the 'workers' bus' had gone in through the back door in Cooper Road. The police had blocked off the road and thereby trapped about 500 pickets, including delegations from the London Region of ASLEF, the Camden Direct Works Building Department and the British Leyland factories in Birmingham.

As usual, after the bus had gone in, most of the pickets wanted to leave. To do so, they had to pass through the police cordon to rejoin their coaches or catch a train from Dollis Hill Station. The police would not let them through. The pickets stood across the road fifty yards or so from the police cordon. They were good-humoured and had applauded a brief speech from Jayaben Desai. They were then attacked from behind by several hundred police officers. The violence stunned everyone. Pickets were hurled to the ground and kicked and punched. Men and women of all ages were dragged along by the hair. Press photographers trying to take pictures were assaulted. A film showed a police officer seize a youth by the hair and smash his face into a car bonnet.

Having cleared the road, the police pressed the pickets back against the walls to the front gardens of the local residents. Using parked cars as levers for their legs, they pushed dozens of pickets through the walls. It was a deliberate attempt to cause damage for which the pickets would be blamed. One householder, a West Indian, came out of his house. 'My wall is down', he complained to a police officer, who promptly hit him. Another local retired resident, and the leader of those in the surrounding streets opposed to the strike, later said that he had been a police officer for over twenty years and that he was ashamed of what the police had done.

That afternoon, Jim Marshall, the MP for Leicester East, who had come to the picket with the delegation from Leicester Trades Council, complained bitterly in the House of Commons of what he had seen at the other entrance to the factory. Merlyn Rees remained impervious to the demands of his fellow Labour MPs for an inquiry. There was, he said, a perfectly good procedure that could be used under the new Police Act for the investigation of any complaint. Earlier, a delegation of the strike leaders, headed by Martin Flannery, MP, had made a complaint at Willesden Green Police Station, as 3000 pickets demonstrated outside against police behaviour. The new Act provided for an independent element in the complaints procedure, but the investigations would still be carried out by a senior officer from another station in the London area, and would be into individual incidents only. 'It's like asking the Gestapo', said one member of the Strike Committee 'to investigate allegations that the SS were anti-Semitic'.

One film crew recorded the whole attack, and the film was shown to an audience of MPs in the House of Commons. Present was Eldon Griffiths, adviser to the Police Federation. He had to admit that it showed things that clearly deserved a full inquiry. But he felt sure that there was an explanation for the actions of the police. A number of papers, notably the *Guardian, The Times* and the *Morning Star,* gave full accounts of what happened, and even those whose normal focus is anti-trade union and cheesecake, labelled the police behaviour 'vigorous' and 'unceremonial' – the kinds of euphemisms that would have described the feeding of the 5000 as a culinary event of some note.

The Strike Committee was bitter. 'Must a trade unionist die at Grunwick', it asked, 'before the TUC and the unions providing essential services use their power to compel recognition and reinstatement?' On the Monday afternoon, it announced that it was calling for a National Day of Action in early December, the date of which would be announced following consultation with the trade-union movement. It hoped for another enormous turnout on the picket line and for lunchtime meetings in workplaces on Grunwick, up and down the country.

Three days later, it appealed to APEX for support for the new 'day of action'. Even if the union were not prepared to back a mass picket, could it not at least support the call for meetings in work hours? To do so, argued the Strike Committee, would be to 'say to the whole trade-union movement that our union is determined to win this historic dispute'. The response was less than enthusiastic. Besides, said Grantham, the Executive Committee of APEX would be meeting to consider Grunwick on Saturday 19 November. He could not prejudge the outcome of that meeting.

Things then began to go wrong. The aim of a further mass picket was still the same – to create the climate for action, either official or unofficial, on essential services. The Strike Committee repeatedly rejected the suggestion that there was any procedural device that could resolve the dispute. It canvassed the opinions of the big battalions that had given the best support. Its intention was for the 'day of action' to be either Monday 5 or Monday 12 December, but it found a certain war-weariness. Christmas, a notoriously difficult time to get a substantial response from the trade-union movement on anything, was approaching; and the view was increasingly expressed that the official machine was not going to be budged. The strikers therefore had to get some form of unofficial response to turn the situation once again in their favour.

Four members of the Strike Committee and the Trades Council had had the responsibility for maintaining weekly, sometimes daily, contact with the workers providing essential services. Now, they were asked to force a decision one way or the other from those involved. Urgent and clandestine meetings took place. The outcome was to be a hammer-blow to the strikers. The phones, they were told, could be cut any time by engineers from the Post Office Engineering Union. But for a company like Grunwick, that would be of nuisance value only. The water supplies could be sabotaged by supply workers from another part of London, but the local GMWU members could not be moved. But again, such action would only be of nuisance value, because the level of trade-union organisation in William Press, the contractors, was poor, and they were the ones who would be called on by the Metropolitan Water Board to repair any damage that had been inflicted. In September, frantic efforts by the Strike Committee, APEX and, particularly, the TGWU, had failed to prevent repairs being carried out by a William Press gang of mainly non-union workers on a burst water main.

The two most important sanctions and, potentially, the most hopeful, were the post and the electricity. Jack Dromey met the London District

Council Officers. Could they move once again? The officers made heroic efforts, but their report was gloomy. West Central would not move, Cricklewood was now of minimal importance to the company, the other local offices were not as well organised as Cricklewood and they would never be able to carry the London District Council into a second fight over Grunwick with their Executive Committee. The local sorters confirmed the depressing picture.

What about electricity? Grunwick may have purchased some independent generating capacity in anticipation, but a move by the electricians would still cause it great hardship. Several meetings took place with local EEPTU members and leading figures from the left in the union in London. A move was possible but the local workers required a guarantee that, if the Board or even their own union moved against them, they would be protected by the threat of sympathetic action elsewhere in London. The climax of these debates was after the November General Council, at a meeting addressed by Tom Durkin, Mahmood Ahmad and Jayaben Desai, where the left tried to get such a guarantee. Shut down Fleet Street, they urged, if anyone touches hair on the heads of those who do the job. They failed narrowly.

For the second time, defeat stared the Strike Committee in the face. Every effort had been made to get action on essential services. By October, it knew that the EEPTU and the GMWU would never make an official move. The only hope of official action had been the UPW. There was strong support for defying the law from within the union, and Jackson was sympathetic. But the Executive, which had refused to back Jackson in declaring war upon the company and the NAFF over 'Operation Pony Express', was cautious in the extreme. It had got its promise from the Government in the Queen's Speech, that the Post Office Act would be amended to give it the right to strike. In response to the call by the September General Council, the Executive had met that same afternoon, Wednesday 28 September. In a seven page letter to Len Murray and the General Council signed by Norman Stagg, the 'axeman' of Black Friday, it set out, as was proper, the possible consequences of official action to black Grunwick's mail a second time: the Post Office might suspend up to 100,000 postal workers and it would cost the movement £15,000,000 per week to maintain them.

The letter asked for a full financial indemnity and for the TUC to call upon other Post Office unions to stand with the UPW if the management did anything silly. The UPW was posturing. It was stating the possible rather than the likely consequences. The demands for support were not unreasonable in themselves, but they were pitched at an absurd level.

The October General Council passed the buck to the Finance and General Purposes Committee, who were asked to have further discussions with the UPW and report back in November. But the strikers' friends in the UPW and on the General Council told them the score. If there was a chance of the UPW moving backed by the TUC, then there was hope that pigs might fly. And, without action on essential services, all hope of reinstatement was lost.

The Strike Committee decided to stage a protest hunger strike outside the TUC against the continued intransigence of the company, and the failure of the TUC and the service unions to act. APEX reacted with a speed which, by this stage, was reserved only for sitting on its members. The Executive Committee on 19 October instructed the strikers not to hunger strike outside Congress House. 'Do it outside the company instead and we'll provide a doctor', said the Executive. 'Ward would let us starve to death', said Jayaben Desai. Very well, said the Executive, anyone who is involved in the strike or any further mass picket will be suspended without strike pay for four weeks. Its statement concluded with the suggestion that, after sixty-five weeks of struggle, the Executive Committee and the strikers should meet to determine 'a long term strategy'.

The hunger strike went ahead. Hours of pleadings by the officers of the TUC and APEX failed to change the minds of the four bold spirits, who braved three icy days on the steps of Congress House. The four, Jayaben Desai, Yasu Patel, Vipin Magdani and Johnny Patel, together with Mahmood Ahmad and Kamlesh Gandhi, were all suspended for four weeks.

The movement reacted angrily. Three MPs visited the four and condemned the extraordinary act of APEX. Dozens of APEX branches poured in protests and some threatened to resign *en bloc* from the union. At a mass meeting at the end of the week, the strikers, after an address by Grantham, gave a unanimous vote of confidence in the six.

But the strikers' desperate last minute plea fell on deaf ears. 'We believe in and are proud of the British trade-union movement', said their leaflet to the General Council. But politely and quietly, the Grunwick strike was buried. The General Council would, however, consult affiliated unions on how the Employment Protection Act should be amended.

Following the General Council, the media tried to give a premature burial to the strike. Strikers and Trades Council members were grossly misquoted by the *Daily Mail* and others. 'We are certainly not considering the best way to pull out', said the Strike Committee on 29 November in a statement refuting the stories. 'We feel bitter that there has been no official action on essential services but there are two factors that will decide our final attitude: the first is the prospect of unofficial action and the second is the House of Lords ACAS judgement …'

Within a week, the final flicker of hope for unofficial action was extinguished with the failure of the EEPTU left in London to move the electricians. Further, there seemed to be no point in action against the telephones and water without a movement on the things that would really hurt the company. Simultaneously, APEX was sabotaging the recall of the 23 August conference, scheduled for 14 December. Grantham refused to have anything to do with the conference, and the TGWU Region No. 1, compromised by being the minor union in the dispute, reluctantly withdrew its sponsorship. The other sponsor, the Regional TUC, could not proceed without the unions involved. APEX turned its guns on Jack Dromey. Grantham accused him of pursuing 'counter-productive policies', and 'death threats' arrived from the TUC. The Regional TUC Executive unanimously dismissed APEX's personalisation. Dromey has carried out the policy of the Regional Council, they said.

These were dark days for the strikers. They were as proud as ever, but their morale was never so low. Some argued amongst themselves and others gave up the ghost and left. After sixty-eight weeks of faithful bookkeeping for the Strike Committee, Vijay Patel, one of only three bread winners for a large extended family, quit with tears in his eyes. At Chapter Road, the management once again taunted the pickets. Alden was particularly obnoxious. He threatened one supporter, a pensioner from the Ealing Trades Council, with an iron bar. The directors knew that they were winning but reacted wildly against those still on picket duty in the morning. They could not understand what kept them going.

The strikers were further depressed by what was happening to their supporters. After an initial favourable acquittal rate before a stipendiary magistrate in Barnet, the 550 arrested were getting four to five convictions for every acquittal. Ironically, all of the labour movement 'officers' were acquitted: Scargill, Emlyn Williams, the leader of the Welsh delegation on 23 June, Dai Davies, a local headmaster and President of the Brent National Union of Teachers, and Councillor Karamat Hussein. They were all cleared on all charges. It was the poor foot soldiers who were going down: savage fines were meted out and a number went to prison for terms of up to three months. The Strike Committee did everything possible to assist. It set up a national appeal to help those who were not assisted by their unions, as some were not. One of those imprisoned, a shop steward from the National Society of Metal Mechanics had his wife and young baby looked after by the National Executive of his union.

Some, like Eldon Griffiths, pointed to the conviction rate as proof of the pickets' wrongdoings. Their thesis crumbled when, on 1 December, the International Marxist Group paper *Socialist Challenge* revealed that a Willesden magistrate, Dorothy Oakley, had told a progressive doctor and the Secretary of the local Council of Social Services, that she was not pleased by the 'very light sentences' the stipendiary magistrate at Barnet had been handing out to the Grunwick pickets. 'We shall have to change all that', she announced, 'and they will get much stiffer sentences'. Subsequently the Court announced that Mrs Oakley would hear no more Grunwick cases. The decision, said the Court, was because she had completed her turn on the rota, and had nothing to do with what she was alleged to have said. Defence lawyers remarked on the remarkable improvement in the acquittal rate at Willesden in December and January.

APEX, meanwhile, was telling the world that it still had several legal shots in its locker. However, within two days in mid-December, those claims were made to look a bit hollow. First, on Monday 12 December, the Central Arbitration Committee published its report on the claim by APEX for improved terms and conditions of employment for the workers of Grunwick. The CAC declared that the claim of APEX under Schedule 11 of the Employment Protection Act was not founded.

The *Sunday Telegraph* and others supportive of the company grossly misrepresented a judgement which, in fact, proved the truth of the union's claims that, at the start of the strike, Ward was paying well below the average in what was already a low-paid industry. The company, in purchasing the loyalty of its remaining workforce, had effected dramatic improvements, which were greater – 25 per cent across the board on basic pay alone – than for the workers at any other company in the country. And all of this took place at a time of a chorus of calls from, amongst others, the *Telegraph,* for a tightening of belts and observance of Phase Two of the Government's wages policy. Ward's response to being accused of having broken the Government pay norms was to say that the Social Contract was an agreement between the Government and the TUC, and that it did not have the force of law behind it. He argued that he, as a law-abiding citizen, was therefore not bound by it. If the Ford workers had similarly 'abided by the law', Fleet Street would have crucified them.

Then on Wednesday 14 December, the expected happened. The House of Lords came out in support of Denning's defence of the Old Establishment, and found in favour of the company in the ACAS appeal. Thus, in true Alice-in-Wonderland spirit, ACAS had been penalised for not doing what George Ward had prevented it from doing – seeking the views of those still at work. In the words of Ken Gill:

> The will of Parliament has once again been undermined by judges using the letter instead of the spirit of the law. Trade unionists will make the inevitable judgement. Only organised strength and collective action will secure the advance of working people's interests.

Within hours, seventy MPs had tabled a motion demanding legislation to ensure that 'obstructive employers cannot shelter behind the protection now given by the decision of the Law Lords'.

It is worth recalling how the case started to see how the propagandists of the right had transformed an action designed to prevent a workforce from freely expressing its views through an independent agency into what the NAFF hailed as a 'triumph for the rule of law over the brute force of union bullies'. When Ward objected to the ballot going ahead in November and December of 1976, it was because he knew that there was a clear majority of the workers inside and outside, for whom APEX was claiming recognition, and who supported the union. Collections were being taken inside the company for those on strike, and in early January 1977, a number of the 'loyal' workers signed a petition saying that they wanted union representation.

Ward delayed the ballot on two grounds; he objected to the form of the questionnaire and to those on strike being balloted. ACAS went ahead with the ballot of those it could reach, after nearly two months of endless haggling over the two objections. In the courts, Ward lost on both grounds but ACAS was still penalised for having tried to do the job Parliament conferred on it. The law was weak, because it assumed the cooperation of both sides, though ACAS had argued that implicit in its powers was the right to proceed with an investigation even if the employer was delaying unreasonably. Widgery agreed but Denning and the Lords did not.

Thus Ward was feted as a defender of freedom and a bulwark against the growth of 'corporatism'. Earlier, Arthur Scargill was castigated by the press for being antidemocratic and muzzling his members, when he argued against a national ballot on a productivity scheme (a ballot the left subsequently won), on the basis that it infringed the rulebook of the National Union of Mineworkers.

Meanwhile, the smoother voices of the interests of the business world were trying to persuade the TUC to forgo its opposition to an American-style framework of law governing British industrial relations. The economic journalist Andrew Shonfield harked back to the days of his minority viewpoint in the Donovan Report, the Royal Commission on Trade Unions of 1965-8. The report had broadly defended the basis of voluntary collective bargaining and laid the basis for the establishment of ACAS. He was right, said Shonfield, when he argued against 'the deliberate abstention of the law from the activities of mighty subjects'. Joe Rogaly, a long time seeker after 'certainty' in industrial relations, seized upon Grunwick to write a book urging the establishment of a new set of legal ground rules. Rogaly was a leading journalist on the *Financial Times,* a paper whose style is devoid of anti-union rhetoric and which is aimed at an audience who want to understand union members, so that it can cope with them better rather than see them burnt at the stake daily by Rupert Murdoch. However, Denning and the Lords rudely shattered any illusion that the trade-union movement could ever expect anything from the judiciary other than pro-employer partisanship.

1977 closed with the strikers in a desperate position. They had set out with three objectives, to secure: better pay and conditions, their reinstatement and recognition of their union. On pay and conditions, they had ironically won, but it was a victory for those still inside.

On the question of reinstatement, their only hope had been action on essential services. There was now virtually no hope of such action. On recognition, fourteen months after the original reference under Section 11 of the Employment Act to ACAS, they had seen their employer crawl through a loophole in the law. The response of Roy Grantham was immediately to ask ACAS to carry out a second ballot, a face saver for Grantham and APEX in the run up to their Annual Conference. But there were grave reservations on the part of some of the strikers and the Trades Council. They viewed the second ballot as a blind alley for the strike, particularly now that Ward had a carte blanche from the House of Lords for endless procrastination. The dispute had either to be won industrially or defeat conceded, full employment found for those still on strike and a permanent black placed on Grunwick through the TUC. It was far better to go down fighting than to allow the dispute to peter out. Besides, they said, the powers-that-be in the trade-union movement want to hide behind ACAS to let the strike die a quiet death, whereas they, on the contrary, had an obligation to the movement to spell out the lessons of Grunwick loud and clear.

But Grantham triumphed. He was late for his Executive on the 23 December and he arrived to find it on the point of wrapping up the strike. He persuaded it to endorse his action in calling for the second ballot. To be fair, Grantham's motive went beyond internal APEX politics. He felt a genuine sense of commitment to the strikers, something that Denis Howell had never felt, and he could not come to terms with having lost at the hands of Ward, who had humiliated him in the Chapter Road canteen in June. In the New Year, on 6 January, he sold the same line to the dispirited strikers. There was no longer any resistance. They had no alternative strategy. They recognised that winning recognition would not benefit them directly and that it would not get them reinstated, but they were still anxious to strike a blow for the trade-union movement against Grunwick. Besides, it was proving extremely difficult for those who wanted to leave the strike to find employment elsewhere. APEX had said that it would help the strikers in the event of a defeat to find jobs. Now, with many of the leading lights almost unemployable, to stick with the union was the only thing between them, and the black list, with potentially years of unemployment.

So, in the early months of 1978, the wheel had turned full circle. The strikers were back to the days of November 1976, handing out appeals from APEX to those still at work, advising them to vote 'yes' to the union. The 'loyal' workers were no longer being bussed in to the company. They walked through the picket lines and many talked to the pickets as if nothing had ever happened. Some begged the strikers to continue their struggle. 'You are', they said, 'our continuing guarantee that Ward will behave himself'.

In Parliament, Ted Fletcher and Ian Mikardo tabled bills to plug the holes in the Employment Protection Act, and to strengthen protection against dismissal for joining a union. Fletcher, an APEX sponsored MP, had drawn first place in the private members' ballot and Mikardo second place. Another backbencher, Norman Buchan, moved to amend the law, with Government support, on the right of postal workers to strike. The strikers welcomed the moves, even though they would have no impact upon their situation.

Elsewhere, retribution was being sought. Ward, anxious to obtain a more favourable image for posterity, was flinging round libel writs like confetti. Roy Grantham, Mahmood Ahmad, *War on Want,* the *Daily Mirror,* LBC, the Editor of the journal of the CPSA, a Methodist Minister from Brent, and the former Secretary of the South East Regional Council of the TUC were amongst the recipients. Moreover, the unkindest cut of all – seven of the officers and members of the London District Council of the UPW were fined a total of £1400, by a disciplinary committee of their own Executive Committee; John Taylor, the District Organiser and an EC member for London, was fined £500. Their crime was to have instigated and supported the blacking of the Grunwick mail during the summer. Thousands of pounds were raised in a matter of weeks, through a fund to pay off the fines established by the London District Committee of the UPW, backed by an appeal organised by Brent Trades Council, signed by twenty-two Labour MPs. 'History will remember those who were fined long after it has buried those who fined them in the anonymity they so richly deserve', said the Trades Council.

Conclusion

May 1978. Brent Trades Hall

The following is a transcript of part of a discussion between the authors and members of the Strike Committee.

The Authors: What are the lessons of this strike?

Jayaben Desai: Stay united. Do not put faith in law and procedure. Rely on your own strength.

Vipin Magdani: That's right. But for most of the time the Strike Committee did all those things.

Jayaben: Not always did we do them.

Bill Henwood: Well, let's face it, Jayaben, many things were out of our hands. The strike's major decisions were made by high up people behind closed doors. Take 7 November. The police decision to knock hell out of us must have been taken beforehand. Rees must have known.

Mahmood Ahmed: Yes, and another example of that was the TUC decision in March [1977] not to black essential services. That really affected how the strike went. If the General Council had voted the other way, perhaps the mass picket would have been unnecessary …

Jayaben: That should be written. It was not the mass picket that made the TUC not support us. They did not support *before* the mass picket.

Kamlesh Gandhi: Don't forget, the TUC itself was under pressure from the Government.

Vipin: As early as March?

Bill: Oh yes, the Government was shaky … Now when was it they were forced to make that deal with the Liberals?

Authors: That was in March.

Bill: There you are then. A stronger government might have made a big difference. Look how the TUC and the Labour Party supported the miners against Ted Heath. They soon put paid to that Industrial Relations Act when they wanted to.

Authors: What about local support?

Jayaben: There were some racialist elements in the local factories, we must admit that.

Kamlesh: That's not altogether true. Maybe one or two places had racialist problems … but the whole mood was defensive, what with unemployment, the wage freeze and all that.

Mahmood: And anyway we gained much more support during this strike from anti-racialist workers than whatever we lost from racialism.

Authors: Let's rephrase the question! Where did things go wrong?

Jayaben: 29 July was a big turning point, when we called off the mass picket.

Bill: Yes, I agree. If we could have resumed the mass picket while Scarman was still sitting, that might have won the strike.

Mahmood: Well, the mass picket would not have won the strike by itself of course. It was a means to an end. And that end was the postal blacking.

Authors: The postal blacking was certainly crucial. In his book, Ward mentions two moments in the strike when he was desperately worried about the prospect of defeat. One was the postal blacking of November 1976, when the NAFF saved him. The other was 9-10 July, 'Operation Pony Express', when UPW support for the Cricklewood action might have finished him.

Bill: It all comes down to one thing: in the UPW, as in APEX, as in the TUC, the left was not as strong as the right, when it came to the crunch.

Mahmood: And there's the leadership problem as well …

Vipin: And we were all so inexperienced of those things.

Jayaben: But we came so close to victory.

Kamlesh: The Scarman Report, of course, was favourable for us, but, by the time it appeared, we'd lost all the momentum of the struggle.

Authors: One final question: what good things have come out of this strike?

Kamlesh: The solidarity we received was marvellous. Workers came from all over the country. They travelled all night, gave up holidays, lost their wages, stood in the rain, got hammered by the police – but still they came!

Vipin: The support from APEX was also tremendous. Up until the summer, that is.

Mahmood: We improved conditions inside that factory. The workers have been treated with a lot more respect since we walked out. And we must have cost Grunwick some money – in wage increases alone.

Vipin: That improvement is only temporary, of course, unless a proper union is established inside there…

Jayaben: In the book, write that we thank all those supporters, from our hearts.

Kamlesh: There's a lot more interest in politics now, in the immigrant community. The strikers certainly learnt a lot …

Vipin: Then there are the bills in Parliament from Mikardo and Ted Fletcher. Perhaps the law will be changed more in favour of the unions, if Labour is re-elected.

Bill: Some strikers have joined the Labour Party …

Kamlesh: It has helped the fight back against racialism and the formation of organisations like the Anti-Nazi League …

Vipin: The strike will change the future.

The Significance of Grunwick

The Grunwick Strike became the focus for some of the most acute controversies of the 1970s. For trade unionists, it was, above all, a struggle for the most basic of rights, the right to organise and the right to union recognition, and a struggle for human dignity. For feminists, it was a desperate rebellion by oppressed female workers. For democrats, it was a campaign against gross violations of the human rights to work, to speak freely and to associate. For many, the Grunwick Strike was part of the struggle against racism and an imperialism that had taken the Gujaratis from India to East Africa, and deposited them in the industrial wasteland of Willesden. Others regarded these aspects as minimal and rallied behind a simple class struggle on behalf of the underpaid.

The importance of the Grunwick Strike was that it roundly embraced all of these issues. That was the major reason for the sustained interest in what started as an apparently trivial dispute. Indeed, it is a tribute to the maturity of the trade-union movement that it was able to organise such a struggle. The Grunwick Strike was a strike of the 1970s, a strike that could not have taken place even one decade earlier. For, at an earlier time, the movement would have been unable to mobilise such tremendous support for a group of black and Asian white-collar workers. It would not have been capable of summoning up such solidarity for a tiny strike that raised not just the traditional economic issues, but also the democratic rights of the working class as a whole.

For Lord Justice Scarman, of course, it was none of these things. For him, it was a technical problem. His elegantly written report rationally dismembered the strike, and pronounced a verdict overwhelmingly in favour of the strikers. In the circumstances, it would have been diffi-cult in the extreme for him to have done otherwise. That was why APEX called for a Court of Inquiry as early as the second month of the strike. Even the Grunwick management and its political advisers had so little faith in their own case that they wisely took the precau-tion, before the inquiry began, of refusing to be bound by its findings.

Scarman, therefore, merely put the judicial icing on the union's cast iron cake, and sought to do what the inquiry was set up to do: provide the basis for a settlement and get the Government out of a corner. In so doing, however, he necessarily skirted the fundamental issues which made the dispute a centre of worldwide attention.

Scarman could well reply that he was not called upon to write a sociological treatise. On the other hand, a less narrow, less tech-nical and less cautious interpretation might have advanced the heated discussion that disputes like Grunwick invariably provoke. Scarman was well aware that everyone in the country, from the centre of the

Conservative Party to the far left, agreed that the strikers had a good cause, and that Ward, the NAFF and their allies were wrong to keep on rejecting mediation. Nevertheless, while condemning the recourse to the postal blacking and the mass picket, the Inquiry offered no proposals that would solve the problem of how to deal with a recalcitrant employer who admits no social responsibilities (Ward: 'It's what I think of me that matters', *Daily Telegraph*, 23 April 1977).

Could the Strike have been Won?

The strike started on the most unfavourable possible terms: none of the first workers to walk out was a member of a union; the strikers never numbered more than half of the total workforce – a factor which was to prove to be a critical weakness; their industrial muscle was limited; and they were up against an employer who would not compromise. However, against all the odds, the strikers, their union and the Brent Trades Council, built a mass movement of immense proportions around the dispute.

That movement was so great that the CGT dockers of Northern France threatened strike action, unless lorries carrying strikebreaking processing materials were stopped from using their ports. Tens and hundreds of thousands of trade unionists rallied to the cause of the Grunwick strikers. Of those who came onto the picket line, card-carrying members of the Conservative Party rubbed shoulders with the full spectrum of the British left. So strong was the sense of outrage at the behaviour of the employer and his backers, and so effective was the work that had been done, that trade unionists came from as far afield as Belfast to show their solidarity. Those who came from Northern Ireland were almost all 'loyalists' and good trade unionists. At a press conference during the second week of the mass picket, their leader expressed his shock at the behaviour of the police. 'A constable called me an Irish bastard', he said incredulously.

After ten bitter months, the mass movement around the dispute, which crystallised on the picket lines after the police attack of the 13 June, created the climate for the unofficial blacking of the mail, and brought George Ward to his knees for a second time. The left approach was being vindicated. Only a high level of solidarity action could crack Grunwick, the left had argued, and that level had now been realised. Victory was at hand for the trade-union movement, in a struggle that many had written off as being unwinnable many months earlier.

But the mass movement was broken. It was not George Ward that broke it; his was a relatively insignificant part. The unpalatable truth is that what enabled George Ward to regain his feet was the intervention of the right wing in the British labour movement. It was that which snatched defeat out of the jaws of victory. The Government, dominated by the Labour right, feared for its future and determined to bring the mass picket and the unofficial blacking to an end. No one doubts that the Government and the TUC wanted to see a union victory at Grunwick, but their first preoccupation became restoring order at any cost, irrespective of the consequences for the Grunwick strikers.

APEX gave in. Some of its leadership did so with various degrees of reluctance: the right in the labour movement, like the left, is not a monolith. Denis Howell did not bat an eyelid. After all, what was Grunwick set against the affairs of state and sport? Roy Grantham, on the other hand, looked on the dispute first and foremost as a trade unionist. He recognised the dangers of cooling the situation too far and mistakenly believed that the unofficial blacking could be maintained without the mass picket. He also believed, in good faith, that no British employer would ever dare defy a Court of Inquiry.

Roy Grantham was a prisoner of his own ideology. Important as it is to recognise the difference between right and right in the dispute, whatever their motives, all those who played a part in winding down the mass movement must share the blame for the defeat of the Grunwick Strike.

A Labour Government – Yes, but ...

The authors are strong supporters of there being a Labour, rather than a Conservative, Government in power. But – at Grunwick – Keith Joseph could not have acted with greater determination than did the Labour Home Secretary, Merlyn Rees, in presiding over a police operation that saw the arrest of over 550 pickets and the use of the Special Patrol Group against trade unionists. Rees claimed that his policy of 'non-intervention' in the police handling of Grunwick was modelled upon his experience in Northern Ireland. However, a democratically elected Government must be held responsible for the actions of its security forces. Rees could have intervened at any time, for example to withdraw the Special Patrol Group, but he lacked the necessary will. A Government must never be allowed to use the excuse that the machinery of state is too strong for it, a tale told by Crossman in his diaries. The state is indeed strong, but people who call themselves socialists must continually battle to expose and transform that machinery or else abandon the claim to be 'democrats'.

The Government's handling of the Post Office was also not helpful to the trade-union movement. The Post Office suspended the sorters, locked them out, and then allowed the company to remove mail from the building and distribute it around the country, in breach of the Post Office Act. If Callaghan and Rees were able to pressurise the TUC and the leaders of APEX, they were surely able to influence the Post Office.

The political justification behind the actions of Rees and Callaghan was simple, and based on the theory that the electorate would be frightened off Labour if it had policies that were left-wing. Yet in Brent, in May 1978, in the local elections the Labour Party actually increased its majority on the Council, in what had been billed as one of the most marginal areas in London. Elsewhere in the capital, the Conservatives made sweeping gains. Councillors Karamat Hussein and Cyril Shaw, both arrested at Grunwick, topped the poll in their wards. The Conservatives even lost a safe ward in Wembley, Tokyngton, largely because of a campaign by the local Indian community, a direct reaction to the Grunwick strike. And, nationally, the February 1974 election saw a victory for Labour, with the most left election manifesto since 1945, in the midst of the Miners' Strike and a wave of Conservative McCarthyism.

Some on the left have sought to explain what led to the reversal at Grunwick in different terms. The trade-union bureaucracy, they say, was responsible. Certainly, bureaucratic self-interest and self-importance in APEX were substantial negative factors. There is no doubt that, once the decision had been taken to run down the mass picket, the APEX officials brought powerful pressure to bear on the strikers. Thus, the supporters of this theory say that the essential problem is one of rank-and-file versus leadership. The conclusion that they draw is that the official structures of the trade-union movement have become dominated by a bureaucracy which has different interests to that of the membership, and that the only path is to forsake the structures, and concentrate on rank-and-file organisation alone.

Such a view ignores the fact that the immense mobilisation around Grunwick was because of the coordination of the official and the rank-and-file approaches: the two ran in tandem. In the same way, the campaign to free the Pentonville Five in 1972, launched by the rank-and-file, spread like a bush fire through the workplaces of Britain and the structures of the trade-union movement, until the TUC was forced to move. When it did, the force of a united movement proved irresistible, and a legal fairy godmother was conjured up to free the jailed dockers.

In Brent, it was recognised that, if the District, Divisional and Regional Committees of the unions could be won, and if they made a call to their membership accordingly, the response from the rank-and-file would be much greater, as would the pressure upon the unions. And if the General Secretary of the TUC gave a dispute the stamp of approval, even if the TUC did little to follow up his call, it would make it much easier for those in dispute to win solidarity.

Thus, at Grunwick, the strikers and the Trades Council took the dispute into every level of the trade-union movement. Throughout, the emphasis of the work was upon a major propaganda exercise in the workplaces and branches, but every effort was also made to mobilise the official movement. The miners would never had made their massive contribution had it not been for the commitment of leading figures like Arthur Scargill and Mick McGahey. The officers and committee members of the London District Council of the UPW were, similarly, crucial to launching and sustaining the action by the Cricklewood postal workers. And it is highly unlikely that the 'loyal' trade unionists of Belfast would have chartered a plane to fly to Grunwick without the call made by the National Executive of their union.

To write off the official structures of the trade-union movement is to invite further Grunwicks, and is to leave the machine in the hands of the majority of the General Council who let down the Grunwick strikers. It is also to ignore that those who retreated under Government pressure are elected and maintained in office by the membership of the trade-union movement. Thus, the problem of the right wing in the British labour movement is not only one of leadership, it is also one of acceptance by the majority of trade union members of that leadership *and its ideology*.

The Grunwick dispute is a milestone in the war of ideas within the trade unions. Many thousands of trade unionists, not only on the left, were bitterly disappointed at the outcome of the dispute, and angry at the conduct of the leadership of the service unions and the General Council. The more astute employers fear situations like Grunwick which, they say, summon up class instincts in the British working class. They are right. In mine and mill, shop and office, the length and breadth of Britain, there are trade unionists who have undergone a dramatic experience which they will never forget. Like the young Kent miners who cut their teeth at Chapter Road on 11 July, like the postal workers of London who reacted so magnificently to a challenge they had never previously faced, like the thousands of immigrant workers who took heart from Grunwick and joined a union, nothing will ever quite be the same again in countless working-class households.

The Law

The partisan nature of law enforcement is nothing new to the British trade union movement. The strikers saw their legal rights flouted and rendered unenforceable by the intransigence of the employer, the hostility of the judiciary and police and, at best, the reluctance of the Government to do anything about it. The company camp, on the other hand, could command the full support and weight of the machinery of state to maintain production. Grunwick re-emphasised to trade unionists that the most effective guarantee of the enforcement of rights is not the legal process, but the exercise of collective strength.

The left at Grunwick rejected dependence upon a legal remedy. Events proved them right. A broader question is then raised: can the law be changed to deal with employers like George Ward? Certainly, in several European legal jurisdictions, Ward would have been compelled to recognise APEX and would have been fined heavily for not doing so.

The TUC, however, rejects the introduction of a binding framework of law for industrial relations. To seek an amendment to the Employment Protection Act to introduce sanctions against a defaulting employer would, inevitably, invite counter-sanctions from a future and more hostile government. And, even if a union were able to compel an employer like Ward by law to recognise it, the American experience has shown that a further law is then required to compel an employer to bargain in good faith. The result there has been protracted litigation in the courts, with the union trying to prove that the employer has not negotiated in good faith.

It is not only the trade unions that are opposed to retreading the path of sanctions in industrial relations. In the aftermath of the 1971 Heath Government and the Industrial Relations Act, there is no significant support for such a course in either of the two main parties or amongst the employers.

The debate within the trade unions has gone even further. There is now a substantial body of opinion even within the General Council, which would take away ACAS's powers to carry out formal investigations into a claim for recognition, where it has failed to obtain a settlement. Others take a different view, and welcome the attempts by Ted Fletcher and Ian Mikardo to strengthen the powers of ACAS to ballot the workforce of an employer who refuses to cooperate, and to increase the protection of workers claiming union recognition. These attempts were thwarted early in 1978 by a Tory filibuster, and by the refusal of the Government to make time available for anything so controversial in a pre-election period.

But if there are two certainties in the situation, they are these: sanctions will not be introduced into the recognition process, and rightly so; and there never was a way of winning recognition and reinstatement at Grunwick through the courts.

Likewise, some have wrongly sought a restrictive reform of the law on picketing, as a result of what happened at Grunwick. However, Grunwick was far from typical. Basing a reform of the picketing law on what happened at Grunwick is like discussing London policing on the basis of the Battle of Stalingrad. On the other hand, the introduction of a statutory right to obstruct the highway for a reasonable period of time, in order to communicate peacefully with those passing through the picket line, might be helpful to trade unionists, and would probably serve to take some of the heat out of picketing situations.

At Grunwick the existing rights of pickets to communicate were denied by the use of the 'workers' bus'. Without the right to stop the vehicle, a mockery was made of the right to picket. But, again, even if the law had been different, the events at Grunwick would have differed little. The mass picket was much more than an attempt to persuade wavering workers to join the strike. It was an act of last recourse to seek a remedy for a proven grievance. Democracy had let down the Grunwick strikers, and the trade-union movement did the only thing it could, in the circumstances, to focus attention on the festering sore of the situation. The mass picket is a difficult weapon, only rarely used and needed, and one which is fraught with dangers, but if the normal channels for achieving justice (for example by focusing media attention on a grievance) are shut off, then society must not be surprised if the trade-union movement takes to the streets as it did at Grunwick.

The Grunwick dispute will have confirmed the trade-union movement's healthy disrespect for the intervention of law in industrial relations. But the analysis of the role of law must go further than simply a gut reaction – however legitimate – against ermine-clad reactionaries. Since the Redundancy Payments Act of 1965, which proved to be a two-edged sword, when it greatly weakened resistance to redundancies and closures, there have been increasing legal interventions to provide the citizen at work with new individual and collective rights. Much of the legislation has been as a result of the pressures brought to bear by the trade-union movement itself, and many valuable advances have been made in the field of individual rights. Further, while the first recourse for the resolution of any problem should always be collective bargaining and collective action, the use of the law may be the only alternative in the under-organised or unorganised workplace. However, to allow the cutting edge of the trade-union movement to be blunted, against the stone wall of legal procedures, is not in the interests of democracy, which demands a strong, independent trade-union movement.

Grunwick and the Immigrant Community

Grunwick was the most important dispute concerning the immigrant community in the history of the British labour movement. It put to rest the assumption that black and Asian workers were not prepared to join unions and were undercutting the wages of white workers. Gone is the image of the passive and unorganisable traditional Asian woman.

There are still problems with regard to race within the trade-union movement, but Grunwick did much to erase the painful memory of disputes in which black and Asian workers were not supported by their white colleagues. For highly-skilled, better paid and highly-organised workers, Grunwick brought home the realities of working life for a large percentage of the immigrant community. And those workers responded with a commitment rarely seen in any dispute. In so doing, they and the Grunwick strikers dealt a blow to the separatist arguments put forward by some in the immigrant community, who sought to write off the trade-union movement. Grunwick showed that white workers could be mobilised on a massive scale in defence of their black and Asian brothers and sisters. It also showed that the trade unions have to develop new organisational techniques, and that trade unionism has to be taken into the organisations of the immigrant community. This was successfully shown by the meeting organised by Jayaben Desai and Jack Dromey for forty husbands of the strikers, when the issues of the strike and the role of the trade-union movement was explained and discussed.

Those who are strong in the movement must help the weak to organise, and the work APEX did in this respect was commendable. Without its efforts, the mobilisation would have been less effective. The support from the Indian community overall was first rate, and important links were forged with the trade unions in Brent and elsewhere. Even the Barnet Community Relations Council, the vice chairs of which included John Gorst and Margaret Thatcher, came forward and asked what it could do for the Grunwick strikers.

The Future

The Grunwick Strike has already inspired a series of strikes by immigrant workers in the catering industry. It will surely inspire many more. For the Grunwick Strike showed how the trade-union movement could fight, not only for economic gains, but also for the democratic rights of all employees, male and female, blue-collar, white-collar, black, Asian and white. It showed the potential and effectiveness of local trades councils – as in the General Strike of 1926 – in organising a rank-and-file struggle. Strong and representative trades councils have a unique local coordinating role to play, not only in their affiliated branches but also in the workplaces and the community organisations in their locality. They have been weakened by the movement of power away from the branch and to the workplace committee. But in Brent, firm links had been forged with the workplaces and District Committees of the unions. It was fortunate for the strikers that the dispute began in an area with a healthy trades council, whose approach was better geared than APEX to coping with an employer like Ward. Grunwick showed how mass pressure, official pressure and parliamentary pressure can be coordinated to produce a mighty movement of solidarity.

It proved to white trade unionists that they need not fear the introduction of immigrant labour.

Grunwick was a defeat for the immediate objectives of the trade-union movement, but a dispute like that at Grunwick is never lost. The strike bulletins often spoke of 'from Tolpuddle to Tonypandy, from the Match Girls to the Miners', placing Grunwick in the best traditions of the British trade-union movement. That it was. However, two of those four glorious chapters in working-class history were, like Grunwick, defeats. What is important is that the right lessons are learnt from what was an epic struggle.

The Grunwick Strike showed that what was true in the days of the Chartists is still true now: it is the combination of democratic demands and working-class interests that is capable of mobilising mass action in Britain. Above all, the course of the strike illustrated, with a vividness rarely seen before, how a section of workers totally unorganised, totally ignorant of trade unionism, totally insecure in a foreign land, can yet develop – in response to autocratic treatment – such militancy, attract in a few months such solidarity, that all the forces of the state, the media, the police, the courts, employers' organisations, racial prejudice and women's inequality can be swept aside by the freshness and dynamism of determined struggle.

> Malcolm Alden: All of a sudden she [Jayaben Desai] kind of exploded and said 'I want my freedom. I am going. I have had enough.'
>
> Lord Justice Scarman: Could you understand what she was shouting about?
>
> Malcolm Alden: 'I want my freedom' is the phrase that stands out in my mind ...